HEART of the Matter

A Lifetime of Survival

JOYCE H. HYNES

The Reading Glass Books
(888) 420-3050
www.readingglassbooks.com
fulfillment@readingglassbooks.com

Contents

Introduction

The Father's Land
Think of me as the wind flowing free in the sky
Think of me as a fluffy white cloud passing by.
Think of me as a mountain ever changing, never still
Think of me as you listen to the song on the Whippoorwill.
Think of me as you watch the faithful rolling sea
Think of me as you view the blowing of the trees.
Think of me as you smell the fragrance of a rose
Think of me as you touch the graceful falling snow.
Think of me as a star watching ore you at night.
Think of me as an eagle spreading wing, taking flight.
Think of me as you feel the raindrops touch your face
Think of me as the moon and sun change place.
Feel no sorrow cry no tears my pain is put to rest.
Sing a song, say a prayer my life's been full and blest.
My spirit will be with you; there's music in the air.
Rejoice for all we've shared.
Even though you cannot see or take me by the hand
I'm present in your life living in The Father's Land.
I'm living as an angel in The Father's Land.

CHAPTER 1

Present Day

My story is about God and faith, the courage of self, the knowledge of others who made my road to health a reality by keeping my heart beating.

Comfortably sitting in my recliner, my eyes of seventy-one years are clouded with glaucoma and strain to focus. My fingers bent, worn from age and "Arthur" struggle to hold and push play on the remote. The blackened screen hesitates flickering back 'n' forth to produce the picture on the screen. I barely make out the grayish formations moving across my wall-mounted TV. GraceNote, my loving cat, standing on my desk, wiggles preparing to jump in my lap as I try to find my comfort zone. No Milk Duds or fresh hot buttered popcorn to munch. I sat back, relaxing listening to the peaceful purr of my cat waiting for the movie to begin.

Looking outside my window, I saw a rainbow appear, transporting my mind. The room darkens as a smokey mist enters under the front door, traveling to every room. Swiftly the area is consumed, and silence takes hold. GraceNote stirs as her ears twitch in several directions. Frozen in fear, my eyes follow the path of the mysterious vapor. GraceNote, on all four, hisses. Her right paw rises as claws appear ready for combat on a moment's notice. Multicolored fur stands as an armored shield protecting me from the mist. Cobalt blue eyes track every motion traveling across the room. An eerie feeling befalls me suggesting I have gone "over the rainbow." My eyes follow the path of the advancing vapor. GraceNote stirs as her ears overlook and twitch in several directions—showing her teeth, spreading her claws, protecting me from the mist. Embers burning in the fireplace softened as chill consumes the room. One loud "pop" sends GraceNote skedaddling down the hallway, sliding into the door. Up in a flash, she runs to her favorite niche hiding until she feels safe. A massive tornado visits, lifting our home skyward. Everything around me follows in a spin. Highly shaken, I realize I am no longer in Portsmouth; therefore, where am I? Hit by an unknown object, I fall . . .

February 10, 1957. Morning sunrays join in a game of peek-a-boo among the clouds. A large group of birds gather for morning sky diving. They swoop, spin, and dodge with precision. Lights shine brightly through the kitchen window. Mommy must have rolled out of bed early as a breakfast of homemade biscuits and gravy awaits on the dining room table. Sizzlin' on the stove, eggs over easily now piping hot topped with cheddar cheese. Mommy sits down to have a cup of hot black coffee with Daddy while Grace and I like ice-cold milk in glass jelly jars. A hearty meal is one of Daddy's delights. Where is he? Is he coming down soon? Upstairs, shaver in hand, Daddy caresses the instrument with the care of a musician. Delicately he knows how to hold and let loose. Too tight he might injure himself, or slackened and the look won't satisfy the ladies. Like playing an instrument, there is not enough pressure on a string and the sound could go sour. Proper finger position produces a sweet sound pleasant to the ear.

Mommy saw me peeking around the corner. My guilty look was hard to deny as I wondered if she noticed my heart jumped up into my throat. Today is my fifth birthday. Later my family will gather for a quaint celebration. The four of us will sit down as family-like all dressed up even though it's not church day. Daddy will have his white shirt and tie on, and he'll look spiffy! Mommy has been busy preparing for the party baking, cleaning, and that's in addition to going to the store and buying everything. Oh, that reminds me: I wonder what she bought me for my birthday, hm?

I cannot play like most kids because I have a troubled heart. I watch the neighborhood kids from a special place in the living room. I sat in a rocking chair that was my grandmother's on my daddy's side, which is why it is special. Grace had it until she got too big, and now it is mine. Running games like tag and red light/green light look like fun, but I am stuck inside watching as I rock, playing paper dolls or *Old Maid*.

I smell good ole' country ham fillin' up the house. Mommy knows how to bring out the flavors of all my favorite foods made from scratch. Biscuits make any morning special by adding a few drops of honey made from the bees down on grandpa's farm. After breakfast, my mouth is hankering to chew. I'm talkin' 'bout *Bazooka Bubble Gum* to be exact—the square glob that smells extra good wrapped in paper with intricate design. The sweet aroma drifts up, tickling my nasal passages. I unwrap and check out the tiny markings across the rectangular piece. I wonder why the creator chose pink as the color. Was he thinking of cotton, cotton candy? The only other "food" item this color I know is "PB" and not peanut butter. I can't remember the name, but Mommy gives me some on a spoon when I have a tummy ache. What is that name? I can't recall. I love to chomp this wonderful hard pink mass and make huge pink bubbles—blowing 'n' blowing until the bubble grows and shatters all over my face. Momentary excitement then .. . my heart paused jumping back into action. Who would have thought this little gem would stir up my ticker? Oh, I'm sorry I tend to talk in circles, but back to the gum. I take the piece, place it on my tongue, move it around again until it is wet with saliva. Start to chew up and down moving it side to side until the consistency is smooth. Now start to blow and blow, but be careful not to force the air. Now you have the perfect bubble! Carefully with two thumbs, take it out of your mouth and pinch the bottom section to seal the end. Oh, so mindful, place it in the freezer until it freezes. Hopefully, Mommy doesn't find it before it is ready 'cause she might have a hissy fit having a foreign object out of someone's mouth in her freezer and have a conniption! You gotta wait until it is completely frozen and then you . . . POP! Watch the Bazooka Gum shatter! Watch as it flies . . . EVERYWHERE! Here it comes in my hair! Oh no! Scissors! Mommy is coming with the scissors. SNIP! SNIP! Be careful and close your mouth as you chew. Oh no! Here she comes! She made me spit out my Bazooka! Too much noise 'cause I sound like a cow chewing cud. Getting a new piece, I unwrap with ease taking my index and thumb fingers and grab the fresh piece. Just like before, excitement builds as my mouth fills with saliva and my nose picks up the scent. My tongue and jaw go into motion. My mouth is voluntarily out of control opening as my eyes intently focus. Placed on my tongue, I close my lips.

My jaws embrace and feel the dryness and struggle to push the mass around inside to chew. I impatiently wait for my saliva to reach and coat the gum I am so eager to chew.

I repeat moving and chomping until the gum is the right consistency to make a great bubble. My muscles are tired, but I am ready to blow. One, two, three . . . "WOOSH!" A bubble appears. My eyes now enlarged feel like shooting from their sockets. They cross and I cannot focus on the wet mass in my "so-called" vision. Taking the gum out of my mouth, I pinch the ends, sealing them together with my fingertips. A round bubble is created, a little lopsided, but it is my creation, and I am "hot stuff," pink hot stuff, that is. No one will believe me, so I placed my trophy glob in Mommy's nice clean freezer for safekeeping. I would not dare tell her I stressed my heart blowing, causing it to skip sideways five times. I feel light-headed and need to sit on the side of the bed.

After breakfast, the neighborhood gang rang the doorbell wanting me to play outside. I could not wait to brag about my invention. With extreme enthusiasm, I tried to explain. A question mark floated over their faces following them demanding proof of my bubble's existence. Since when do friends call for proof? These are the same friends that convinced me to believe in Santa Claus without a hair of evidence from Santa's beard. Why all the questions? Hurrying inside, I grabbed my creation from the freezer, careful not to destroy the bubble. Mommy will have a double hissy fit knowing I put a pink glob fresh out of my mouth into her nice clean freezer, not to mention the stress on my heart blowing it up. This would account for double whammies making her very unhappy. Three hours later, I withdrew my bubble—POP! Bazooka Bubble Gum in my hair, nose, glasses, everywhere, again!

My relationship with Bazooka is on edge. Mommy is constantly asking me to close my mouth as I tend to chew open and loud. Having had enough of "gum" horseplay, she has banned me from chewing. No more! Not listening, this morning I found a large pink glob stuck solidly in the back of my head. Oh, brother! Now I need scissors after sharing my bed with a piece of escaped gum. I am nervous and up with the chickens. I do not have any, yet I am awake before the sun and chickens decide to show themselves. I need a solution, a secret solution to the gum that's taken residence in the nap of my neck. I got it! I'll wake up Grace, and together we will get that gum outta my hair. Darkness is still out my window, so instead of a few more winks, Grace and I, or I should say, Grace will cut the gum from my hair. Breakfast was fair, and now Grace and I have kitchen duty to wash, dry, and put away the breakfast dishes. We are not getting along and have argued since crawling out of bed.

"Joyce, don't forget to put on your white ankle socks and your Mary Jane shoes."

"Yes, Mommy. "

Daddy is outside tinkering on the family Ford. We will be leaving soon as a family to go to my appointment at Dr. Craft's. Daddy is doing something that looks important, but I have no idea what that is. His hands are greasy, and sweat is dripping off his nose. Mommy is gonna yell at him for getting black stuff all over his new pants she bought at JC Penney's. She is inside doing stuff mothers do. Grace is staying home with Daddy to watch ***The Mickey Mouse Club***. All she wants to do is watch boys flirt with the girls and dance. What's so fun about all that? This morning Mommy and I are going to Dr. Craft's, my regular downtown doctor for my checkup. Riding in the back seat, my nose reaches two inches above the window, fogging up the glass as I breathe. I cannot wait to grow up enough to see the whole picture outside. Right now, as I look out, all I do is fog up the window. In front of the office, a large sign appeared: **Today is Doctor's Day. Give your Doctor a Hug!** I can do that! Everyone showed up today causing a problem with parking. Mommy dropped me off at the front door while she searched for a space. A mother and daughter got up to leave as Mommy entered. Having called my name, Nurse Rachel escorted Mommy and I back to a patient room. She helped me up on the table, and now Mommy and I had the pleasure of waiting once again for Dr. Craft. Restless, I jumped three feet when there was a knock. Slowly the knob turned; a left foot sneaker entered the room but was interrupted by a nurse. Ten minutes later, there was another knock, but there was no hesitation. The sneaker came in followed by the matching right foot attached to a six-foot man reddish-brown head of hair man wearing wire-rimmed glasses. A smile the size of a ten-inch pizza was attached to my doctor, Craft. The door opened, and Dr. Romeo Craft entered with his Rosie's Pizza smile.

Dressed in a white coat, black bow tie, white shirt, black pants, size 13 sneakers and highlighted bright orange shoelaces completed his professional attire. He asked me to be patient. What is he talking about? I am the patient, and I'm being patient. He should be a patient on the "funny farm." He spoke a few words before pulling out his trusty-non-dusty stethoscope from his right-side pocket. Placing the instrument on my skin he heard my heart going "lub-dub-lub-dub-(silent)-dub."

"Hello, Joyce, I am Dr. Craft, and you must be Mrs. Noffsinger. Pleased to meet you both. Joyce, do you know why your mom brought you today?"

"Something about my ticker not ticking too good, I think. Is that right?"

"Good, I would like to take a listen to your ticker, if that's OK."

"Guess so."

Dr. Craft looked over at my mommy as she smiled nodding that it was "OK" to listen. He lifted my gown, positioning this thingamajig around his neck on my chest which was ice cold. Closing his eyes, he listened intently to the sound of each beat. Was he picturing the "lub-dubbing" in his mind? A visible expression of concern flashed as his eyebrows rose, taking a second sound check of my heart.

My eyes tracked his every move. Dr. Craft asked if I would like to listen to my heart, which tickled me to be included in his thoughts. Dr. Craft took off his "ear" thing and carefully replaced them in mine. Feeling odd a whole new means of sound started coming into play. I am sure my eyes lit up like trees during the holiday season. Besides my heart beating, I could hear gurgling and other weird sounds. Turning my head toward Mommy, I noticed her eyes tearing as she watched me listening to my own beating heart. Is she crying? I should be bawling, but a little voice inside my head told me to be silent. Wrapped up in the moment, I did not realize I was in the room alone. Mommy and Dr. Craft had slipped out for a private chat. "Mrs. Noffsinger, I will review my findings with my colleagues and call next week with our recommendations. I heard something unusual and would recommend a trip to New York. Go home, let her play. Talk soon."

By the time they returned, I had counted all the ceiling holes totaling nine hundred ninety-nine to be exact plus drifted off for a snooze. Mommy caught me hanging off the end of the table catching me by the seat of my pants. Dr. Craft waved goodbye as Mommy and I left the exam room. As he walked away, I never realized he stood straight as a yard stick, and his left foot dragged due to an earlier car accident while in medical school. I followed Mommy to the car carrying my dolly close in my arms. The stress of it all was getting too much. My heart began skipping, limiting my air, preventing me from calling her by name. Finally, Mommy turned around, and I was stunned. Her beautiful blue eyes were swollen from intense crying; redness overshadowed the whites. Her complexion, once clear, is now blotchy and covered with rough patches of Rosaces. Her nose was dripping with fluid and needing a soft hankie to cleanse the delicate tissue now highly inflamed. Someone or something had upset her. Mommy is pouring out her heart, and I do not know what to do. I guess adults would say she is an "emotional" wreck. She needs a hankie; she needs a friend. Sharing my dolly put a much-needed smile on her face and made me feel better. I watched Captain Kangaroo and his buddy, Mr. GreenJeans, while my dolly did her magic. Ooh! My heart fluttered back, but this time it felt good.

Finally, we are back home and starvin'. Mommy decided to fix fried chicken for dinner. She told me the right skillet gets the best crisp. Daddy got her an electric frying pan last Christmas that does the job right. Preparing the chicken involves several steps. First, you gotta skin the meat, rinse then dip in egg yolks beaten until light-yellow 'n' frothy. Isn't the yolk already yellow? Yes, Joyce, but this is more of a "creamy yellow color" if you can make sense of that. You repeat that step before sprinkling with breadcrumbs, carefully placing it in hot oil. Mommy always told me to never use "fat back," but she did not explain who's "back" or from where it came. Smelling good! Turning the temperature down a smidge, Mommy stepped outside for a chat with next-door neighbor Bonnie. The front yard filled with the fragrance of fresh frying chicken. After fifteen minutes, Mommy went inside to check on the cooking progress and was alarmed. The kitchen is engulfed with a thick heavy smoke. Her vision impaired, she managed to reach the sizzling stove and unplugged the electric skillet. Reaching over to the sink, she turned on the faucet, drowning the pan and our dinner. No fried chicken tonight, but soggy is available. Instead grilled cheese, tomato soup, and salad with Peppercorn dressing. As the smoky mist cleared the room, we took a few minutes to settle down before getting to work cleaning up.

My big sister and I did the dishes while Mommy and Daddy enjoyed coffee before going down to the "nitty-gritty" of cleanup. Everything was going fine until renegade suds got into Grace's hair, starting a massive battle between her and I. However, the life of a bubble is short otherwise this could have gone on and on. Mommy and Daddy chipped in, taking care of any wall or floor cleanup. Lastly, the trash was taken out, and we were ready to retire. Well, that's what Mommy said 'cause I was not ready to go to bed. My inner voice was active, keeping me awake while Grace was comfortable and asleep in her twin bed. I would be in "dreamland" if my inner voice would shut up, curl up, and leave me alone.

I love music. I was tickled finding out you can listen to music while eating breakfast. I look forward each morning to hearing the first three notes of a musical scale in my bowl, however, not every box will serenade you. How can anyone start the day without a song? Even the farmer wakes up to the rhythm of six/eight time. The rooster in his glory stands at attention, lungs full of air, and with a deep breath, he awakens everything within hearing distance. In the Noffsinger household, morning music has been moved to afternoons by something no longer in a cereal box. My sister decided to make music and spread her fingers out among the eighty-eight keys of a piano. Mommy is excited about her decision 'cause she learned violin as a child living in New York City. I do not know if she played Carnegie Hall, so it must have been on Broadway. However, when Grace practices, I cannot tell if she's playing "Twinkle, Twinkle" or "Mary Had a Lamb." Every evening, she sits on the bench running her fingers up and down the piano keys pretending she's Liberace, but no sound comes forth. Everything she plays sounds the same and it is **BORING!**

Periodically a song keeps playing relentlessly in my mind and will not stop. Also known as the Song Stuck Syndrome, this little bugaboo wedges in my mind not letting go or giving me peace of mind—a simple catchy tune with clout that needs to let me go.

The doorbell rings and the neighborhood gang is fired up to play marbles under the large oak tree in front of our house. I might be the youngest of the "California Street Kids," but I can play a mean game of "thumb shooting" glass balls. This is the perfect form of fun for me—no required running or strenuous activity. I flew out the back door heading for the game by the railroad tracks. Yes, I did say "flew," and no, I did not grow wings, but I got there on time despite being called back by Mommy. One would think I committed a mortal sin by slamming the side door. Mommy had me return home, open the slammed door, close it properly, and apologize to her before I could return to the marble game. Tired, out of breath, but I knew I could win if I could get to the game. I may be small, but I can shoot little round glass balls outta any circle with my right thumb and power. My air is limited inside my lungs, keeping me from playing other games, but watch out when my thumb meets a glass ball. However, if I have a coughing spell, I must leave because I cannot breathe. I did leave one time when my breathing was fine only because I was chasing a runaway marble. Sometimes I do go after the little rascal far from the dirt field due to having a coughing fit. Time to get the gang together and the game going. However, looking up at the sky, we had better get going, now! Looks like the storm will be here soon.

Walter drew a circle with a stick found earlier in a section of dirt cleared for marble playing—smooth, level, and the texture light and airy. Excited, I grabbed a handful of the soil and rubbed it on my face. The rest of the gang followed my lead by asking no questions. Had they been brainwashed? If so, by whom? Marbles were placed near the center and arranged in an "x" pattern. Players flick a shooter into the center, knocking a marble out. The player with the most marbles wins. Being the youngest, I always go first. I lined up my shooter perfectly by setting my thumb at a right angle when a forceful cough came out of nowhere. I thought for sure my head was going to be blown off my shoulders. The strength of this one must have traveled from my little toe. Every bit of energy stored in my body was drained. We finished round one as several clouds approached the neighborhood. We decided sitting under a tree was not the best place to be during an approaching storm. We gathered our marbles and hurried home before the rain.

Mommy was in the kitchen, talking on the phone, having her usual coffee and Danish. The morning *Huntington Gazette* was on the kitchen table undisturbed while the voice continued on the other end. At that moment, the room was enhanced with energy. Mommy's antique tea kettle started whistling on the stove. Outside the sky opened up with fierce thunder and lightning. One strong bolt startled Mommy, spilling the warm brew held in her left hand all over her housecoat. Hearing her scream, I came running from the living room dragging Betsy McCall by her ponytails to see if she was OK. Mommy looked up at me with her loving blue eyes before shooing me out with a right-hand gesture. She has never ever asked me to leave while talking on the phone or any other time for that matter. Was something wrong, or was it a secret? Secret? We were not supposed to have secrets in the family. Mommy's orders! How can she have one, a secret that is and not me? Her face, the expression on her face was concerned. No smile! No frown! Flat face! However, her eyes spoke seriously. You know "the mommy look." An example was just yesterday when I tripped and skinned my knee on the sidewalk. Mommy heard me crying and came running out the side door to my rescue. That "look" I spoke of happens each and every time I do something stupid causing me to cry. She worries so much because of my sick heart that every little bump or scratch puts her in a tizzy. In my infinite wisdom, I listened in on the conversation and eavesdropped on a lesson I learned after watching Dragnet on TV:

"Mrs. Noffsinger, I am Field Nurse Helen from **Peds** of Huntington. I have a message saying a cardiac catheterization should be considered for scheduling on your daughter, Joyce. St. Mary's Hospital in New York is the only hospital on the East Coast performing this procedure at this time. Our office will make all the arrangements and get back with you. Dr. Craft will be in touch."

I tried to be quiet hanging up the phone nice 'n' slow. Busting with the news, I had to get all this outta my mouth and off my chest. This "stuff" is causing heaviness inside me, upsetting the delicate working of my heart. Confused and ready to explode, I went to my trusted friend, Betsy, for a chat. Unfortunately, she did not know any of the big words or know what to do either, but at least I felt better.

Mommy ended her conversation with **Peds** of Huntington and stepped away from the telephone. Five minutes later, the phone rang repeatedly. Dr. Craft, on the line, was anxious to speak with Mrs. Noffsinger about the need for a trip to New York for a cardiac catheterization. She was reluctant at first but received reassurance from Dr. Craft. Mrs. Noffsinger then gave permission to his office to secure an appointment date for Joyce to have the procedure at the earliest date.

I have never known my mommy to be at a loss for words, but nary a word escaped from her lips. She looked pale and tears fell softly from her eyes. I put my arms around her waist giving her a hug, hoping that she would replace the twinkle in her eye washed away by tears. I grabbed a few tissues from the blue box to gently wipe her face, then we said our goodbyes and headed for home.

Playing outside the next morning, Mommy called me in to change clothes, brush my teeth, and comb my hair. Dr. Craft had called requesting to see me within one hour in his office. Little did she know I was covered in mud beyond her vision, needing a good scrub down. Oh, the famous look as she snatched me off the ground, grabbed my earlobe, rushing me into the shower. A quick sloshing around, a washcloth across my face, and we were ready to jump out of the tub, dressed in a flash, into the car, and arriving downtown where there was no parking in front of his office. Hesitantly, Mommy let me out at the curb going in alone while she searched for a space. Recognized at once by medical staff, I was escorted down the hall to one of the patient rooms. Mommy arrived at the office after parallel parking around the corner. Directed back to where I was waiting, Dr. Craft joined us with his recommendations:

"I know Nurse Helen spoke with you, but I wanted to personally talk with you about the importance of the procedure and your daughter's health. Here in Huntington, we do not have equipment needed to diagnose correctly Joyce's heart issues. A trip to New York's St. Mary's Hospital in Manhattan would give the answers and improve Joyce's quality of life."

I woke up the next morning to the tune of Mommy informing me there was no time to dilly-dally. I picked up Betsy from the floor, got dressed, and struggled putting on my black-and-white saddle oxford shoes. I called for Grace as to which string goes first—right over left or left over right. She hesitated but eventually helped get the string and bow looking correct. Mommy was waiting patiently at the front door with keys in hand until the shoe bows looked perfect. I side-stepped to the little girl's room just as Mommy was ready to go out the front door, which did not make her happy. Daddy honked the horn many times making me nervous, and hurrying tinkled a little in my panties. "Everybody ready to take a trip? I thought it would be a great idea to venture through the beautiful West

Virginia mountains and on up to New York. How does that sound? Joyce, do you have your dolly?"

"Yes, Daddy, got her right here in my lap."

I was so busy talking to Daddy I did not realize the difference in the back seat. Nice, clean, and something strange. The floor was missing! Instead, below was a mattress that was as comfy as my bed with a pillow, top sheet, and coverlet. What is this all about? Usually, my feet dangle down, yet now rest soft on light blue covers. 'Tis a puzzlement.

Grace was not blabbing like usual 'cause she wants to be the first to tattle-tale when something is new. Is Daddy gonna give her a whippin' if she blabs?

Daddy explained the bed he made fits down over the hump in the back seat. When traveling, I can lay down comfortably and sleep. Pretty neat, huh? Blankets provide cushions and comfort just like a mattress. Meanwhile, Grace can curl up on the seat reminiscent of being in her own bed. I say that's pretty neat!

While traveling, Grace and I can play games, look out the window, color, and do whatever keeps us out of trouble. Mommy made activity bags filled with crayons, cards, colored pencils, snacks, and various other stuff to keep us contented. "Moo!"

The mountain roads are narrow and scary. Big trucks pass forcing you either to the outer edge of the road or so close you could kiss or lick the dripping water off the rock. Looking up from the game board, I noticed the heavy white fog hugging the mountain low this morning. "That's God's blanket hanging down from heaven keeping us warm," Mommy explained. Miles of beautiful trees topped off with a mist against a beautiful perfect sky captured my attention.

Everyone complained about starving, so Daddy pulled into a little place called Jack's Drive Inn for lunch. The server, dressed in shorts, funny square hat, ruffled apron stained with mustard, short-sleeved top gliding on roller skates, arrived at our table. Daddy was impressed as she twirled around at our table before bumping into the fresh flower vase. She introduced herself as Barbara Jo from Red House. The menu was simple—just burgers, fries, Cokes, coffee, and iced water. Mentally recording our selections, she then skated back away, returning a few minutes later with straws, silverware, beverages, napkins, and ketchup. No mustard? I got a brief whiff of the hamburgers on the grill and anxiously waited for the arrival of my junior bacon cheeseburger. Another server delivered a pitcher of iced tea, mayo, salt, pepper, and several packets of yellow mustard. Yes! Last but not least, the burgers and fries arrived majestically on foot. The burger, at least a quarter pounder, tomato, lettuce, onion, and sesame bun, arrived with ample crinkle hot, hot fries to our liking. Hmm, hmm good! A vanilla milkshake topped off our lunch, and then it was time to get back into the car. Who would have thought that a "rinky-dink" off-the-beaten-path place like this served food tasting "out of this world" on a West Virginia mountain?

Back in the car, key in the ignition, Daddy hesitated to put the car in gear.

"Girls, your mother and I need to tell you something. We should have told you earlier, I am sorry. Dr. Craft has scheduled an appointment for you, Joyce, at St. Mary's Hospital in New York. At that time, they will evaluate your heart for a congenital defect. Previously, he heard something that he would like other doctors to hear. People travel from all over the world to see the doctors at St. Mary's."

Early Monday morning, Daddy was behind the wheel, eyes clearly focused on the road. Mommy was flipping through pages of *Gardening Today* magazine, while Grace's nose was permanently stuck inside this month's *Teen*. I, on the other hand, was quiet as a mouse, trouble free, cuddled with Betsy resting safe 'n' sound. I asked Mommy at breakfast if the doctors could fix Betsy's arm. The stuffing was falling out of her arm and needed attention. A puzzled look flashed across her face, but hey, grown-ups don't know everything! Going into the big city of New York, we planned to stop for dinner and take a little time to relax. The car needed gas, so Daddy would like to make a "one-stop, fill up, eat" and be on our way. I didn't want to go in, sit, order, and wait 'cause I was ready to eat, stretch my legs, and climb into bed.

Daddy found an Esso station three miles up the road. His plan was to fill up, pick up snacks, and continue down to the Sheraton Hotel across the street from St. Mary's Hospital. Eating, well, whatever happens to be on the right side of the road will be dinner. Once in the hotel, Mommy and I can tidy up tonight and be clean for my appointment in the morning. Daddy will relax and read the paper or snooze while Grace can watch TV or whatever.

By the time we reached the city, all four of us were ready to get out of the car. Evening was fast approaching, the day had been hard on each one of us, especially our driver. The rest of us could hang loose, sleep, but Daddy had to always be ready for anything. Traffic in the city was heavy, busy, and some not nice. Daddy pulled into the hotel going inside to register. Intrigued by the lights across the streets, I looked out the back window mesmerized! My eyes were glued to the huge red building across the street. Surrounded by lights, the vision took my breath away. Grand and mysterious yet welcoming to the eyes and a little spooky. Tomorrow Mommy and I will venture over to St. Mary's Hospital to see a new set of doctors who will listen to my "ticker." Hopefully, these "wizards" and I say that because these guys are supposed to be special heart doctors above all others. Do they have a crystal ball or something that the others don't have? Maybe a crystal ball that solves heart problems? Anyway, the place is calling my name for good things to come.

Daddy returned to the car after being in the office for a long time. I was afraid there was no room; however, he returned smiling, holding a key in his right hand. Our room was found on the left side of the hotel. Daddy unloaded the car as Grace, and I got comfortable stretching out on one of the beds. WOW! Two beds, a nightstand, and a tall lamp. I called this pretty fancy. I spoke up at once calling the bed space by the bathroom, making Grace unhappy. She usually yells out first, but I beat her this time. Mommy and Daddy never have a problem figuring out who sleeps where 'cause since saying "I do" they sleep in the same position. I turned on the TV to watch *Denis the Menace*, but Daddy changed the channel to the news. At first I was upset, but then realized he had been driving all day, so I figured it was best to let him have his way since he paid for the room. Besides, I am only five and do not have the nerve to tell my daddy to change the channel.

Four showers taken, four sets of teeth brushed, and it was time for the lights to go out. Tomorrow will be busy, and everyone needed a good night's rest. Cramped up in the car all day, I was restless and full of anticipation. Every hair on my head was standing straight up, and my eyeballs were wide awake. Grace and I got into bed, covered up, and within minutes, I thought she was asleep. I had too much nervousness inside me even though my eyelids refused to close. I needed my rest; my heart needed rest; now if only I could shut my eyes and rest! I began my usual antic of rolling my head back 'n' forth, left and right, picking up speed. Unfortunately, all this made me dizzy and angry at my sister. She yelled at Mommy which made her yell back at me. Now everyone was awake and getting zero rest.

Plan B: I positioned myself on my stomach and started kicking my left foot thinking it would be less disturbing. WRONG! That did not go well.

Plan C: Counting sheep went over like a deflated balloon. My brain must be all straw 'cause something just ain't right. Does the hospital carry new brain material?

"CLICK!" Lights out, but that didn't help with sleeping. Outside lighting entered the room, bringing in shadows from various sources. Now I definitely can't sleep! Then Daddy started to snore. It sounded like the winds of a tornado. My sheets would be off if I did not have a good grip on them. One more time I will roll over, hold on tight, and close my eyes. One thousand one, one thousand two, one . . .

"Ring! Ring!"

What already? It can't be morning!

Grace stirred but rolled back over. I looked for Daddy, but he was nowhere in sight. Water was running in the shower, so I figured he was in the bathroom. Mommy nudged Grace again, instructing her to hurry as the alarm clock was blaring. Moving at the pace of a slug, she continued toward the bathroom, but Daddy was in there. Now what? Traffic jam! Hurry up and wait. Grace and Daddy can sit back and relax, but Mommy and I needed to get ready. The bathroom was filled with steam thick as a milkshake from *The Creamery*. Stepping in, I could see nothing but steam yet could hear, "Joyce, get moving and hurry up! You know where your mouth is; now brush!"

Yes, I know that, but where is the brush? Since I couldn't see, I did not stay in the shower and was in and out in a flash. The doctors over at St. Mary's won't ask me to say, "Ahh!" We had an hour to get across the street to the hospital for my appointment. I wet my two index fingers with water, dabbed them on my face, and I was ready to go.

Downstairs a Yellow Cab was waiting to take us across the street. I had never ridden in vehicle like this. The back seat had enough room to take a nap in or fight with Grace, whichever came first. Weakness and a strange flutter came over me as the cab pulled up to the curb. The door opened and I froze. Guess I am not as brave as I thought. Mommy grabbed at me, but I refused. I sat down on the floor and would not budge. The cab driver informed Daddy that there would be a charge if I continued to sit. His facial expression said it all, convincing me to move, or he would fix my heart another way without anesthetic!

Standing outside you could hear Grace laughing her head off. At this point, Daddy was aggravated, but I am not sure with whom he was more upset. His expression said it all, and it was in my best interest to move forward and get out of the taxi. Stepping into the lobby, my breath escaped me not due to my medical condition but by the sight of the tall white marble statue. Christ's eyes stared directly down at me, calming my nerves to a standstill. As I gazed upon HIS FACE, my fears withdrew. HIS arms reached downward, directing me to come forward and have peace. A gentle sensation flowed over my face and well beyond my toes. No longer anxious, I stepped forward with a smile. We walked beyond the statue following the white marble flooring. Three elevators listed all the areas of the hospital. Eventually we reconnected with The Halcomb Unit and Elevator Five.

Heading down the hall, we found a large reception area to the right. A nice lady dressed in a crisp white dress and cap greeted us at a desk in the corner. She was friendly and warm like a summer evening directing us to the nurse's station down the long hallway.

Giving Joyce's name, we were directed toward room number 25. She helped me up onto the table and informed Mommy and I, Dr. Wilson would be in before either of us could spell "Mississippi."

Dressed in one of "those" fashionable gowns with an open back, I was fussing and complaining when a tall, bearded face approached wearing wire-rimmed glasses and entered the room grinning.

"Hello, I am Dr. Wilson. You must be Mrs. Noffsinger and daughter Joyce, correct? I am so glad to meet you both. Joyce, do you know why your mommy brought you here?"

"Somethin' about my ticker does not tick right. That is all I know."

"That's good, Joyce. Is it all right if I take a listen to your heart with my stethoscope?"

"I guess so. Ask my mommy."

"Mrs. Noffsinger, is it OK if I listen to Joyce's heart?"

"Sure, Doctor, go ahead and take a listen."

Dr. Wilson lifted my gown and took this thingamagig hangin' 'round his neck, placing it on my chest. He closed his eyes as he listened intently to my beating heart. I started to speak, but he hushed me, placing his right hand on my mouth. Was that rude or what? Was he painting a picture in his mind of the "lub dubbing"? Could he draw me a picture of what he was hearing? I want to "see" what he heard.

I got to "see" all right, all the way down the hall to the next elevator. Two flights down for more x-rays. I won't have to worry about getting lost in the dark. I have had so many pictures that I should be able to provide my own lighting; I'll glow in the dark the rest of my life! Arriving in the x-ray department, the tech helped me out of the wheelchair and lifted me onto a long black table with a glass top. Cold as ice lying down, shivers went all the way up my spine. The tech, named Susan, rolled a huge camera over my chest. She walked away and hid behind a protective wall. Before she pushed the button, I waited for her to say "Cheese," but she only asked me to hold my breath. "BUZZ!" "You can breathe now." Rolling back the machine, I was helped off the table and aided back into the wheelchair. A nursing assistant whisked me down a non-familiar hallway to a different area. I kept thinking people come and go quickly in this place, not like Huntington where everyone moves at a slower pace.

CHAPTER 2

1960

Monthly visits to Dr. Craft's office in Huntington, WV, for the last four years show my heart condition has not improved. Dr. Craft and I have talked many times becoming good friends. He communicates with Mommy, but the doctor/patient relationship is something unique. In fact, he makes house calls when I'm feelin' poorly, and I do not know of any other doctor making special efforts such as these. Mommy only has to give him a call and he's by my house within an hour or two. Dr. Craft seldom refers to me by my given name preferring to call me "Miss ESP," standing for extra special patient. Is that because he knows my phone number by heart? St. Mary's in New York keeps open communications with Dr. Craft so that my records can be studied simultaneously. My heart and body is still growing, and when I am a little older, I will return to New York for further evaluation.

I just had my eighth birthday. I will attend Sacred Heart School where the classes are small, and teachers will stay with you the entire day. ALL DAY! YUCK! During recess, most of the students go out to the playground, but I stay inside to straighten up the books in the library or wash the blackboards. I wonder why they call it a "blackboard" when the color is green?

Tonight, while eating dinner, an event took place outside the dining room window. I noticed a bunch of dancing bugs outside. No, they were not waltzing or doing the jitterbug, but I was so excited I almost lost my breath. Securing my napkin under my belt, I mistakenly added the corner of Nana's holiday tablecloth. I could not control myself; running to the window, the cloth, my plate, and a few extra items followed, crashing into the floor. Meatballs started rolling as spaghetti strings darted from the sides of my mouth, not pleasing my mother's eyes. I knew the chocolate pudding was all over my face, but I headed for the large window in the hall. I had to get a close-up view of the performance outside featuring the bugs! There, beyond the swing set a group of light bugs began their routine, magically prancing around turning their lights on and off. Rhythmical geniuses floating in darkness with a hint of light at the right time. Beaming with so much excitement, I should be lighting up myself. Spitting on my two first fingers, I scrubbed my face and hands clean with Ivory soap before scurrying out the door. I never creamed Mommy would be upset after doing all that! Her anger produced large droplets of fluid that started running out her nose. Her blue eyes turned ruby red, setting my hearts flutter into hyper speed. Due to the "bug" mission's importance, I was unconcerned I had left a beautiful spaghetti tattoo on newly bought white guest towels. Swinging the door open, I darted out cupping my hands together, catching five little critters all anxious to escape. Keeping my hands tightly together, peeking in I saw one beady-eyed critter staring back. My hands opened as their little feet tickled the insides. Suddenly their lights came on. The little bug lights started flickering as though talking in their own electrical code. I had to tell my family and ran inside to share.

"Mommy, hurry and see."

"What is wrong, are you OK?"

"Look what I got."

"Joyce Helen, you know better than to bring insects inside the house."

"Mommy, these are not insects; they are bugs, special bugs that light up! See them got batteries."

"For heaven's sake, Joyce. They have no batteries. God made them perfectly. Now take these, these perfect . . . whatever outside and go wash your hands. Now!"

"But, Mommy—"

"But Mommy nothing."

I had something else to say but changed my mind and did exactly as I was told. The sad faces of my little friends slowed my heartbeat; was it going to stop? I needed to tell Mommy, but she was already upset enough for one night, so I kept quiet.

Wanting to make her feel better I offered to clean the kitchen. Declining my offer, Mommy gave me a mason jar to collect bugs for later after my homework and kitchen cleanup was completed. I accepted, tiptoed past Daddy sleeping in his chair, and went to work. The evening air was cool and so distracting I almost forgot why I was outside. Zipping by my nose, one of those cute lightning bugs reminded me of my mission. I needed to get up and scoop up the critters.

Evening was upon us and my name would soon be echoing throughout the neighborhood to come inside. There she went; time was up, and I only had two critters in my jar. Oh well!

Mommy was waiting on the back porch under the yellow light. My mason jar was glowing with two little bugs. Stepping inside, Mommy's hand dropped down halting my step inside.

"Where do you think you're going with that jar, young lady?"

"To my room, Mommy, to my room."

The phone rang, stealing Mommy away from my presence, giving me the opportunity to hide the jar of critters under my bed. Twenty-five minutes later, returning she kissed me good night. Her right big toe slammed into the jar, sending it halfway across the room. My heart skipped not one but two beats! Three beats! I was in a heap of trouble. My two little critters started lighting up, sending emergency messages: "Help! Help! Help!"

"What is this, Joyce Helen? Outside where it belongs!"

"OUTSIDE? But, Mommy, it is cold outside."

Immediately her famous stare was heading my way.

"Joyce, you don't understand. I buy bug paper for cabinets, fly paper for the air, and traps for the house all to keep critters out! Take this . . . this jar and its contents outside and turn off the lights. Get ready for bed and do not forget to brush your teeth, wash behind you ears, and say your prayers."

"Can I sleep outside with my bug friends?"

"Joyce . . ."

"Mommy, I cannot sleep thinking my tiny light friends are alone on the porch; they might get scared. Can I ask another question?"

"Yes, ask me anything."

"Where is the switch to turn off the bug's light? I did not find one."

"Joyce . . ."

Reluctantly, I took my little friends outside. Before leaving them on the porch, I apologized,

kissed the jar, and sat the jar down. My eyes teared as I returned inside.

I could not sleep thinking about my little bug friends out in the cold. I dreamed about them shivering and freezing outside. I tried to paint a dreary picture to make Mommy feel like a bad wicked witch. However, she was definite about keeping them outside, and even if she were a good witch, there was no way I could change her mind.

The sounds of morning were in the air. Early birds singing reminded neighborhood creatures it was time to crawl out of bed, get moving, and sing. Daddy's fingers were gripped solidly around his cup of steaming hot coffee as he read over his AAA travel map. Soon his eyes would be fixed on the roads leading out of Huntington to Manhattan. Hey, I'm a kid needing a cuddle from my dolly, Betsy, who always helps me rest no matter where I lay my hair, curled or straight. Mommy was ready to go with her magazines in hand. Soon she would be here in the front seat, sittin' 'n' flippin' through the pages of the current *McCall's Magazine*. Every month she spends hours dreaming her house was picture perfect like the ones in the advertisements. No chance of that 'cause little munchkins living under this roof mess things up while she's not lookin'. I'm not sure who she's referrin' and blaming for the chaos. Grace, on the other hand, was hogging the bathroom putting curlers in her short brown hair. I did not understand why she needed to be "dolled up" sitting down in the backseat of the car traveling to New York. Who does she expect to see on the side of the road? Elvis or somebody important? Well, all this excitement was for me, and Mommy did not bother to curl my hair. We were on a mission to see the great "ticker" doctor in the big City of Manhattan. Am I special or what?

The three of us were loaded in the car as Daddy was ready to turn around at the bottom of the floodwall. Holding Betsy close, I noticed a large hole in her right arm. Immediately I started screaming, "Mommy, Mommy, we can't leave now! I have an emergency!"

"Joyce, what's wrong, honey, are you in pain, bleeding, or something?"

"No, Betsy's arm has a hole. Is there a dolly hospital somewhere?"

Here comes the look! Ignited on Mommy's face headed my way coming across the front seat to the back. I could not tell if her answer was "yes" or "no," so I quietly sat back down in my seat and waited.

Silence, total silence surrounded the four of us sitting in the car. Was the car suddenly broken down, or was Mommy and Daddy beyond mad at me thinking my dolly's arm problem would stop our trip to New York? Grace and I were told to get out of the car and go inside. Mommy and Daddy remained talking, sometimes yelling for another fifteen minutes. I wanted to peek through the bedroom door but dared not to be nosey. Well, both of them came inside. Mommy grabbed the pitcher of iced tea from the refrigerator as Daddy made a trip to the little boy's room. As usual several cubes of ice escaped from the metal trays as Mommy raised the cold handle. Within ten minutes, four

Welches jelly glasses of tea disappeared. Mommy, Grace, and I went back to the car except Daddy who answered a phone call adding fifteen minutes. I thought sure I was gonna have to go back in and go potty, but I heard the front door slam. Returning, Daddy opened the driver's side door, stuck in his head, then pointed his right thumb at us like a hitchhiker saying, "Out." Unknown to Mommy, Grace, and me, he had received a phone call while in the house from work demanding he report within the next few hours. Now a different means of transportation to New York was needed as soon as possible.

Everyone got out of the car again and into the house for a family powwow. Grace was all upset 'cause her face was all dressed up and now there was no place to go. Mommy was in a tizzy not knowing how we would make the appointment date on time in Manhattan. Well, being a kid, I got my dolly and went back to my bed for a snooze. A lot had to be worked out before Daddy reported to work that evening. Mommy fixed a pot of black coffee so they could work things out as Grace sat in the living room looking at herself in a mirror while watching the *Rifleman*. She later informed me Johnny Crawford was not too bad to look at, so the day was not a total loss. Within a few hours, everyone was cool and calm as the family crisis was solved. Mommy got on the house phone searching for a means to Manhattan. However, she was unsuccessful in finding neither cheap nor quick. As luck would have it, neighbors Bonnie and Jim volunteered to take both Mommy and I down to the train station later that evening to catch the B&O FLYER to Manhattan. The trip would be long, but we had to get there in our scheduled time for my procedure.

A change of plans at the last minute was a hair-raising experience for all of us. Daddy hated that he was not going to take Mommy and I up to get my procedure. Grace was upset because she had planned on being away, and none of her school assignments were completed. The three of them were running in all directions and me, well I am trying to figure out where in the world my dolly was.

Daddy was no longer working on the waterfront. He had secured a new position with General Motor with over-the-top medical benefits. However, one drawback required him to be on the road twenty days a month. Unfortunately, because of this requirement, he will be unavailable to take Mommy and I to New York. Grace will stay with neighbors Bonnie and Jim overnight until Daddy gets home. They live next door to us, and Grace has a house key to get whatever she needs.

The ride to the station lasted twenty minutes. A nice guy unloaded our suitcases from Jim's car and took them inside the large station on Cooper Street over to the ticket counter. Mommy gave him fifty cents, and we were on our way. Once inside, they announced our boarding call. The voice echoed several times high in the ceiling. Walking toward the train, my bladder made an urgent call of its own, needing immediate attention. I slipped away to the little girl's room without disturbing Mommy deep in conversation standing in line with another passenger. She had no idea of the trouble I was having, and more importantly, she didn't notice I was gone. The line continued boarding as tickets were taken and seats assigned. Alone in the station bathroom with that last bit of paper on the roll, I heard our final boarding call.

CHAPTER 3

"All aboard Train #257, Track #3. All aboard. Last call."

Tugging away at my waistband, losing my balance, I fell flat on my face. My eyes and nose were inches away from the floor as I noticed a multitude of ants marching by two by two. My baby blues crossed yet focusing on a piece of gum positioned on the cement floor. Unable to stand, my antics had managed to produce filthy hands, new white socks dusted in soot, and sneakers an interesting tinge of black. I know, I know a kid of eight usually doesn't have much thought on "life," but give me a break, I do. I escaped from the walls of the bathroom climbing out on all fours. Stepping out beyond that door, I was grabbed from behind, jolting my sick heart into cyber-speed. Dizziness and weakness caused me to faint. Two gentlemen caught me before I crashed to the floor as paramedics arrived. After their medical review, I was released from their care then handed over to the anxious arms of my mommy. Our eyes met; she grabbed my right hand, and we scurried to the train. Can she read my mind and know my secret? Boarding the train, the conductor helped us up the two steps. Mommy handed our tickets to the tailored gentleman in the blue suit. A rush of steam lifted my dress, causing a blushing of my face. The kind words spoken by the conductor calmed my fears. Out of breath, I struggled to continue. The conductor inquired about my health, but

Mommy assured him I was fine. On the other hand, my heart was no longer in slow motion. I felt dizzy needing a chair before I collapsed (again). A porter named Jon came to my rescue, helping me to the first set of seats directly across the refreshment area. I thanked him with a single blink and nod of my head. Non-friendly words began building up inside Mommy, and I did not look forward to immediate conversations. Talking to the head conductor, Mommy quickly found a place beside me. I was glad to be aboard the train and moving but not ready to sit down beside Mommy not knowing what she was going to say. I could almost guess but didn't want to.

Embarrassed, Mommy's face was redder than a circus clown's nose. Was she about to blow, not her nose I might add? I pretended to be clueless as to why she was so upset but knew I would soon find out one way or another. The whistle blew signaling we would soon be in motion. The conductor informed us of The Club Car three cars back serving hot dogs, fries, and soda. I am not interested in eating, but curious enough, I went down for a look. A short nap was first on the "to-do" list being extremely tired and having been warned about the consequences of not getting enough rest. I had already tried to hide my breathing problem, and a few minutes of rest sounded good to me. Winded, I took her up on her suggestion and, within five minutes of closing my eyes, was dreaming high class. Shut-eye over it was time to check out the Club Car. I grabbed Betsy just as Mommy was walking toward the door.

Talk about scary! Opening the sliding door watching the moving train cars below gave me the "willies" causing my heart to quiver. Looking down seeing the two cars shift back and forth I froze in my footsteps. The conductor came to my rescue by whispering sweet words in my right ear, "Ice cream, you scream, we all scream for ice cream," several times clearing any hesitation. Instantly I forgot about the MC problem (moving cars) and strutted across with ease eyes closed heading for my two scoops, please.

The Club Car had four round tables and seats attractively decorated with flowers and pre-folded napkins standing in clean glass goblets. Fancy, fancy, I thought but Mommy considered it extra "fluff" for extra money, nothing else. Did I mention the tables were "higher uppers"? Kids like me must be "booted" up to sit down. Sounds funny, doesn't it? Booted up to sit down, what a plan. By golly, which was what they had to do for me, but not for Mommy 'cause she's a grown-up. I saw a lady wearing a fancy mint green uniform that was short. The fabric wrapped up above her knees. Mommy would not let me out of the closet in somethin' like that—NEVER! EVER!

A tall lady approached our table handing out menus acting like "hot stuff." My impression was she appeared more of a "cool" cucumber. I thought she might need oxygen because of her height. Returning to take our order, I struggled to contain myself, yet I could not make a sound. I was on the edge of losing my "WWL'S." You know wits, words, and burst out laughing. Oh, I forgot to tell you she wore this hat with a feather that topped off her uniform giving me a good belly laugh. Mommy always told me to never hold back a sneeze, so I figured a laugh was the same.

I needed to let the laughter out. My insides were about to burst. Mommy sensed I was about to come unglued, so she firmly placed her right hand over my mouth preventing the slightest peep. I missed twirling, eating, and sipping from the curly straws in The Club Car. Mommy whisked me up and out so fast I did not realize we crossed those crazy wiggling cars. Once back in our seats, I was to sit, go to sleep, and NOT blink an eyelash unless the train derailed, or my bladder exploded. She was madder than the little kitten I dunked in the rainwater barrel last summer.

She yelled so loud that other passengers gave the evil eye "look" our way. I am not sure if the "eye" was directed at me or Mommy.

Being a kid, keeping track of time is not on my to-do list. Having to change trains, I worried my favorite PJs and Betsy would end up separated or lost from the rest of us.

Tired, I wanted to lie down, but we did not get the four seats. I had to rest sitting up, which was not comfortable. Finally, relaxed and ready to close my eyes, I heard the conductor: "New York Station fifteen minutes. New York Station is fifteen minutes. Gather your possessions."

Already? I rushed to put my shoes on but had to search for the one that had fallen under the seat. Oh, Mom's piercing blue eyes. Gathering my dolly and all her stuff, I noticed her right shoe was missing. I cried and again those "blue eyes" glanced my way as we moved to exit the train. Mommy sensed I was ready to come unglued, placing her hand over my mouth leaving my nose intact, free to breathe. This simple gesture prevented me from twirling, eating, and sipping from the curly straws—a triple whammy in one simple gesture.

She grabbed my right earlobe whisking me through the train car so fast I do not remember crossing those crazy wiggling cars. Can you believe that! Back in our seats, Mommy was so upset the veins in her neck were bouncing in and out creating a massive commotion among the passengers. I think she was beyond furious. Sitting across the aisle from us, another passenger stood up and looked our way with an "evil" eye. Is that a "mommy" thing? I could not decide if this person was lookin' at me, but I felt vibrations in my chest. A flutter of sorts and I knew it was time for me to relax, but how?

Once the cabin dimmed, the clickety-clack rocking motion of the train made falling asleep easy. However, a brief time later, my mind started to harass me with constant irritating thoughts. I even woke up Betsy McCall to see if she had a solution to shut my mind off and calm me down. I admitted to her about those thoughts were private and she was not to blab to anyone on the train. I had been telling everyone I was brave, but deep down inside, I was scared beyond scared.

Morning was approaching and we would be at the station., getting off and taking the cab over to St. Mary's Hospital for my "cath-er-other" something. Oh, here comes the conductor. He's yelling about something.

"Grand Central Station, ten minutes. Gather your belongings."

"Grand Central Station, ten minutes. Gather your belongings."

"Wait! I cannot go! My dolly! She is missing a shoe!"

The conductor came over saying he could not hold the train for a doll shoe as there was a schedule to keep. I was an inch away from an emotional disaster. Nonetheless, my dolly was now minus a shoe. It was a good shoe as I paid ninety-nine cents at Woolworth's. I was beyond mad but forced to be silent. Oh, brother, now I am nervous! I think I got wet my pants. Guess I am gonna have to go around wet. Mommy and I shared the bathroom brushing our teeth so my breath would not stink when the doctors say, "Open up and say, AHH!"

What about my panties? Do I tell her or go to the hospital wet? I was hoping to have breakfast before going over to "the big red house," but we just passed the little café. Was Mommy losing it? I didn't know what she wanted to do about eating or anything else. I was so confused, and Betsy was in no position to offer any suggestions. Since losing her shoe, she couldn't think or act straight. I was gonna do my best to keep quiet, but I did not know how long. "Ooh! I feel the wheels slowing down. Guess we have arrived at Grand Central Station."

"WOW! Look at this! Grand Central Station is somethin' else!" Outside taxi cabs are lined up ready to take passengers to places of their choice. The gray skies just unloaded several buckets of rain, and massive puddles of water lined the street in front of the station. One of the taxi drivers pulled up to the curb stopping to load our luggage. Unfortunately, in doing so, the dirty street water was splashed all over Mommy and myself. Safely inside the cab, we were informed the Sheraton and St. Mary's Hospital was about two blocks on the left. Not bad but the streets were lined with bumper-to-bumper traffic, meaning a quick escape out of my wet panties would not be possible. I asked why all the traffic. The driver informed us a new sports arena had just opened up and a major basketball team was playing in a few hours and "go figure the rest." Go figure! Do you mean a basketball team is the holdup? I'm sitting in wet underclothes and can't get to the hotel 'cause of basketball. Horsefeathers! Ninety minutes later, which seemed like days in wet panties, we arrived at the Sheraton. A nice bellhop unloaded our things, bringing them inside to the front desk where Mommy registered. Signing-in providing all the pertinent information took forever. The sun was starting to escape behind the tall buildings and the brisk evening air was settling down. We followed the nice young man into the elevator stopping at Room 239 at the end of the hall. My eyes were glued looking out the large picturesque glass window. I was about to lose my religion trying to keep my mouth zippered. Mommy planned for a short rest period, but time had marched faster than I thought, and now it was time to report over to St. Mary's. The front desk would go ahead and send our luggage upstairs while Mommy and I went across the street.

Mommy called her neighbor Bonnie asking if Grace could spend the night while Daddy worked out of town in his new position with General Motors. She didn't want Grace to be home alone while we were in New York for one night.

Mommy and I were up with the chickens; here we go again with the invisible poultry. I kept waiting for Mommy to stop at the coffee place well hidden in a nook at the hospital, but she made no effort. She surprised me by going directly to the outpatient area for my catheterization. I started to get nervous as we rode up the elevator, yet I wanted to get this over with so I could go snuggling with my dolly.

We headed up to the surgical floor to check in and speak with Nurse Diane. Within minutes, I was arm-banded, re-dressed in a high-fashioned gown with no personality, holes and an open back! Whoever designed this piece of clothing needs to go back to the drawing board or be flunked out of design school! Now I must hang around with my backside hanging out! What kind of place is this?

The x-ray picture was taken right on schedule, then over to the lab for blood work and lastly a place called the EKG room. Here in this room, they connected my heart to a machine that wrote a message in squiggly lines. Who says I can't write legibly? Again, I'm in the room alone wishing I had my dolly to keep me company, but now I wonder what they did with my mommy.

"Knock! Knock! This is transportation looking for a Miss Joyce. May we come in?"

"Why not, you're going to anyway."

"Let me check your wrist band, please. Thank you."

A long bed on wheels entered through the curtains, and two staff members went ahead to slide me over to the bed on wheels. Laying down I was covered with green sheets and secured (strapped) on the bed. Within a couple of minutes, the two dressed in green, and I went through several double doors into a well-lit ice-cold room. Brrrr! Don't they pay for the heat? I think the room should at least be warm. Why don't they turn it on? Numerous staff roamed around with a specific purpose and were busy. Positioned over onto a very narrow table, I was wired for sound, breathing, temperature, and other vital statistics. Do the machines measure my shivering rate? The surgeon, Dr. Webb, walked over introducing himself and then we had a little discussion over the matter of sleep. While we were talking, nursing managed to insert an IV in my right arm and then my shaking slowed as I started to feel the effects of the anesthetics. I was curious about what was going to happen as I wanted to watch. Dr. Webb disagreed, telling me I could not be alert under any circumstances, putting me into a rage. My response was noted in my chart prompting Dr. Webb to increase the amount of sedation. Once again the medicine was injected into my arm, drifting me into a deep sleep so Dr. Webb and his team could begin the cardiac catheterization.

Two hours later I woke up feelin' like I had been run over by a sixteen-wheeler or been out drinkin' 'n' now drunk. I only knew one thing: I felt "turrible." I never, ever want to feel this way again! Why would anyone drink too much knowing they would feel this way? My unfocused eyes were blinded by the extreme overhead lights. Gentle footsteps walked my way as a soft voice asked if I was in pain. The only problem she could help with was my need to sit up. The nurse gently responded that I could not move for at least six hours. SIX HOURS! I think six minutes is too long! My legs and head wanted to move on their own, and I had no control! The incision in my leg from the procedure ached and the surgical dressing was bulky and uncomfortable. How was I going to have a decent night of rest feeling this way? I have never been still this long unless asleep, but sometimes my legs or head move, having a mind of their own. Oh, and what if I need to, you know? I was given a "puddle pad" underneath me, so if I have to "go," I am to let it go!

All of it! Here comes one of the nurses. I did not think I could make a sound 'cause my mouth was so dry. I was in serious trouble not able to talk or scream, whispering, "Can someone bring me a milkshake, banana split. Pretty please with sugar on top." In comes one of the nurses with ice chips. She began feeding me like a baby. Although it felt refreshing, I did not understand why. I admit it felt good because my mouth was as dry as a desert. Just then a song popped into my mind:

"Dem bones, Dem bones, Dem dry bones. Dem bones, Dem bones, Dem dry bones. Dem bones, Dem bones, Dem dry bones, Now hear the Word of The Lord." Can you hear me? I grabbed the glass dumping those chips all over my face sending goose bumps all over. Why are they called "goose" bumps? "HONK!"

I really would have preferred a banana split with a dip of vanilla, chocolate, and strawberry ice cream and topped with a cherry! I can feel my throat closing thinking about that.

The day has been long and looking at Mommy over in the chair, I think she's half-half. Half asleep and half somewhere else, that's for sure.

Given the OK, I started to sit up with Mommy helping. Sitting on the edge of the bed, it took about five minutes before I felt comfortable to step down.

Slower than a turtle moving across the road, Mommy helped me get dressed. A nursing assistant came in the room to help me get ready for discharge and gather my belongings: one bunch of balloons and one bag of personal items to be taken downstairs. A knock on the door yielded Dr. Kneil. She had come to give us the results of the catheterization. Mincing no words, she went right to the point. "Joyce has a congenital condition known as aortic stenosis. Her aortic valve does not close properly meaning adequate oxygen does not flow correctly through the body. A certain amount of oxygen is needed for proper function of each organ every minute of life. Physicians in Huntington will have to keep a close watch on her until corrective cardiac measures are available. We can discuss options later. Feel free to contact us here at St. Mary's with questions or concerns."

Mommy thanked Dr. Kneil for stopping by and that we would see her soon.

I continued to keep my leg up in bed as we waited for nursing to complete the discharge paperwork and a ride to take us downstairs.

Discharge paperwork completed, now we wait for our ride downstairs to catch a taxi to the train station. Where are they? Did nursing forget to call? Mommy was back sitting in the corner chair by the window sleeping. Where are they?

I sure hope she doesn't fall out, and then what are we gonna do? Wait, I hear footsteps coming down the hall. I bet it's nursing coming to take us downstairs.

"Mommy, Mommy, wake up! It's time to go downstairs!"

Coming in the door was not nursing but Grace and Daddy! SURPRISE! I almost fell out of bed. Daddy had to catch me before I hit the floor. Betsy McCall followed right after landing on top of my head. All the commotion stirred Mommy enough to wake her, and boy was she surprised finding Grace and Daddy in the room. Her baby blue eyes widened as far as possible, and her smile was the size of California! Daddy went over to her and planted the biggest kiss on her, and I thought they would never come up for air.

Daddy explained business had slowed down on the road giving him a break letting him to go off to be with his family. Gave him a break, letting him off to get us here in New York.

Grace picked up my suitcase, Daddy grabbed the handles on the back of my wheelchair, and Mommy followed along as the four of us walked down the hall. I waved goodbye to nursing as the doors of the elevator closed. Momentarily I had trouble breathing realizing I was going home. Finally on the main floor, Daddy let Grace take the handles of my wheelchair as he walked ahead to fetch the car. The fresh air and wind felt so good on my face. I stuck my tongue out like some of the creatures do just to be silly. I have only been in the hospital a few days, but being outside felt like heaven. Daddy drove up to the curb, got out of the driver's side, and guided me into the backseat. Mommy and Grace got in the car while Daddy returned the wheelchair to the hospital lobby. All doors locked, we were on our way to the serenity of the mountains.

"When we gonna get there, Daddy? Are we there?"

Mommy had to remind me that travel by car took longer than traveling by plane. Although excited at first, I found out my "special" bed in the floor wasn't cracked up to be what I thought it was gonna be. Hard as cement as who wants to sleep on the sidewalk? Not me!

However, it was me when it was time for Grace and me to sleep while Daddy drove through the night so he could get back into town. He's scheduled to report to work tomorrow night, so he'll need to sleep sometime after we get home before reporting back to the city.

After being in the "big" city, all of us were looking forward to breathing clean air, quiet nights, and gazing at the stars from atop the floodwall on California Street. Neighborhoods in the area were friendly, sharing cups of sugar or butter in a heartbeat and eager to help one another any time of day or night. People living in New York don't do things like we do. Why is that?

The skies are even different in New York. Hidden by massive lights and buildings, the people miss all the messages sent by twinkling stars, songs sung by The Man in the Moon and who knows what else. New York can be noisy, crowded, and full of obnoxious "me-I-tis" drivers.

You know the ones who think they own the road. Forget about laws and do what they want whether it's wrong 'cause it does not matter. It's like they have no "heart."

Daddy's eyes were clearly on the road leading toward home. Mommy had "reprogrammed" and decided to watch the road helping Daddy stay safe.

On the other hand, Grace had not done a thing, meaning she still drooled over the guys in her teen magazines. For the life of me, I did not understand why she would do something so silly, but I was just a kid, what did I know?

Once out of the city, Daddy pulled off the main road where Mommy unfolded a large map stored underneath the front seat.

"What do I do, Harv? I can't read this."

"What language is this anyway? These lines go in all directions making no sense. Are we lost?"

"Here, Daddy, here let me help!"

A voice from the back seat was taking control of the situation and taking it fast.

"Daddy, we are 'this far' from the Howard Johnson Restaurant where we can have lunch before going on down the road."

I showed him the distance between my thumb and index finger of my right hand measuring about one inch firmly planted on the map. Daddy glanced, shook his head, continuing to drive no questions asked.

Although we had ventured out of the city, traffic was a nightmare. Bumper to bumper and the air was filled with exhaust. I didn't say anything to Daddy, but I believed we were lost.

You could hear yourself breathing. In the car everything was still, except my heart! It's beating a little awkward to get my attention. A little voice inside my head said, "You better button your lip and stop acting like a know-it-all. It is time to settle down and keep your thoughts to yourself.

This is hard stuff, yet I think it was the right thing to do.

Daddy finally got us back on a main road, and by that time, my stomach started to roar asking for something to fill the empty spaces. Daddy drove around, refusing to ask for directions. Signs displaying various food choices were seen on rooftops and advertising billboards.

Feeling lightheaded, I told Daddy I was in dire need and would eat at the first place he drove up to the side of the road. Grace looked at me, rolled her eyes, and remarked, "Daddy, are you really gonna drive up to any old place and eat?"

Daddy drove on about a mile or so then I spotted a sign. "Wait! There's a sign!"

> *The Corn Husk five miles on the left.*
> *Country pikin' at its best.*

Well, this is it! Daddy drove until we reached the place, and a fallen sign was covered in dried mud:

> *John's Spaghetti House where meatballs are tops!*
> *Two miles left at the light, Y'all come!*

Daddy whipped the car around so fast I thought we were gonna flip over. Two miles and left at the light the road looked like a dead end. He glanced at Mommy as if he wanted an "A-OK" before turning down the dirt road. Driving with caution, we reached a run-down wooden building with a large wraparound porch. A worn and tattered sign read:

John's Spaghetti House

Daddy pulled into the parking lot, stopped, turned off the engine, and stared. Mommy reached over, touching him on his left shoulder.

"Harv, Harv, are we going in?"

From the outside the building looked like it belonged to an Alfred Hitchcock movie. The sky was filling with darkening gray clouds, adding mystery to the air. Going in, a gentleman greeted us dressed in a black coat, tie, crisp white shirt, and black slacks. He provided us with a window seat fully dressed in a pressed fabric cloth, crystal seasoning shakers, and a small vase having three fresh white daisies. Harriet, our server, handed us a large menu that was perfectly designed. Slipping from my hands, the menu tipped the container of flowers all over my sister. Her smile flipped upside down into an ugly frown. Mommy's keen brown eyes never drifted far from my sight, making sure I stayed on my best behavior.

Grace was instructed to collect extra napkins to clean up the mess. Being the "perfect" child, she went into action clearing the area of flowers, drying wet areas, and resetting any dishes affected by the spill.

Once again we were all seated anxiously to enjoy a family meal. One server returned three minutes later with a basket of piping fresh rolls and beverages. The aroma drifted up into my nostrils, sending a unique message to my taste buds. My mouth overflowed with saliva as my tongue desired to smack my lips, yet Mommy was quick to remind me of my manners. Struggling to reach the table, our server walked to the right side carefully serving each of us managing to not drop a morsel. A plate of long thin noodles topped with juicy meatballs was placed in front of me. I was tempted to scoop up a bit with my fingers, but I knew that would land me in a heap of trouble. Mouth open, saliva flowing, and then all motion ceased. Mommy again reminded me to act like a lady. But I was just a kid.

Did she expect me to be perfect?

No desserts will be missing from the glass cabinets and heading for my stomach.

My funny bones quit laughing as I climbed in the back seat after hitting my forehead on the car door. OUCH! This actually worked better at resetting my heart rhythm than any method they have tried at the hospital. I will have to tell the doctors at the hospital about my new inventive procedure.

All night my insides were tossing and turning thinking about going across the street to the "big" red house. I began my usual antics of rolling my head back 'n' forth to encourage sleep. Picking up speed with each flip-flop motion aggravated Grace as well as making me dizzy. Hollering at Mommy adding to the noise ended up waking up everyone. I tried the quieter method of counting sheep: One, two, three . . . Wait! This little guy looked heavy! He would never get off the ground. Grace was fussing at me because I was making noise taking care of the sheep in my dream. She thought she was a know-it-all! Well, I had an idea. Plan B: Roll over on my stomach and kick my foot! That's bound to get back at her for being disrupting. That went well. Not exactly. My foot went to sleep while the rest of me remained wide awake. Silence and then the unexpected noise startled every hair on my head. My eardrums went into a roll sounding like an entire percussion section of *The London Symphony* playing inside my head. Mommy started to snore with such significance. I knew the walls would soon be moving to the rhythm of the tango.

I could not get up and put a plug in her mouth, but I wanted too! I was too embarrassed to tell her about the noise, but rest was nowhere in sight. I might as well give up on sleeping 'cause now my heart was racing, my legs were kicking and scared, I was scared!

Morning? It can't be morning! I had no sleep; my mind refused to settle down and the moon smiled back at me from my bedroom window.

Today, full of emotions, Mommy and I leave for New York one more time. Flying out of Huntington was not for fraidy cats, those prone to throwing up or have weak tickers.

Well, guess what, I fit into all those categories and here I am. The twisted, narrow, two-lane mountain road will put hair on bald heads or jump-start slow heart rates. That's me with the exception of bald head. The sweet mountain air is delightful and can keep a heart beating if The Big Guy upstairs agrees.

"Why would anyone want to travel on this old road, Mommy?"

"Joyce, you know this is the only airport serving Kentucky, Ohio and our wonderful state of West Virginia. The weather conditions on this mountain affect air travel. The forecast today reads 'cloudy' so passengers on today's flights can expect a bumpy ride. Be thankful you are able to travel today in order to get to St. Mary's. Most children are not as fortunate, so tonight be sure to get on your knees and thank Jesus for all His blessings on you."

Local churches and schools were planning blood drives to raise the B+ blood needed for my surgery. I am blessed because my blood type is not the more common one.

Proceeds from bake sales and other events as this will also help families such as mine.

Football and basketball game proceeds will go into the "heart" fund to aid families with medical bills.

Seated and strapped in a wheelchair, airport staff pushed me down the long corridor and into the plane cabin. Mommy followed behind aided by the flight crew for our trip to New York City.

The captain introduced himself as Robert B. and First Officer Walt C. Various information was shared such as weather reports, air speed, arrival time, and finally, the plane was cleared for takeoff.

I wanted to watch as the road dropped off, but the "chicken" in me wanted to run. However, my seat belt prevented me from moving and my heart started to race. Was it trying to keep time with the engines? I reached for Mommy to tell her I was lightheaded, but her eyes were buried in a dime store love book. I do not think I have ever seen her "in touch" with a book.

At the end of the runway, the plane turned as the engines switched to the highest speed. Up! Up and away into the sky.

My eyes closed as I breathed deeply inward. I was afraid to look out the window, but I wanted to. Just a peek?

Mommy did not notice, but I placed my nose on the small window to see what was down below. To my amazement, I watched the hills disappear as we traveled above the clouds.

WOW! I was impressed and definitely not depressed.

The two-hour flight ended with a rough landing at the New York Airport. At the gate, we were greeted by hotel staff providing a wheelchair to transport Mommy and I to the waiting taxi. Another employee informed us that our luggage would automatically be sent over to the Sheraton. Opening the door to the backseat, Mommy climbed in and then it was my turn.

The staff member whose name tag read Matthew folded back the leg supports of the wheelchair and grabbed my left hand as I stepped forward and stepped into the taxi. The ride from the airport took about forty-five minutes. I was overwhelmed at all the hustle and bustle of the big city. Downtown Huntington consists of only one main street, and I mean one. No crisscrossing streets to get lost on during holiday shopping.

Once inside the Sheraton, two familiar faces waved "hello" as Mommy registered for our room. Two hotel employees recognized us from earlier visits making me feel at ease. At this point I needed familiar faces, besides family ones, to ease the butterflies taking up residence in my belly. A bellhop approached asking me if I would like a wheelchair in my room. Another day I would have declined, but the day was taking its toll on me, and a ride sounded mighty good.

Finally, inside our hotel room, I kicked off my shoes, changed clothes, and was ready to relax and watch TV. Stations in New York offer more variety than the ones in Huntington. I could not wait to search through all the selections to find something new and exciting to watch. Unfortunately, Mommy had other plans for the evening. Exhausted from the day's events, we would order room service for the dinner meal. The choice wasn't the greatest, but I was able to order my kid-proof hot dog, fries, and ice-cold milk for myself.

On the other hand, Mommy wanted something more traditional: petite steak, medium rare, butter with her baked potato and salad with French dressing. Please don't forget the Coke or else we will all be in trouble.

Brushing my teeth was next on my agenda, which doesn't take but a jiffy for a kid since my teeth are small and not dirty. Mommy followed, but she takes longer than me. All was quiet until a blood-curdling scream came from the bathroom. Rushing out of bed, I went to check on Mommy knocking on the door. A roach had run across the sink while she was brushing her teeth. The locked door prevented my entering and lending a hand. Feeling helpless, I decided to scream along so Mommy would not feel alone until someone answered our call for help. If there is any doubt about the beating of my heart, well let me tell you—it beats fine! Right now, it is going at the speed of lightning after the visit from that four-legged varmint. I think we should forget about tomorrow and go back to West Virginia. My stomach just went into hysterics. Grumbling and roaring, I didn't think I've eaten all day!

I am nine and tomorrow my life will change big time. I have been pretending to be brave and tough. Guess I will see how "tough" I really am in the morning, but now it is bedtime.

Lights out!

Hall lights in the hotel outlined our room door. The footsteps of other guests sounded like giants. I didn't know if they were green, but they sure didn't know how to walk light as they go from room to room.

Mommy was sound asleep, cuddled up and rolled up on her side. I should be so lucky. I climbed out of bed going down on my knees folding my hands in prayer. It was a bit rusty, but I made the sign of the cross. I prayed to Jesus that tomorrow will be a good day and everything will be OK. A hymn came to mind, "God Will Take Care of You," and started playing in my mind. No amount of head banging or leg thumping could help me fall asleep. I laid in every corner, inch of the sheet, and both the foot and head of the bed to no avail. Sleep would not come, and the little voices inside my brain would not shut up!

Counting to one thousand made no difference; my sheep were jumping, and my eyes were wide awake.

How could my mommy be rude and sleep through all this? I expect those chickens will make their presence known soon. Here chickee! chickee!

The hallway noise began at the same time as morning sunlight creeps around the curtain frame of our hotel room. Mommy thought we had woken up at the same time, but in reality I did not have a wink of sleep. I can honestly say it wasn't the chickens, but my mind kept on and on, and now I do not remember what kept me awake.

Mommy and I shared the bathroom brushing our teeth and combing our hair. I went looking for my dolly and could not figure where she could have run off to during the night. What kind of problems can a doll have? She doesn't have any reasons to be afraid. Not anxious to get downstairs until Mommy suggested we have breakfast at the small café' in the hotel. I have been wanting to eat there since coming to New York.

To my amazement, that little suggestion perked me up completely, practically letting me forget about the next twenty-four hours and get some rest.

Mommy decided to have eggs, bacon, and wheat toast. The pictured biscuits 'n' gravy called to me, but I opted for the lighter side of two slices of rye toast, whipped margarine, strawberry jelly, two soft-boiled eggs, and cold milk. My glass of milk must be iced cold, freezin' cold 'causse that makes it good.

Mommy paid the check, and then it was time to take a cab across the street to St. Mary's Hospital. The hotel manager called the cab not realizing one was already waiting at the double doors. Walking out the front doors, Mommy and I found two cabs waiting to take us across the street to St. Mary's.

"Look, Mommy, two cabs; one for you and one for me."

"Joyce, now don't be silly; we will only take one cab to the hospital."

We both got into the first cab, and as the driver closed the door, I knew then there was no turning back.

Reality settled in riding across the street the morning of May 19, 1961. I had known I needed surgery, but I never took it seriously. As the cab stopped at the hospital entrance, my heart went into a major flutter. I didn't understand 'cause I had been coming here since 1957 for cardiac checkups, but today was different. No longer did it look like an enchanted castle, and today I would not be going home right away.

The driver opened the cab door. Mommy stepped out, but I did not. I may look calm, but I was very much afraid. Did I mention my legs were stuck like glue to the seat? Have I turned chicken? There's that word again! The driver mentioned to Mommy that the meter would continue to run as long as I remain seated in the cab. She said not a word, but her facial expression convinced me to change positions. I decided it was in my best interest to leave the cab even though I wanted to sit. As I was helped in a wheelchair, the warmth of the sun had an amazing effect. My spirit was renewed, and my attitude changed.

The storybook castle I have visited for years was once again before me. I looked at Mommy wondering how a wheelchair and I would climb those many steps. Puzzled, several other wheelchair patients arrived having the same concerns. Then a group of hospital employees arrived by bus. Without further waste of time, one by one the employees exited the bus, helping the wheelchair patients up the stairs. One gentleman, dressed in a fine suit, greeted Mommy and I graciously and took control of my chair from my mommy. Turning it around, he tilted the chair backward then guided me up the stairs like a pro within a couple of minutes. He disappeared as quickly as he arrived at the bottom of the stairs. Neither of us got his name to thank or give him a tip. Asking around, we later found out that my transporter was the director of cardiac surgery, Dr. John Smith.

Stunned that a man of his importance would take the time out of his schedule to lift a patient up one hundred steps "floored" both me and Mommy. What a blessing to start off the day.

Going through the double doors, Mommy and I were a bit unsure of ourselves after our brief encounter with an "angel." Both of us were having trouble navigating our surroundings until a familiar sight jolted both our memories to make the right turn needed.

There, there stood the tall white marble statue of Christ. Again, taking my breath away just like the first time in 1957 four years ago. Today, as our eyes met, I was again touched by His Presence. No matter what happens tomorrow during surgery, I will not be alone. Free of all uncertainty, I was stronger than I had ever been before. Then Christ winked at me! I needed to keep this to myself 'cause no one will believe me, but HE winked! Do you know why I know? Because God is God, and He can do anything!

We continued our journey down the hall as the sun's rays glistened off meticulously polished marble floors. Taking my hand, Mommy and I entered the elevator stopping on Halstead, the children's floor. As the double doors opened, the nurse in charge greeted us.

"Good morning, can I help you?"

"Yes, I am Mrs. Noffsinger, here with my daughter, Joyce."

The greeting area on the fifth floor was massive. The Lance Unit is divided into several sections depending on the level of care needed by your child. Pediatric cardiology was the biggest section straight down the hall. Boy was I now getting nervous as the nurse checked her admittance schedule finding my name on top of page 2. Getting on her phone, she called for a Candy Striper to show Mommy and I to my room. An ID bracelet was placed on my right wrist before the Candy Striper arrived to show us to my room. I hoped no one had heard my stomach 'cause it sounded mighty unhappy. Reality had set in, and there was no turning back. Taking the elevator to the fifth floor, you could still hear the moans and groans.

Am I gonna throw up in the elevator? I sure hope not 'cause that would not make a good impression. At least let me throw up in my room! Getting off the elevator, I was surprised to find the area colorfully decorated with lions, tigers, and sea creatures covering several areas. However, I was not sure if I was on a safari or needed a pair of goggles or swimsuit.

Art supplies were available in one nook for up-and-coming artists of any age. I was ready to escape this medical jargon and go draw but . . .

"Hello, I am Nurse Jamison, and I will be your nurse today. Follow me."

Mommy and I followed the nice lady. I did more than lag behind; I was not about to miss a step and mentally made notes of the layout just in case I needed to escape. Nurse Jamison checked me in then showed Mommy and I into my room. Situated close to the charting and refreshment area, I figured I could get anything I wanted anytime. However, I later found out that was not the case. I was disappointed realizing my room was not private and the view consisted of the loading area. Some views! While Mommy went searching for ice, I changed into my (old) new pink PJs and jumped into bed. Hard as a rock!

This bed had no bounce just like the one over at the hotel. Do beds not come comfortable anymore? I bet they bought them at the same time as the hotel at a discount price or GOB (going out of business).

KNOCK! KNOCK! Two white coats entered asking for Joyce. Mommy informed them I was in the bathroom. Back in bed, they checked my right wrist band then a large rubber band was placed tight around my left arm. I thought my eyeballs were going to jump out of their sockets. I was asked to make a fist, but at this point, I was feeling pins and needles in my arm, and I really wanted to do something besides making a fist. I didn't faint, but I was not feeling normal. I survived the withdrawing of blood, but now all I wanted was to be left alone. But that didn't happen as we headed toward another area of the hospital.

Downstairs the halls were bustling with activity. The area was filled with staff and patients going in all directions reminding me of storms we had at home in the mountains. My driver, who happened to be the wheelchair pusher, was a nice young person dressed like a candy cane, you know, red-and-white-striped jumper. She checked in at the desk, put the brakes on, and said goodbye. I sat there, this time patiently, until the technician named Pam pushed me into a room with a semi-cushioned bed and pillow. Naptime? My hospital gown was folded back, and cold metal stickers were stuck to my skin. Talk about cold and weird. Did they forget to pay the electric bill 'cause it sure is chilly? A wire connected to stickers were hooked to a balloon-looking gizmo. This long arm attached to another machine with wires wiggling like it was nervous. These so-called arms wrote funny penmanship on moving paper. I thought my writing was bad. Sister Agnas would be yelling and screaming if I turned my homework in looking like this.

After the test, a stretcher came by as my pickup. I got to hop up and lay down on well-pressed green sheets. I thought this was odd needing three "green" dressed people to get me. Are we going to Mars? The more I thought about this, it was all very odd. Traveling down a narrow hallway, it dawned on me I skipped breakfast.

"When does a kid get to eat? I am starved and could . . . let me see, I do not think I want horse meat, but a steak that would be cow and I eat cow. Yes, that would be nice."

"Sorry, kid, no eat ng or drinking at this time. You are NPO."

"No, I am not! Are you outta your mind? I can eat whenever I want!"

"Not this morning, kid. Doctor's orders."

Within a couple of minutes, the green gang and I wert through several double doors into a well-lit room ice cold. Numerous staff roamed around each with a specific purpose and busy. Positioned and over to a thin table, exceptional care was taken to slide me to the exact spot. I was strapped on, hooked up to various machines reading my heart rate, breathing, pulse, and other numbers. Several other staff members entered the room taking specific places in front of different machines. My surgeon, Dr. Webb, entered walking over, asking me if I were comfortable and that within a few minutes we would be starting. The anesthesiologist spoke, telling me that I would soon be feeling a warm sensation in my arm, making me drowsy. I told him I was a nosey child and wanted to watch, but he disagreed, telling me it was not surgical protocol, and it would be best if I slept. I disagreed this time demanding I wanted to watch. I kept telling him I wanted to be a surgeon one day, and why not get an early start on watching surgical techniques? The room was getting a little warmer, but I still was arguing that I wanted to be alert and see what was taking place.

Once again he disagreed telling me I could not, putting me into a rage. My response was noted in my chart, prompting Dr. Webb to increase the amount of sedation. Slowly injected into my arm, I drifted into a deep sleep so the doctors could begin the cardiac catheterization. Two hours later, I woke up groggy 'n' sore. Feelin' I had been run over by a sixteen-wheeler or been out drinkin', I only knew how bad my head was throbbing, and all I wanted to do was sleep. I felt bad and never wanted to feel this way again.

My unfocused eyes were blinded by the extreme overhead lights. Gentle footsteps walked my way followed by a soft voice asking if I felt any pain. My only problem was the need to sit up. The nurse's response was that I could not move for at least six hours. In shock, I knew being still that amount of time would be impossible. Even while sleeping I bang my head or slam my leg up and down 'cause they have a mind of their own. That did no good for Mommy's tone of voice was frightening.

Dr. Webb stopped by to speak to my parents, but they had stepped out of the room to get a bite to eat in the cafeteria. They planned to return in about thirty minutes knowing I was to be discharged and then head back to the mountains of West Virginia. Sure enough, thirty minutes later, Dr. Webb returned as promised with my folks following close behind "snug as a bug."

We managed in all our "closeness" anxiousness to hear the report and get on the road. Dr. Webb got right to the point explaining I have a congenital condition known as aortic stenosis. Since my valve does not close properly, adequate oxygen does not flow correctly through my body. Her pediatrician should watch her closely and keep us posted for any changes. Feel free to contact us with your questions or concerns. See the receptionist for your next appointment."

All said and done, Dr. Webb quietly walked out of the room. The stillness was so powerful I heard daddy's tummy gurgling from across the room. I wanted to LOL (laugh out loud) but I knew I better not.

Nurse Rachel came into the room saying that Dr. Kneil had just released Joyce from the hospital and that we were free to leave after Joyce received her midday medications and discharge papers were signed. "A cab was called, and they will meet you downstairs when you are ready."

Mommy completed all the paperwork, and three hours later, Nurse Teresa aided me into a wheelchair. The three of us headed for the elevator and then . . . I needed to go potty. Mommy got me into the stall, but not a minute too soon. Back on the main floor, I was once again in the presence of the statue of Christ. I especially made sure to turn around to see HIS FACE.

Mommy and I were upset about leaving but ready to go back to the mountains of West Virginia. Then, just then I saw it; Christ winked at me! I will need to keep this to myself 'cause no one will believe me, but HE did wink! Do you know why I know? Because God is God and He can do anything, and HE did wink!

After that excitement, I noticed my hands were empty—my dolly was missing! I put my foot down hard on the floor dumping myself out of the wheelchair. There I sat on the cold floor and would not budge until one of the nurses went back to the room to fetch my Betsy. I began screaming creating a major scene. One of New York's finest came over to help, but I assured him everything would get under control as soon as I had my dolly. He must have a daughter 'cause he understood, nodded saying, "Someone go get this fine young lady's dolly," and that was the last I saw of him. A passing nurse's aide called up to the children's floor insisting someone find the doll and bring it down to the lobby STAT!

Waiting for the taxi ride, I was feeling sad and happy. Can you feel both ways at the same time? I do. One hour had passed and no sign of my dolly, Betsy McCall. How could I go home without her? Daddy could get me another one, but that would not be the same. The decision was made that we had to leave without the doll. Tears and lots of them, but no vocal outbursts. Our ride arrived, and as they were getting me into the vehicle, I heard a voice, "Wait, wait. I found her; I found your dolly. I got your dolly! Wait!" I heard the voice, turned my head, and saw Betsy before I got in the vehicle. I was so relieved. The nice lady brought her right to me, gave me a hug, and then she was gone. I hardly got to thank her. Was she an angel? Now we were all ready to head for the mountains.

Leaving the city around 3 PM, traffic had already stopped in many areas. Daddy wanted to get away before we make our first stop for lunch. Rats! Lunchtime was 'bout over; we missed eating! We will no doubt have to double-up on our next meal.

Traveling down the highway for about two and a half hours, we noticed an advertisement for a place called *Home Fries*. Not having heard of this place, Daddy thought we would try it.

The parking lot was full giving us a good feeling and the aroma outside was heavenly. Walking inside, we were greeted with a bright smile from Heather, the cute receptionist. Seated in the center of the room, I got a "bird's-eye view" of all the customers. Personally, it did not matter, but Grace, my sister, wanted to make sure she could see all the action. Mommy helped me read the menu consisting of unfamiliar fancy words. Even "fries" means potatoes, but flavors and non-traditional cooking styles might make them unrecognizable.

Daddy, extremely hungry, ordered their version of a cheeseburger, extra hot curly fries, and iced tea. Mommy wanted something light ordering a chef salad with French dressing and tea.

Grace was impossible but finally deciding on a breakfast choice of waffles and sausage links with chocolate milk. When it was my order, I went completely blank. The server stood calm, but her feet started moving up and down soft 'n' easy into a mean loud tapping. I still had not decided then blurted out, "Raisin bran cereal with white milk, cold—ice cold!"

Embarrassed, my face turned red, alarming the server into dropping her writing pen. She went into an apologet c rant, no longer making eye contact and complete.y coming unglued.

Determined to make things right, she refilled our water glasses, delivered our food on time, and offered free dessert to each of us.

Our nasal passages and taste buds were jumping for joy as each plate was precisely placed in front of us.

Daddy hurried us along to finish eating so that we could get back in the Ford, continuing down the road home. Route 60, a narrow and busy two-lane road, cuts through the mountains, requiring drivers to be alert and prepared to stop at all times. We arrived back home around 8 PM safe 'n' sound. Daddy decided to leave everything in the car except personal items so that all of us could get comfortable and sleep in our own beds. Betsy and I were glad to be back in our regular bed after being away in New York. I had no trouble falling asleep as my skin drifted into familiar lumps in my mattress problem free. Mommy and Daddy must have drifted into a deep slumber, not hearing a word or grumble from either of them until morning. On the other hand, my sister, Grace, spent the night arguing with herself. I am unsure of the subject line or who won the dispute, but eventually she shut up and fell asleep on her own. My inner voice was going a mile a minute reciting the alphabet, keeping me awake. I heard the alarm strike twelve, but that was all until . . . robin red breast landed on the edge of the window. Her melody began to flow filling the air with song.

Downstairs, dishes rattled in the kitchen loud and clear. Mommy must have whipped up her famous "blue" pancakes after seeing the batter in a glass bowl. I started to drool out the side of my mouth, then the sizzle of the bacon captured all my attention. Four slices of wheat toast popped up together out of the toaster signaling breakfast was ready for the taking. Mommy called us to the table, and after a prayer for thanksgiving, we began to enjoy our meal.

Wake up! Smell the fresh air as dew lingers on early morning clover. The crispness flowing through your lungs invigorates every cell in your body. There is no time to dilly-dally for a second cup of coffee because there is work to be done.

On the other hand, Mommy was searching for the newly purchased ant traps after finding a complete group of worker ants invading an open box of graham crackers. Daddy was planning on tinkering on the Ford after finishing his morning drink, and I hoped he was careful 'cause Mommy will yell at him if he gets grease on his new pants.

I cannot believe he was wearing pants with somebody else's name. Who is Dickie?

"Joyce, we are going shopping downtown before visiting Aunt Helen, so please put on your Mary Jane shoes. Have you brushed your teeth and combed your hair?"

"Oh, and do not forget your ankle socks. Do not dawdle, we must be getting on the road."

"Yes, Mommy."

Grace was instructed to turn off the T.V. Thoroughly involved in *The Mickey Mouse Club*, Mommy asked three times before gaining her full attention. Grace's beautiful blue eyes glued to the TV, watching the guys wearing the funny hats with ears. The TV was off, and now Daddy was blowing the horn and now everyone is ready to go to Joyce's doctor appointment. Mommy did not inform Joyce of the scheduled EEG so that she would be calm as possible.

I could not believe Daddy got a front-door parking space at Dr. Craft's office. We were able to step out of the car and got right into his office. As usual, Grace and Daddy waited in the car while Mommy and I spent time together with twenty anxious kids. Nurse Rachel called my name and went ahead to escort Mommy and I to an examination room at the end of the hall. A few minutes later, Nurse Rachel returned. Dr. Craft was on a phone call and will be in shortly. I was here every four weeks, and it had been a drag. I thought it would be fantastic if doctors would make house calls. I got so tired waiting around in these small rooms, and at times, it was hard for me to breathe. Mommy instructed me to sit down and be patient. Seems that this is one word that follows me everywhere.

"Be patient, Joyce," a little phrase that keeps repeating in my mind. Over and over and frankly it was making me sick, or should I say "sicker" 'cause one month from today Mommy and I would leave for New York to have my heart surgery. Later today, the Huntington Merchant Association would be holding a blood drive to raise twenty-four pints of blood needed for my open-heart surgery.

Employees of Silver's and the Huntington Store pledged pastries and beverages for all taking part in the drive to be held in the Huntington Store's parking lot from 9 AM to 6 PM on Saturday. Another activity was scheduled at the Catholic Academy on the second Sunday in April from 12 to 2 PM in the church hall.

Tomorrow, the *Huntington Herald* will interview me for an upcoming article, making me feel like princess for a day. I dislike having my picture taken as I tend to close my eyes. I was anxious to see myself in the paper and hoped it would be on the front page, then I would feel like "hot stuff." The reporter read me a few lines from his article:

Nine-year-old Joyce Noffsinger of Huntington is scheduled to have open-heart surgery next month at St. Mary's Hospital in Manhattan, New York. Anyone interested in donating blood can contact the local American Red Cross for further information.

My mail carrier had been delivering cards and letters since my story appeared in the newspaper.

Everyone had been nice, wishing me the best. I never imagined receiving all these cards and letters from strangers. Here was one as far away as California; how did they find out about me?

Mommy said she would help me start a scrapbook with all news articles and cards. I appeared strong and brave telling everyone that my operation would be like baking a cake. I like chocolate, so let's pretend it will be instant and simple. Mommy and Daddy were worried, but I have faith that everything will be OK because the Bible says, **"Be Not Afraid."**

Today Mommy dragged me along shopping for stuff to take on our trip. The day was long, but worth going to the soda fountain at the five-and-ten store. I have never sat at a real soda fountain seat. There were eight round seats that twirled. A long narrow table was lined with salt 'n' pepper shakers and pearly white napkins stuffed in a shiny box. Behind the napkins a crisp shiny pictured printed menu of all the food. Reaching across for the menu, Mommy quickly grabbed my hand.

"Mind your manners, little lady. Wait!"

A uniformed lady wearing a silly square hat walked over giving us a menu. A few minutes later, she returned taking orders. I've never been without a word. However, this time all the words were stuck in the left corner of my mouth. I was about to lose my wits and burst out in laughter. Mommy constantly told me to stop holding back a sneeze. She went into a big explanation, but I didn't care! Everything she was saying drifted. I was not listening 'cause it is going out the other ear; a laugh would be the same. I hear laughter is the "best medicine," so why not laugh and let it all out?

Mommy sensed I was about to burst. Placing her right hand over my mouth figured that would prevent even the slightest peep from escaping. Well, she was wrong, and I let it out all right. I missed my chance of sitting on the twirling seats, eating at the soda fountain, and sipping cold drinks through the curly straw. Mommy whisked me off the seat grabbing my ear lobes, and we headed home down Route 60 also known as "the scenic" route because depending on the seasons is what you're gonna get. Nothin' bad, only beautiful.

Traveling down the road, we passed an advertisement for a place called **The Pig House.**

I thought it was interesting that their menu was covered with hamburgers.

"Mommy, does hamburger meat come from pigs?"

"Honey, no, the meat comes from cows, everybody knows that!"

"Then why do they call 'em ham-burgers?"

Mommy was speechless. She turned her head sideways, scrunched her nose, then threw up her hands as to imply, "I don't know."

I was hungry and needing to eat. The hamburger picture on the menu incited a riot in my stomach as it churned singing "Old McDonald." I wanted to sing-along, but my lips were stuck together. Now of all things, I needed to go potty. I could not tell Daddy 'cause I had an accident earlier on the backseat I forgot to tell him about. I was in a heap of trouble, and I did not see my way out. Oh, there goes my stomach singing, *"How dry I am, nobody knows, How dry I am."* But that's not true because I was w-e-t!

My friends Paula and Linda came over after school today, but Mommy turned them away, insisting I relax. She did not want me to be too active and insisted I be rested for my surgery.

I had been lounging, coloring, playing with dolls, and doing all this "nothingness," and I thought it was time for a kid to have a little fun.

I was going to Dr. Craft's today getting a checkup for the big surgery next month. My sister, Grace, was the one who needed a head checkup 'cause she continues to block the door to our room. I might punch her one day if I get mad enough, and if I get Mommy involved, she'd make Grace say six *Hail Mary's*. I would have made her say at least ten to twenty. Even though she is my sister, sharing a room with her was a chore. Her dolls and stuff were always on my side of the room, and then I get blamed for the mess! She told me the oldest kid should have her own room. She whines saying I get all the privileges and I'm always underfoot. WHAT?

Her feet stink, so why would I want to be under them? I've got my own two feet. What is her problem?

Grace seems to think I get more attention, and it affects her privacy!

I just tell her "Horsefeathers!" She looked at me then mouthed back, "Horses don't have feathers! There, Miss Sassy Britches!"

Grace huffs and puffs, then walks down to the room we share. Thoughts of the conversation between Mommy and Daddy replays in her mind. Her eyes started to tear.

Footsteps were heard coming toward the bedroom door. Grace found me leaning in the door of our room not sure whether to enter. A deep voice inside my head began to give me a lecture:

"Why are you waiting? Go on in, it's your room too! Well, at least half of it is. Are, are you afraid? Scare-d-cat!"

"I am so confused; OK, I'll go in. Here goes nothin'."

Today, I feel low, and my life is a mess. Dr. Craft told me not to, but I need to play. My daily routine involves taking this med, swallowing this pill, taking naps, eating, and going to bed.

What happened to life, MY LIFE? Mommy had even stopped me catching flying bugs saying it stresses me out; I think NOT. What kid does not like bugs? Catching bugs calms me down!

Betsy McCall was upset because Mommy will not put her in the washer. She was afraid Betsy had germs that would infect ALL my stuff which would interfere with my surgery, making me sick. Now I can't sleep or play with her, and that's not all. My friends can't come over, and I can't go out! Really! Playing by myself makes my heart sick. Isn't it already sick?

We go back to New York in a few days. Will I really be normal after all this hoopla?

"Mommy, what is normal?"

"Go look it up in the dictionary, Joyce."

I couldn't believe it! Grace had decided to take down the room divider thinking it would make me feel better. I had gotten used to it by now, and besides, we just had an argument. Is she worried about my surgery and chicken to admit it? Oops! There's a chicken again! Here chickie, chickie!

Our mailbox had been overloaded since the article first appeared in the newspaper. Cards and letters keep filling up our little mailbox every week wishing me good luck and speedy recovery from the upcoming surgery. If I'm getting this mail before my operation, what's it gonna be like after? Do I write back to all these people? What is all this excitement? It's just an operation, right? Why am I so special? I'm just an ordinary kid with a heart problem.

It's like finding a leak in your house and calling a plumber, don't you think? I think so. We'll go to New York instead of climbing under the kitchen sink. Problem solved. Lots of people have problems like this except mine is a little odd because it's in my chest. Can we get this over with? I need to play with my friends, go places other than to the doctors.

Tonight, I will get down on my knees and give thanks, sleep peacefully knowing I will board a plane in the morning.

I was gonna sleep peacefully last night, but guess what? Every brain cell in my head was on high alert keeping me awake! I heard the bugs breathing outside my windowsill and the sneeze of the Hootie Owl. My ears fine-tuned would not let me sleep.

Consequently, I will not be "Miss Bright-Eye and Bushy-Tailed" today. I will try to be on my best behavior, but I know how I act when tired.

This was May 18, 1961, I turned nine in February, and since then, I had been bombarded with emotions. So much had been going on, it was too much for a kid to manage.

I've been spending gobs of time at the doctors, forbidden to play with my friends, restricted to play inside and that's a lot to deal with. Agree?

Right now, Mommy and I were on our way to the mountaintop Tristate Airport. Serving West Virginia, Kentucky, and Ohio, the insane hair-pin curves will straighten Shirley Temple curls, or jump-start a slow heart rate.

Once on top of the mountain, all are welcomed by a view like no other. Shades of green rolling hills extend for miles paired with the contrasting blue sky. White fluffy clouds appear like icing on the cake with the sun's rays bouncing upward brightening the sky.

The airport terminal is small with only three gates, so there is little chance of a mix-up.

Boarding of our flight was just announced as passengers said their good-byes to family and friends. Mommy and I waited our turn, which wasn't long since only five other passengers had tickets. Once seated by the window, I planned to watch the plane take off, resting firmly against the window as much as possible. Taxied to the end of the runway, the plane turned sharply, stopping only briefly. The air speed increased as we traveled down the runway, and within seconds, the cement dropped off. A beautiful showcase and menagerie of colors flashed below. I didn't realize that my mouth was open until the saliva started flowing down my chin.

Boy was I glad Mommy was taking a snooze 'cause she would have been after me drooling all down my face in front of all "those" people! Not much to see now that we have climbed to twenty thousand feet. Nothing to see except gentle white cotton balls of various shapes and forms. Occasionally, a little blurb of blue sky peeked through, but most all white.

During our flight, I felt my heart go into a quivering mode, but I think everything was A-OK. Mommy was relaxed enough to catch a few winks, so I didn't want to wake her, but I was frightened. I tried to relax, but you know my mind.

Not until landing in New York did I realize how small my airport is yet able to serve the communities of three. After thirty minutes of circling, we landed followed by fifteen minutes getting to the terminal. Baggage claim was a nightmare. Tiredness had settled in by now, and we had no idea when our luggage would show up on the "turn-a-round."

Beyond being tired, Mommy decided to pay a little and have our baggage sent to our hotel.

Finding a taxi was no problem 'cause they are everywhere. Twelve drivers stopped by before I decided which one was the best looking. Mommy spotted the "one," and after getting his attention, he took us to the Sheraton. He unloaded our luggage, opened and closed the door for us going inside to check-in to the hotel. I was so glad to be here 'cause I don't think I could have walked another step, and looking at Mommy, she's about to fall over.

Conveniently found across the street, St. Mary's Hospital which will make our visit in the morning easy as pie.

Arrangements had already been made for a cab to take Mommy and me across the street for an early morning admission to the hospital.

Exhausted from travel, Mommy decided we would stay in and let our food come to us via room service. The menu was full of choices making it hard to decide, but eventually our minds were made up, and all we had to do was order then wait for room delivery. Mommy opted for a medium steak, baked potato with lots of butter, or should I say butter with potato, salad topped with Thousand Island dressing. Hot dog with fries was enough for me knowing I would be going to bed. I don't sleep well in strange places, so as expected, I tossed and turned. My mind would not shut off thinking about the events that would occur after walking across the street.

A little voice inside my head kept telling me I would end up with more than a "plumbing" job. I tried my old antics of rolling my head back 'n' forth, kicking my foot, but nothing would settle my anxious spirit.

Three little words kept haunting me, running circles in my mind. All night over and over again it played: call a plumber.

Is that silly or what?

Coming to my rescue, a prayer Sr. Amelia taught us:

> *Heavenly Father, I come to You*
> *Wanting to walk in Your Ways.*
> *Give me strength and love*
> *Beside me come and pray.*
> *Heavenly Father, I come to You*
> *Tomorrow hold me near.*
> *Hold me close; keep me safe,*
> *Release me from my fear.*

I woke up before the chickens! Ha! Ha! Beat Ya! Excitement was in the air.

Mommy was running around like a chicken without her head; Oh no! Flittin' around putting everything except the kitchen sink in my suitcase. She's all done, but something was missing,

Betsy McCall. Mommy said we could bring and keep her in my suitcase for a few days. I already missed her hugs and kisses and didn't want to wait. How was I gonna sleep tonight without her?

This is the day I will check into St. Mary's Hospital for the long-awaited open-heart surgery. I just felt my heart jump trying to climb into my throat, but I think it was just my nerves.

The City of Huntington gave me a ticker-tape parade celebration before we left with well-wishes, marching bands, and blood donations in addition to all the other activities. Never in my wildest dreams would I have imagined all these events in my honor all because of my heart.

Conveniently across the street, St. Mary's Hospital. All we needed to do was hop in a cab for the short ride across the street for admission.

The morning air felt good to breathe through my nostrils and mouth. Riding in the cab, Mommy and I had no idea of the surprise we were about to see. Stepping out of the cab, we were stunned.

Red, flaming flowers—hundreds surrounding the hospital grounds.

"Look, Mommy, beautiful flowers! What kind of flowers are these?"

"Honey, these are poppies, magnificent red poppies more beautiful than I have ever seen. Truly a work from God's Hands."

My heart started to flutter, but I knew we would be inside soon among medical staff if needed.

Looking at these flowers, I felt a peace come over me like a comforting blanket, like a drug effect.

For years I have known about this surgery, but being a kid, I figured I would go to bed, wake up, and my heart would be well. However, here I was.

I had been coming to St. Mary's since 1957, and now it was May 1961. One month ago, I was here for a catheterization to confirm my diagnosis. I wanted to wake up rested this morning, but that did not happen. I tried rolling my head back 'n' forth, kicking my foot, but nothing would settle down my "thinking" mind until walking by the tall marble statue of Christ. His outreached arms once again brought harmony and peace to every restless inch of my body.

Mommy and I continued to walk the hallway toward the elevator leading to the Lance Unit or on the fifth floor. I pushed the button, and we went upward. The elevator doors opened, and I felt my heart skip several beats and pressure build in my chest, but I was not afraid.

Walking up to the reception desk, Mommy and I were greeted by Nurse Marli. Registration forms were pulled out from under the desk needing only a signature for completion.

Mommy pulled out her special pen kept secretly in her purse for signing special papers. My mind rumbled as an ID bracelet was placed around my right wrist. We were directed five doors down from the nurse's station into a private room. Immediately, I jumped into bed pulling the covers over my head. Head Nurse Matt could not believe my enthusiasm. I was overjoyed not having to share the room with another patient. My present state of mind changed when a member of the medical staff came to call:

"Knock! Knock! Hello! I am CNA Cindy, here to take your vitals. May I come in?"

"Sure, come on."

I did not know why Mommy let this person in because this is MY ROOM! Cindy what's-her-name entered pushing a cart. Before I knew it, she had stuck a glass stick in my mouth and walked away. She sure had nerve! Returning, she then took the stick out of my mouth.

She placed the numbers on a piece of paper. An hour later, a lab technician knocked requesting entrance needing four vials of blood. I sat back consenting to the procedure but squirmed as the tech pulled the rubber band tight around my arm. My little veins decided to play hide 'n' seek and not cooperate. Unsuccessful after four tries, I felt like a pin cushion with tears rolling down my cheek. The technician gave up, waving goodbye to go down the hall to his next (victim) patient. Head Nurse Suzanne later spoke to Mommy about the procedure requested by one of the surgeons. The most recent x-ray showed an area of concern requiring another catheterization ordered by Dr. Kneil. The actual heart surgery would follow.

The expression on Mommy's face was pure shock hearing the need for another procedure. I feel weary listening to all the discussions and cannot imagine how Mommy's dealing with the information. As I watch *Lassie*, Mommy was determined to take five minutes to call home and give Daddy the latest medical report and ask for another long-distance kiss. I was sure the "real" thing would have been better, but this would have to do for now.

Mommy arrived to find my bed empty. One of the aides noticed her concern and mentioned that I had scooted down the hall to play Monopoly with two other children. I was sure she was going to take me back to the room, but I was not ready. "I cannot leave now, Mother; I have all the hotels and am not leaving 'till I win it all!" Having all the property and money, I was more than determined. I wanted to brag and tell all my West Virginia friends that I beat "everyone" in New York out of everything, fair and square! However, Mommy gave me five minutes, but Nurse Jamie forced me to leave right then for an EKG. Game over and no win posted. MAD like a snake, I yelled and screamed at the top of my lungs all the way back to my room. Mommy decided to stay an extra thirty minutes to make sure I calmed down within a reasonable amount of time. Whose reasonable amount of time is questionable, but of course, it was different from mine. I noticed a new piece of equipment in the room and demanded to know what it was. The EKG machine was ready for me; however, I was showing so much emotion that a correct reading would not be possible. The technician talked me into a relaxed state that would give a correct reading. Leads were connected to patches placed on areas of my body that read the electrical activity of my heart. In a flash, the test was over, and the staff member quietly left the room. Total silence embraced the room, frightening me so much I wanted to turn the TV volume on full blast, but instead screamed loud and clear. Nurse Jamie ran down the hall, crashing through the door like a bat out of you-know-where.

"Joyce, what is your problem? Turn down that TV!"

"I was winning and had to leave all for this stupid test!"

"Well, this stupid test, as you call it, will help the doctors in making decisions related to your surgery, so it is not so stupid. Don't you agree?"

"I guess so."

Nurse Jamie promptly left the room after our discussion. Lunch was being delivered, but I was beyond upset to be hungry. The meals had not been to my liking, so I was not eager to uncover the mystery food served today. To my surprise, the lunch servers bypassed my bed, and no lunch was delivered, yet my roommate received a tray. I could smell exactly what was underneath that round plastic covering: hot dog on a stick, onion rings, applesauce, chocolate chip cookie, and white milk to drink. It looked good, smelled good, and I bet it even tasted good. I rang my nurse's bell wondering if my tray had taken a wrong turn. Shortly after my request, two nurses entered my room with a surprise: two shots! I had planned to snooze after lunch, but it was not like this.

I was asked to roll over on my side, and by now I know better than to object. I managed to color two pages as my eyes started getting heavy. Nurse Cheryl knocked on my door and entering gave me a few words of wisdom.

"Miss Joyce, I am sorry you had to leave the game of importance to you. However, we needed you back in your room for medical reasons which happen to be a smidgen more important than your desire to 'cream' everyone in Monopoly."

"Got it?"

"Got it?"

What I didn't know was I was to be taken for a second catheterization, and the doctors felt it would be less stressful to not have my mommy present and to sedate me without me knowing and, after the test, to continue with the actual open-heart surgery.

Waking up in the recovery room, I felt like I'd been run over by a sixteen-wheeler or out drinking and now drunk. The only thing I knew was I felt bad. Never, ever want to feel like this again! Returned to my room, Mommy explained she rested over at the hotel during the second catheterization. Rested, she could now be present when the doctors came to discuss the results. I myself needed to rest now that the surgery had been changed to tomorrow. Lunch trays arrived with a choice of applesauce, hot dog, French fries, chocolate chip cookies, and milk. I planned to watch TV and rest after eating. Dr. Kneil arrived shortly after lunch before my afternoon snooze. She explained a questionable area showed up on the most recent x-ray that had to be clarified. Now that the issue has been clarified, surgery will take place in the morning.

"Do you have any questions before I leave, Mrs. Noffsinger?"

"No, I can't think of any at this time. Thank you, Dr. Kneil. I will be here early in the morning before she goes into surgery."

Soon after Dr. Kreil said goodbye, Mommy decided she would head over to the hotel to have dinner, shower, and get to bed early so she would be rested for her early morning call.

Little did Joyce realize her evening would not be one for rest and relaxation. The lab let Nurse Webb knew they would be arriving within an hour for a chest x-ray of her patient, Joyce. No big deal except Joyce was asking if the lights went out would she be glowing.

Nurse Webb had to deal with her small patient in room number 106 who was not only being difficult but now trying to be a comedian. Suddenly the call bell down the hall started ringing continuously. A young nursing assistant entering the room was surprised by a flying water jug sent airborne by Joyce in frustration for her long wait.

"Have you forgotten my dinner? I need more than soup and Jell-o!"

"I'll get Nurse Webb; she'll explain."

"I don't want an explanation; I want my dinner!"

I was ready to get comfortable in bed, but in came the nurse with something for me to drink.

Well, I drank it, but they must have somehow melted a bunch of sidewalk chalk 'cause that was what it looked and tasted like. About an hour later, I almost did not make it to the bathroom. Rushing I ran smack-dab into Mommy as she came around the corner entering my room. My stomach was "full of itself," or should I say empty after all all the time sitting on the potty. No time to visit with Mommy since I was running to the bathroom, but at least she was there for company. The phone rang, and it was Daddy calling from Saudi Arabia to wish me luck on my adventure. Mommy grabbed the phone, and we said our goodbyes. Teary eyed, I got an extra-long hug from Mommy; plus, an airborne kiss she blew across the room as she went out the door. Before Nurse Webb arrived, a lab assistant needed more blood. Again, problems in finding an adequate location occurred. After twelve attempts, a technician got a successful draw, and the entire unit could hear:

"GET MY MOMMY!"

Nurse Webb knew it was time to call Joyce's doctor. She was emotionally and medically in trouble. Unable to reach Mrs. Noffsinger, a message was left at the hotel desk. Dr. Kneil initiated a new order for a minor sedative hoping Joyce would receive relief. Mrs. Noffsinger was down in the hotel restaurant having a slow and peaceful dinner knowing a stressful day would follow at sunrise. She kept thinking about her daughter and the difficulty facing her. Returning to the hotel, a staff member at the desk did not deliver the message from the hospital. Mrs. Noffsinger showered, watched the local news, then retired for the evening unaware of the tough time Joyce, her daughter, was enduring over at the hospital. Turning down the finely quilted cover and fluffing the pillows, Mrs. Noffsinger completed her evening calling the front desk for an early wake-up call. Lights were turned out, covers drawn up over to her shoulders, and she was ready for a full night's rest. However, her quiet night did not happen as planned. Over at the hospital, Joyce received a light sedative calming her restless spirit, enabling her to sleep the entire night.

Unfortunately, her mommy was crying after speaking with Harv because she really needed the real thing.

I just had a thought! If my memory serves me, didn't my blood drive raise blood to use for me while I am here in the hospital? Why or why do they keep pestering me for more blood?

What happens when my blood dries up? What then?

"Joyce, please don't worry. Everything has been taken care of."

CHAPTER 7

(Surgery Day)

Monday, May 22, 1961

I was born with congenital aortic stenosis, and St. Mary's Hospital has been a frequent destination since I was five years old. Today, the surgeons will repair my valve, allowing enough blood to travel through my heart's main artery, the aorta, improving my quality of life. Open-heart surgery requires major preparations, many skilled staff beyond the surgeons, and a facility prepared to undertake the entire plan of care for the patients.

Medical staff entered my room on a regular basis after midnight. I wanted to wake up rested, but that's not gonna happen due to the constant monitoring of temperature and blood pressure readings every fifteen minutes. Mommy showed up early as promised asking if I needed anything before they started with medications. The medical staff started coming in soon afterward to harass me by turning on the lights, changing IVs, visitations from anesthesiology, surgical nursing, radiology, and medical students to check me out. I did not realize I was so special nor the seriousness of my operation. I should have charged admission and had everyone sign the autograph dog my daddy sent me. I bet Mommy didn't think about this either. Oh well, I'm a kid; what do I know? I guess I should be asking for ice cream 'cause that's all I hear. When any of my friends have gone into the hospital, they talk about how much ice cream they had; it sounds good to me. I hope I get to have some after my dinner. I guess my answer is "ice cream."

Nurse Rachel walked into my room followed by Nurse Jamison carrying a trayful of goodies. Not my favorite candy but five needles! Roll over, Miss Joyce. *"OUCH!"* Taken without a fuss, minutes later, I started feeling funny as Mommy leaned over giving me a kiss. Two staff members transferred me into another bed as Mommy hurried and kissed me again before being whisked down the long hallway toward the surgical elevators. Knowing the seriousness of the procedure, she was determined to take one more kiss. The nurse revealed to her the surgery would last approximately six hours without any complications and she should rest over at the hotel. Hospital medical staff would keep her informed at all times and call if an emergency took place.

Two orderlies scooted me to another bed then whisked me down a long hallway toward the surgical elevators. A bump, slight jerk then we entered a room where the air was different. Clean smelling and cold. Two staff members helped slide me over to a hard, narrow bed with no pillow. What kind of bed has no pillow? I think they just strapped me down like I planned to go somewhere. I tried lifting my head, but I was too dizzy. Earlier shots were causing my eyelids to fight to stay open as sleep was fast approaching. I was blinded by bright overhead lights but cannot shield my eyes due to my arms fixed downward with IVs.

Footsteps and voices surrounded me, but it was difficult to tell how many were in the room.

"Wait a minute! Somebody please tell me what is going on."

I tried to fight as someone placed a mask firmly on my face. Breathing in, I felt relaxed as a voice told me medicine will flow freely down my arm bringing on a deep sleep.

Under anesthesia, my surgery would last at least six hours or more. During open-heart surgery, the heart/lung machine allows oxygen-rich blood to be received by the body during surgery while the heart is stopped. Sounds neat; wish I could watch! Surgeons gained access to my heart by splitting the large bone in the center of my chest known as the sternum by spreading it apart. *OUCH!* On second thought, count me O-U-T! I won't watch!

I was asleep and unaware of what was taking place. My doctors were using their knowledge and skill to correct the sick heart with which I was born.

As if six hours wasn't enough, later that evening I had to return to the operating room due to bleeding coming from an unknown source and a drop in blood pressure. They reopened my chest, corrected the problem, and sewed me back together like a dolly. Did they use a straight or zigzag stitch? Mommy refused to leave my bedside even though I was in intensive care. That night she slept in a reclining patient chair not more than three inches from my bed. I myself didn't sleep due to the constant flow of staff, but I guess that's to be expected in my delicate condition. Several of the neighbors from California Street drove all night to be with my mommy since my daddy was detained in Saudia Arabia on business.

My sister, Grace, remained in Huntington staying with Aunt Kay until my doctors said I could have visitors.

Mommy later told me I took those shots like a soldier, and she was so proud of my actions.

Everything was going as planned until my blood pressure dropped, causing a major alarm among all the doctors. Internal bleeding rushed me back into the OR requiring a reopening of my chest to fix the issue, resewing and then given more B+ blood. Covered in tubes, heavily medicated, on a ventilator, and listed in critical condition, but I made it! I was not alone as Mommy was at my bedside and I felt God's presence giving both of us strength. I cannot talk being on a ventilator which was hard, but I could hear everything going on in the room. I was alive and that was what counts. Dr. Kneil sat down with my mommy last night and explained everything. My aortic valve, the main valve, doesn't open and close like it should. This doesn't allow enough oxygen to flow making me tired and easily out of breath.

The surgery opened up the airway allowing more oxygen to travel throughout my body. Under general anesthesia, the heart-lung machine breathed for me while the surgeon corrected my cardiac issues. The machine stilled my heart while recirculating the fluids away.

Tonight, my daddy called, and there was a possibility that I might be getting a private nurse. Then Mommy might take time to rest and that will make me feel better and not worrying so much about her. Speaking of rest, it was time for my nap. Sure, I wished they would get rid of all the rubber tubing hanging around me. I was afraid I might get caught up in it as I was still on the critical list at the hospital.

Tubes in my mouth, I was unable to speak and respond to what the nurses were saying. They were not helping matters saying I look like "death warmed over." Really! Have they forgotten I could still hear what they were saying?

Tonight, Mommy refused to go over to the hotel. She slept in the recliner patient chair not moving three inches from my bed. I do not know about Mommy, but I did not sleep due to the constant flow of resolute staff coming in and out, but I guess that's to be expected in my delicate condition. Where is my Mommy? Did you sneak down the hall for a quick bite to eat in the hospital café? I hope so and then maybe she gave up on the chair and went over to the hotel to get a good night's rest. I can't thank the people who donated blood enough for sharing a part of themselves so I could have this operation. I know God will bless you for your kindness.

My first night after surgery was rough, but by the grace of God, I made it. I lost count of the number of staff checking on me. The annoying beeping of the machines were a constant reminder I'm breathing, and Mommy hasn't suffered sleeping in that chair for nothing.

Tuesday, May 23, 1961

Oh, what a beautiful morning somewhere but not for me. I struggled to breathe, and my physicians had decided I needed to have a tracheotomy requiring a third trip to the OR. Mommy had been informed and had kissed me before being wheeled down for surgery. I felt like an old pro now and at least I knew the routine, knowing what to expect. The doctor made a small incision at the base of my neck. I was already asleep due to the medicine given earlier to my arm. A curved metal tube gently slid in the incision at once improved my breathing. Having this tube, I can talk but with little volume. I heard Mommy crying outside my room discussing my present condition with the surgeon, Dr. Liken. Needless to say, not everything had gone perfectly.

Dr. Lyken encouraged Mommy to speak with a member of Pastoral Care, Father Mike, whose office was on the first floor. My condition must be serious because within one hour Father arrived fully robed in sacramental dress of the Catholic Church to administer the Last Rites of the Catholic Church.

Mommy was so upset that my bedrails held her up as tears flowed down her face. She slept again in the patient recliner to be close as she could to me. Daddy called every day for encouragement and his special delivery "long-distance" kiss. For a brief moment, the non-contact smooch restored the twinkle in Mommy's eyes that used to be present every day.

She talked daily to Daddy, but she'd prefer him beside her. No one predicted me needing so much care requiring Mommy to be away so long. My case was supposed to be *a piece of cake*. Must have been an angel food cake 'cause they've sure been watching over me. Isn't there a song about God taking care of us?

Wednesday, May 24, 1961

Here I go again being blessed making it through another night; however, the situation was still touch and go. I had lost count of the number of staff coming in checking my vitals. I was breathing so maybe Mommy sleeping in the recliner was doing some good. That angel cake must have been made with real angels, and I bet they were flying around somewhere. I was awake for small periods of the day smiling at those coming to care for me. Although I was hurting today, it was not an excuse to give them a frown.

Another medical issue developed as a new day dawned. My kidneys had stopped working and now I needed the help of a kidney machine. I was awake at small periods of the day smiling at those caring for me knowing how hard their daily tasks must be. I imagine some patients scream and complain; I tried my best to be cheerful and have at least one smile a shift.

I was hurting; the slightest movement and each little cough was excruciating. The staff kept encouraging me to cough, but it was something I would rather not do. I wished to live and continue, but worrying about my mommy drained my strength. She was a strong person, but even mommies have a breaking point. If Daddy were here, she would be stronger, more energetic, and her beautiful smile would light up the unit. By God's grace, I made it through another night. In the recovery room, I made it through. No one expected all these problems, but I will get through this glitch in my life's story. This heart stuff was supposed to be easy, but I do not know who started that rumor.

I think Mommy feels everything I feel; don't know how much more she can take. I was having trouble going to the bathroom, and my tummy was swollen making me look fat. This afternoon, Nurse Jamie inserted a tube to relieve the pressure, and do you know what? I was still smiling! DO you know it takes more muscles to frown than smile? Have you noticed that my mommy has a great smile? Well, she had not been smiling much lately because of me, but when she does, the room lights up when she smiles.

Fighting for your life is demanding work, yet I smile at those who work hard to keep me alive. Mommy was here daily looking at magazines and talking to staff members thanking them for their help and shared magazines. Dr.

Kneil made daily rounds, but the dialogue was the same. Staff members insisted that Mommy go to the hotel in the evening and get rest.

Thursday May 25, 1961

A new day as the sun rose, but I did not know the date. God blessed me to have another day and grateful to be alive. I certainly can't do much from my bed.

What did I know, I was just a kid. Daddy called last night saying I might be getting a private nurse to give Mommy time to rest. Speaking of rest, I need sleep. However, all the tubing made me feel smothered. Remember that "piece of cake" from a while back?

What happened? Must have been German chocolate 'cause I do not understand.

Friday, May 26, 1961

Dr. Kneil continued to make her daily rounds but was concerned with my lack of progress. Mommy gave in going over to rest at the hotel under the condition she would be notified immediately if a change in my health occurs.

Fighting for my life was hard, yet I smiled back at those who continue keeping me alive. Mommy visited daily looking at magazines and kind staff members have brought in other books. Staff members persuaded mommy to spend nights in the hotel for adequate rest and a decent meal. They promised to call if any change in my condition occurred.

Late Friday night, Mrs. Noffsinger received a call over at the hotel. No alarms were sounding, but my internal temperature was on the rise. The nurse would push fluids and continue to keep a close watch.

Saturday, May 27, 1961

My kidneys were refusing to do their job. Doctors were discussing the possibility of going on the artificial kidney machine. I cannot imagine being hooked up to another gizmo. OK, Lord, you said You would never give us more than we can manage. I am a kid who has grown up quite a bit since coming to St. Mary's, but I am at my limit, and most of all, I know my mommy has reached hers too.

Sunday, May 28, 1961

It is official! The artificial kidney machine and I were one and a new medical diagnosis had been posted. The new critical list had my name as bleeding has started from my bowels.

Hey! It is OK 'cause I am alive, and God still has me in the palm of His Hand. Is there any other better place to be than in God's Hand? If you can think of one, please send me a note and let me know. This was really too much for a nine-year-old, but God gave me strength every day as I traveled down my road to health. Mommy's looking chipper, so I know God had spent quality time by her side. Thanks God.

Monday, May 29, 1961

The bleeding in my bowels continued to be a problem. I overheard the doctors speaking to Mommy about the possibility of the "O" word and I sure hope that does not happen.

Remember the "limit" I talked about earlier? Well, I might have tiptoed over it, but please do not tell anyone if they are not aware.

Tuesday, May 30, 1961

The artificial kidney machine had gotten my urine flowing and the medication had slowed the bleeding, "Hip! Hip! Hurrah!" Things were looking UP! I was beginning to feel like a permanent member of the staff having been here so long. I needed to get out of this room, but at least it won't be the OR. Alleluia! However not the playroom either, bummer. Rats!

Wednesday, May 31, 1961

My urine flow was going pretty well, and the bleeding had slowed down, and medical staff hopes were high. However, I was still surrounded by a bunch of strangers in my room and wondered why they visit every day.

Thursday, June 1, 1961

All this time I have been on a respirator and unable to talk. Everything seemed brighter today. My doctors had informed Mommy and Daddy that I was "going to make it now."

Taken off the respirator and taking in fluids like normal felt strange. Mommy sat back in the easy chair for a nap. Her face appeared more relaxed. Think I will do the same however in comes the cleaning staff mopping the floor, cleaning the bathroom, and collecting the trash. They always have the best timing. Nap time interrupted and my entertainment for the day was keeping a keen eye on the room. What else could I do? I could not talk or sing, but

I could watch and blink answering yes and no! This was exciting! Not too long ago I could not even do that—that was progress. Thank God!

Friday, June 2, 1961

I had a good night sleep except for bleeding from the bowl then . . .

Unexpectedly, into convulsions and back on the respirator. Dr. Kneil thought that a clot formed somewhere, but no one knew for sure. Mommy was hysterical and not able to eat, drink, or rest. One of the doctors suggested a sedative for her, but she flatly refused, wanting to be alert as much as possible if anything else took place. Nurses on the floor were concerned she might need a room of her own and they have agreed to keep an eye on her.

Saturday, June 3, 1961

I was on again and off again, the respirator that is; 7:30 this morning off the machine and thrashing and unable to settle down. Staff members were puzzled as to what was taking place. My breathing was impaired, and the decision was made to put me back on the respirator. Later it was noted that bleeding was again coming from the bowel area, adding to my complications. Dr. Kneil and other physicians were gathering today for a major discussion and further care planning.

Sunday, June 4, 1961

A rough night for all. I was bruised around the temples from extensive thrashing around in bed. A new diagnosis of pneumonia had been recorded in my chart on top of everything else. Mommy was constantly by my side once again sleeping in one of the hospital reclining chairs. Presently she was outside my room speaking to someone in the medical field and the conversation did not sound pleasant.

The IVs had managed to work themselves out with all the thrashing about. My doctors wanted to sedate me to protect me from injuring myself, but my mommy was against the idea, I think. I understand things happen. I remember this procedure was supposed to be a "piece of cake, chocolate as I recall" and then I changed it to angel. Well, I am not sure anymore as now things are a "horse of a different color."

Monday, June 5, 1961

Drugged heavily so that I could heal or be still and out of trouble? Well, it was working because word around the hospital floor was I was no worse or no better than before. Again, the respirator was removed to see if my lungs can function, and breathing can take place on its own. I know God loves me because He MUST have big plans for my future. I was still here regardless of all the wicked turn of events. Which doctor needed more practice? I would like more practice in getting out of this bed!

Tuesday, June 6, 1961

I believe I was improving, but they would not let me start packing. My recovery would be long. How much harder can it get 'cause so far this has been really tough? My breathing was still a major issue; and could you believe it, I was back on the respirator!

This time to save my strength. I never realized the amount of energy it takes to draw in air and push it out, but it does. Is there a prize for the most time on a machine?

During the night, I thought my left leg felt strange, but nothing had been normal during my stay here at St. Mary's.

Wednesday, June 7, 1961

Yes! Doctors changed their minds and did not put me on the respirator but kept me drugged and relaxed. No thrashing or moving about in bed. Today I transferred to Halsted 5 into a private room with special equipment including oxygen. Miss Jamison, a private duty nurse, would be with me on a regular basis plus keeping Mommy and Daddy fully informed.

Thursday, June 8, 1961

Today everyone was awaiting the latest blood test results. Dr. Kneil came into my room without her familiar smile. Tests confirmed that I had blood poisoning which explained why I felt so bad. My folks had been assured the medical staff were doing everything possible to control the infection for a full recovery. None of the physicians can pinpoint the source of the infection and have nearly set their brains on fire searching for the answer.

Mommy continued to have the courage of a lion which she should win an Academy Award. Deep down I know she was struggling and needed prayer for strength.

Friday, June 9, 1961

Call the Fire Department! Someone please pull the fire alarm!

I was on fire! Mommy was trying to convince me this is due to my troubled mental state. I wish they were as hot as I am. H-O-T! I am H-O-T! Somebody Please call the Fire Department!

Was I having another setback? I wanted to go forward for a change! Where was my dolly? I needed a hug!

Nurses put me on a bed of ice to bring my temperature down and convince Mommy felt calm enough to slip across the street to the hotel to shower, grab a nice dinner, hotel to shower, grab a nice dinner before returning to my room, finding me sound asleep and peaceful.

Saturday, June 10, 1961

I felt miserable and confused. There were people in this room I did not know. Who are they? They talked about me as though I was not in the same room. Am I in trouble? How could I? I was in the hospital; do I look as bad as I feel? Where is my Mommy? Why doesn't she ask them to leave?

Sunday, June 11, 1961

Waking up, I thought I had a good night's rest. My room was filled with God's beautiful sunshine. Over on the night stand, I noticed a beautiful vase of flowers, but I did not know where they came from. A nurse's aide had just come in to change my sheets and agree to read the card.

"Get well soon, Paula Sue."

Paula Sue was one of my friends on California Street living two doors from my house. We went to the same school and played together all the time. All this excitement had made me tired; I needed to take a nap before Mommy comes from the hotel across the street.

Monday, June 12, 1961

"Wake up, Joyce. It is Nurse Mary. Time for your medication." There's got to be something else going on in this world except my medication, Can't they say, "Good morning, Joyce"?

I cannot believe you woke me up to get me medication to help me sleep! I did not need or want a shot! Why would you do something like this? I heard Dr. Weller's voice talking on the phone mentioning my name. Mommy says I do not hear well but I heard what he said.

No change in my general condition. Since when did I become a general?

Tuesday, June 13, 1961

"I want to go home! I want to go home! There's no place like home!"

"Can you hear me? Anybody, can you hear me? Can you hear me? I got money!"

My trach was out, so now I had the freedom to talk and say what I want and that is I wanna go home. My throat was scratchy and say what I wanna say and that is "I want to go home!"

Wednesday, June 14, 1961

Oh dear! Something was going on with me. I felt strange. My hand was shaking, and I was in a daze. Shivering, I just started shivering all over. Mommy had that worried look all over her face and rushed down to the nurse's station to get their attention. Two nurses arrived and figured out the possible problem. Somehow, I had lost two pints of blood; don't know where and don't know when or what happened. Help me, O God!

Thursday, June 15, 1961

Hearing voices this morning to find out seven doctors surround my bed at 6:30 AM. Thought I will give them a great big Candid Camera smile then they will know I have not given up.

Feeling better, yet I was weak, on the mend, and wanna go home. Now will not be soon enough. Free this morning of IVs, respirator, and I would fly out of here if I could. I did not know where I'd go, but it would be somewhere other than here. I wondered if they would let me sit up in a chair for a minute. I had been attached to this bed long enough. God is good!

Friday, June 16, 1961

What a wonderful day! Mommy looked fantastic and relaxed, and I was feeling surprisingly good. How long had it been since I said that? News coming down the hall stated there will be a plug coming in the hole in my neck soon! YEAH! I wondered what they use. I have a bottle of Elmer's Glue at home or Rubber Cement might work. Just let me know and I will tell Grace so she can bring a bottle before the celebration starts on the unit. Will my voice sound strange after being silent for so long? I got a special visitor today. My Daddy was here, and having both my folks here was incredibly special to me. I wish we could have a humdinger of a party, but I figure that's not allowed.

Saturday, June 17, 1961

Ice cold milk and warm cinnamon toast tickled my morning fancy which was more than I can talk about the eggs. They were definitely hospital quality and not like the ones my mommy makes them—light, fluffy, and delicious. When we finally got home, I thought that will be the first meal I would ask her to fix. I had just taken a bite of toast when the new group of cardiac residents stepped off the elevator to make rounds. Before I had time to blink, my room was bombarded with wall-to-wall doctors asking questions. Mommy and Daddy have yet to arrive, so maybe they had an enjoyable time last night and slept in late.

When the nice doctors left, they were somber and quiet, which concerned me hoping to go home soon. I had been here so long, and I was beginning to blend in like a picture on the wall.

Sunday, June 18, 1961

Good morning! Word floating around on the unit was "better." Feeling better but now a bit of home sickness had settled in. My desire to be back on California Street was so extreme I never realized the seriousness of my illness. But that is what this kid is wanting NOW!

Sleeping often helped me briefly forget the mountains. I needed to see the mountains and draw strength from them. Since they were not near, my dolly can give me strength. Can someone bring me my dolly? She will lift me up with her special touch.

The afternoon went uneventful as far as medical stuff was a blessing. Mommy called down to West Virginia to check with Aunt Kay and Grace letting everyone know the status of my health.

Monday, June 19, 1961

Breakfast trays collected by dietary staff were swift yet noisy as Mommy arrived from the Sheraton Hotel. Dr. Spencer, staff cardiologist, arrived for the morning rounds planning a detailed discussion carrying my extensive chart in hand. Flipping through the last ten pages of notes, he stressed that progress had been made despite all the setbacks. He was honest in saying there was no guarantee that everything would continue along the same path.

Later that afternoon, a fever of 102.5° spiked and my stomach was upset. Is this the beginning of something else? Only God knows.

Tuesday, June 20, 1961

Here I go again! Hot with fever once again. I was beginning to sound like a broken record.

Today Nurse Jamie brought in another fan to cool me and reduce my fever. My chest was hurting due to the buildup of fluid in my lungs. Dr. Spencer told Mommy that later they would insert a tube in my chest to drain off the fluid.

I hate to admit this, but I miss my sister. We argue, fight, yell, and scream, yet we love each other.

If something were to happen to one of us, we would be terribly sad. Mommy told me she will check flights from Huntington to New York after lunch today. There was a possibility the group from Huntington was planning another trip here as soon as all the arrangements can be made. Goodness Gracious! I just got the best jolt of happiness in my chest; I thought I could jump out the window and fly! Oh! There it goes again.

After dinner I experienced pain in the right side of my neck and back. I picked up my dolly earlier than usual hoping to see if the pain would go away. Mommy stayed a little while longer before going over to the Sheraton Hotel for the night.

Wednesday, June 21, 1961

I cannot sleep but I am champion at throwing up! I thought I was making progress. What was wrong? The nurse took my temperature: 103°. This is not a number on their preferred list, and they brought in a fan for my room. I am not cool, but the force of the fan could blow me away. Nurse Mary was not happy with me and "my" attitude. She said that this was NOT a hotel and my demands for service were out of line. The pain in my neck and back was giving them pain somewhere else. What ever happened to that "piece of cake?"

Thursday, June 22, 1961

My attitude had improved because I had a good night's sleep. Mommy told me the group from Huntington will be arriving today, and I was excited! They would be staying at the same hotel as my mommy, giving her someone to share meals with. A knock at the door and a staff member is present to take me for an EEG. I was hoping the test results will show I can be released from two medications, but we will see what the numbers and doctors have to say. Got my fingers crossed, don't you?

Friday, June 23, 1961

I slept well and that felt terrific! I do not remember when I felt this good, but it had been a long time. Grace and the West Virginia gang plan to be up here sometime today. An aide was just here taking my vitals and noted my temperature was up a smidgen, but I did not consider that a major issue. Do they?

Saturday, June 24, 1961

"Hail, Hail the gangs all here!" That sounds like a song! Everybody knows that song!

Everybody managed to cram into my room again. That was OK but could all this "togetherness" cause my temperature to rise? Having a ride down to x-ray this afternoon for a picture of my chest. This afternoon my stomach was uncomfortable and I'm still not feelin' well.

Sunday, June 25, 1961

Peace and quiet returned to my bedside as the West Virginia folks headed back to the mountains. Mommy and I were once again enjoying the emptiness of the space. I am not saying we did not enjoy their visit. My hospital room was so small it gets overwhelming with more than three people in the room. The aide took my temperature which registered near normal making me relieved and putting a smile on my face. I figured my muscles had forgotten how to perform that function, but I was glad that they hadn't.

Monday, June 26, 1961

Sick! Oh no! Today I am sick with germs from the West Virginia gang? That was not a known fact, but no one around here had been sick, but the staff thought my symptoms came from my visitors. I had had so much going on I did not notice Betsy missing.

However, one of her nurses found her hiding under the counter at the nurse's station and brought her back to me. She was home snuggling with me ready for a nap. "There's no place like home," even for a dolly.

Tuesday, June 27, 1961

Hello morning and sunshine! I am glad to report that my breakfast went down without coming back up! Yes! A beautiful way to start the day. I should begin glowing in the dark soon as I had another x-ray before lunch of my chest. I can imagine going into a closet and being able to count my ribs or anything else inside. I am glowing because I am alive!

Thanks God!

Wednesday, June 28, 1961

Dr. Johnson came in for a blood draw and was successful on the first try. I think he should be the only one coming to get blood from me. Let's keep him on staff and only have him stick me! He should mark the spot with an "x" for future reference. Busy asking for coloring supplies, as not all requests must be authorized by my doctors. Can you believe my doctors must approve my coloring. Medical clearance for coloring? Really?

I sure must be upset 'cause my lunch just came roaring upward all over me and the bedding. At least now I get something that might taste better. I know getting new linens will make the aides happy having to remake my bed.

Thursday, June 29, 1961

Oh brother! I wish this pain would go away. I have gone to the bathroom three times, and nothing is happening. Well, I just told you a fib. Something is surely happening and that is pain. Everything is stuck inside me not wanting to come out. Nursing came and gave me something to get things "moving." Excuse me, I got to get out of this bed 'cause something was trying to move! "AAH!" Seven BMs later, I feel normal and a whole lot lighter. I believe a miracle happened as a result of swallowing a "bottle" of liquid bubble gum. A knock at the door and a Candy Striper young lady delivered a basket full of cards from people out of state. Wasn't that nice and thoughtful! I could have used them a few weeks ago, but I can use them now!

Friday, June 30, 1961

I don't believe what I woke up to! Fever and x-ray, what a combination to start my day, yet I felt bright and chipper. My stomach could use a bit of cheering up as breakfast and lunch had reversed themselves out of my body. Do not know exactly what that means except call the clean-up department.

This is exciting news to share: I was sitting in a regular chair today and it felt weird! Who would have thought sitting in a chair could feel strange? Since I have been here, I have felt a lot of things on the weird side. Dr. Wells popped in this afternoon for a chit-chat. His face was stern, and I was afraid he had some sad news for me. Guess what, it must have been a woman's intermission, or whatever that is called. I was right: Another infection was hiding in my body. I asked him if it was "over the rainbow" and he smiled. He then asked me if I would like to receive the Sacrament of the Sick which I agreed to. Father Mike was called to my room responding within thirty minutes. Traditionally dressed, rosary and the Holy Bible in hand, he began with a special prayer and ended with the *Our Father*. Anointed with the Holy Oil concluding with an added prayer before leaving the room.

I feel different now that Father Mike has left. Does this nine-year-old finally realize the size and seriousness of her illness? Does she not understand how blessed she is?

Saturday, July 1, 1961

This morning, I ate despite my chest and stomach giving me a fit (hurting). Dr. Spence thought I have an abscess in my stomach or chest causing my present fever. Not again was my first thought, but they won't listen to me 'cause well I am a kid, no "MD" behind my name. The doctors wanted to sit tight, wait before taking another step. Waiting for what? I sat in a chair for ten minutes today! A big step forward which is a record from my earlier notes.

Oh no! Here comes the "blood" wagon! Where can I hide? I might as well give into them 'cause they always win, and I have no place to go. Is this a "step" backward?

Sunday, July 2, 1961

Feeling better but sick again after breakfast and lunch. This is getting awfully old! Slept all day while Mommy watched TV or looked at magazines. I bet she could recite everyone by heart. I knew she was tired of the old shows. I told her to go home or do something, but she refused all the time. She never complained; 'cause she is an angel. My temperature was on the rise again, and tomorrow more x-rays and blood tests to figure out the source of infection. I was waiting for the next glass of milk or water to leak out from all the holes in my arms any day now. Little ole' me has the entire cardiac staff baffled and on their toes.

Tippy toes, not tipsy toes.

Monday, July 3, 1961

Confused? You bet I am! I felt good, yet I got sick after eating. Today I tried to stand but my legs gave way. I am kid blessed by a higher power. I cannot and will not give up and let Him down. I am thankful to be alive!

Tuesday, July 4, 1961

Happy birthday, America! I did not have air enough to blow out all your candles! Today one of the nurses was listening to a baseball game at the nurses' station. As luck would have it, she was my nurse today. I mentioned my mommy loves to watch "her" team, the New York Yankees. Later the nurse brought in her radio so that my mommy could hear the game, which I thought was "over-the-top nursing." Mommy was so surprised that she was speechless! An exceptionally good day for both of us.

Wednesday, July 5, 1961

UP! Today I stayed up fifteen minutes in a wheelchair which felt fantastic! Later however, I vomited taking all that good feeling completely away. More x-rays and by Halloween I will have a nice glow and will not need any flashlights to see in the dark. I will light up the whole neighborhood. Everyone can follow me and not get lost. Well, that is if I get home and out of this place.

Thursday, July 6, 1961

I took an early wheelchair ride and feeling my oats. Ate breakfast and keeping my fingers crossed everything stays down. Before lunchtime, my stomach was acting strange, and right after eating lunch, you guessed it, I got sick again! I spent the afternoon in sleeping because Mommy told me the West Virginia group would be coming late afternoon for a visit. This time the group from Red House, including Uncle Kenna, Barbara Jo, and Mike, would be arriving around 4:30 PM. Dinner trays were advancing down the hall as Barbara Jo and the gang entered my room. They visited and watched me try to enjoy a bowl of beef stew, biscuit with no butter, warm milk, green Jello, and unbelievably soft vanilla ice cream.

I was sure their stomachs were yelling after seeing the fine meal I had. Debra, the nursing assistant, picked up my dinner tray and straightened out the blankets on my bed. I decided I would try for forty winks while the gang went out to dinner giving Mommy a much-needed break. I got Kenna's attention and told him to try and convince Mommy to stay at the Sheraton tonight so she could get a really good night's sleep. She deserves one!

Friday, July 7, 1961

My stomach stayed unsettled, but my temperature was down which was a blessing. The most recent blood test said my white blood cell count was high but did not raise any red flags with the medical staff. My long ride in the wheelchair was wonderful but wore me out to frazzle calling for a long afternoon nap.

Saturday, July 8, 1961

Early a knock at the door. To my surprise, it was the respiratory team coming to take out the trach. There was nothing to it except one small tug, but it almost made me sick, I am a pro. I feel much better now that I can talk, but now, I have nothing to say. I am drawing a blank; never would have imagined me at a loss for words.

Sunday, July 9, 1961

"I want to go home" and I kept repeating the words. I was tired of all this hospital mess, but my temperature was up, my back hurt, and I needed a change of scenery. This hospital room was the pits. I was looking forward to West Virginia! There was no place like the mountains of West Virginia. I have no bad reports today, so my brain was steady at wishing myself home.

Monday, July 10, 1961

I was in a good mood until a Candy Striper showed up to take me downstairs for a test I never heard of. I thought for sure I already had every test in this hospital having been here over two months, but I was wrong. This one was new: a liver test whatever that is, and do you know what? I got sick later that evening. I was about to believe every test they gave me made me sick. My temperature was down making me incredibly happy for a change. I had to go potty and started hollering for some help. Mommy came to my rescue trying to lift me off before I fell in, but she ended up hurting her hip and getting a serious lecture from nursing about the dangers of non-personnel helping patients. Luckily, neither of us was injured during this little fiasco, but nursing was NOT happy.

Tuesday, July 11, 1961

I felt like a piece of Swiss cheese with all the holes from blood tests and the attached wires. When will it all end? Is there any tests I haven't had? Everyone tells me how I am getting much better, but by golly, I feel like a mess. I kept throwing up and my stomach hurt. Is this the way it's gonna be from now on? I was only nine, and I sure hoped my life was gonna get better. I wanted to get back to the business of smiling and having a cheerful outlook. I was tired of being in the hospital; I wanted to see my daddy. Where was the "yellow brick road" of health I have heard about?

Wednesday, July 12, 1961

This morning got off to a rough start or should I say a familiar start: I got sick. Repeatedly, it happens. I wish I knew how to make it stop. Nurse Mary told me there were no tests scheduled today so I can take it easy. I needed to build up my strength from being in bed so long by taking a few steps by myself; however, I do not have the energy to do so. My crayons were within reach, and **Lassie** is one of my favorite shows on TV while in color.

Thursday, July 13, 1961

My fever had passed, and I had been up a total of sixty minutes and that is my new record for being out of bed! One of the volunteers took me downstairs for a test on my left leg this morning after breakfast. I had been complaining of pain and the test revealed I had a condition known as phlebitis which is painful inflammation and swelling. Two episodes of vomiting this evening, in which Mommy decided to retire to the hotel this evening for dinner and much-needed rest. Everyone hoped I was not taking steps backward and tomorrow all this would have passed.

Friday, July 14, 1961

Big Day for Joyce! Four steps with the aid of the nurse without falling over! Boy, that felt good. I got so excited about those four steps that later I threw up! The excitement must have been too much because later . . .

Running a slight fever of 100.4° this evening. I sure hope all this is the result of excitement and not of something medical to come. I only wanted "good" stuff to come from now on even though I knew I have no control of what happens. Here's something good: I sat in the chair for 2 1/2 hours this afternoon, a new record!

Saturday, July 15, 1961

This morning after breakfast, the nurse carted me down to x-ray for new films of my kidneys. During the night, my doctor ordered a round of IV fluids but as usual they never tell me anything 'cause I was just a kid. I was feeling better, but all of a sudden, I had an episode of throwing up, I wish I had a spicket on the side of my neck so I could turn it off whenever throwing up started. Guess I would look kinda funny, wouldn't I?

The doctors were concerned again about what was going on inside me and I was constantly wondering if I will ever be well. I wonder if Mommy felt she can never go home.

Sunday, July 16, 1961

I felt good having had an uninterrupted night's sleep and a good breakfast. All this throwing up was wearisome. Looking down at my feet, I noticed I walk on my tippy toes like a toddler. Is that because I have been spending so much time in the hospital bed? The nurse told me today to try and take more steps if possible. YEAH! I did so and it felt GREAT! I was finally doing so good the private duty nurse will be leaving.

Monday, July 17, 1961

The private duty nurse said her goodbyes today making me sad. Now when I need something, I will have to use the call bell and not have someone bedside. Mommy was concerned that not having a private nurse might hinder my recovery, but I will get "over it" and recover because I am strong and have faith.

Tuesday, July 18, 1961

Today is not a good day, and it is only 6 AM. Crying and nauseated at 9:30 AM. Is this a reaction to my private duty nurse leaving? I doubt it, but why is this happening?

After lunch I felt well enough to go down to the playroom to make blue flowers out of clay.

I had the energy to stay down there making something to give to my mommy. She will be so surprised. I had such a fun time that I wanted to go back after supper.

I was exhausted, but Mommy was so impressed, tears rolled down her face. In her mind, she figured that would never happen but now she has seen that prayers have been answered. Nurses on the floor clapped for joy seeing my accomplishment. Everyone was so happy that it had almost ignited a riot of happiness.

Wednesday, July 19, 1961

This was a nightmare! Sick again! Sick morning and night! Moved to another room and this one was HOT without a window! No air conditioning! My right leg was hurting, but I have no fever. The nursing staff was lousy. What is happening? I was glad my daddy was not here because he would blow his top with the lack of nursing care and the cost of what he was paying.

Thursday, July 20, 1961

More x-rays but this time of my liver. I think I noticed a little glow in the dark the other night. Come October I should be ready. Physically my temperature was doing fine, and my white blood cell count was within normal limits, so I am fine! Right? Mommy was down the hall at the nurse's station, and I heard her voice giving them a piece of her mind. She was NOT happy with my care and with the amount of money being charged. She also requested physical therapy to gain strength in my legs lost after so much time bedbound. Hearing my mommy raise her voice and upset was out of her character, but today she did what was right.

Friday, July 21, 1961

Physical therapy was to begin today—how is that for fast acting all because Mommy raised a little "Cain" at the nurse's station? Susan, the PTA, came to my room to check my level of ability and set up a plan of care. The entire therapy team encouraged me to eat in order to regain my strength. My appetite was poor and looking at the food served did not encourage me to eat.

Saturday, July 22, 1961

Overjoyed! Went down to the playroom and made a potholder! I gave it to Mommy and she loved it! No therapy on the weekend, so I will have to wait until Monday. Still not hungry, but if someone walked in the room with an ice cream cone, preferably chocolate, I would gobble it down in a flash. Mommy said the two little colored boys from down the hall call me "sleeping beauty." She also said they are genuinely nice and asked me to play with her.

I had been in bed too long and now my legs are weak. I walk for exercise and strength. Someone must tag along with me in case my legs give out. Nobody wants me to fall and split open my chest incision.

Sunday, July 23, 1961

Thank you, God, for this beautiful day! Mommy took me to the fifth floor to visit the nursing staff. I wanted to see the nurses who took care of me right after my open-heart surgery. I needed to thank them for such loving care and let them see how much I had recovered from those early dark days when everyone thought I would not survive.

Monday, July 24, 1961

I enjoy being on the other side of being sick. I hope I never have to go through surgery like this again. I know without God's loving Grace I would not have pulled through. I am truly blessed; I hope I never, ever forget how blessed I am.

Went to therapy and they told my mommy I have made tremendous progress. I watched the movie *Lassie Go Home* in the playroom and cried my eyes out. Walt Disney movies are the best. I also like Donald Duck and Friends because they remind me of myself always getting in trouble.

I felt I was finally on that "yellow brick road" leading to health. Could a plane ticket to West Virginia be in the near future?

CHAPTER 8

Tuesday, July 25, 1961

I walked by myself for the first time today, and everyone on the floor shouted for joy(ce)! I was so happy I could (almost) jump for joy! But I was afraid I might wobble and then, you know . . . fall down. Having a fantastic day and to top it off, Mommy and I went down to the cafeteria and had pizza for lunch! What a treat for my insides. Thanks, Mommy!

Wednesday, July 26, 1961

Walked again by myself; what a thrill it is to do something by yourself! Staff members hooped and hollered at my accomplishment. I received a package from my daddy today.

I opened it and a stuffed white dog with a fountain pen hopped out of the box! Not exactly, but he did say "autograph me." I want to make sure all the staff sign their names so I don't forget anyone who took great care of me while at St. Mary's.

Thursday, July 27, 1961

I started the day with a bang by putting both feet on the floor at the same time! WOW! Am I ready for a marathon? I think I better stick to one foot at a time and stay at a slow pace for now. Everyone told me I was doing a fantastic job, so I wanted to take my time and not mess up anything. There was a rumor going around that I would be going home next week. I'll try and not get myself all excited until Mommy and I hear it from my doctors. Look, see I get goose bumps just thinking about going home.

Friday, July 28, 1961

Everyone says I am going home but not saying when. Mommy spoke to Dr. Kneil today to see if the gossip was true. She didn't want me getting all worked up and then have a major letdown. One of my doctors decided it was time to set the record straight with my mommy.

Looking at her directly, the doctor said, "Mrs. Noffsinger, we will take x-rays and a few tests later today. We know that Joyce, your daughter, was close to death many times. Before she leaves these healing walls, we want to make sure nothing will keep her from the road to full recovery. The doctors working on her case have commented on how it lifts their spirits to see how well she has recovered and that she is definitely a 'miracle' child."

Saturday, July 29, 1961

This morning something amazing was taking place in my room; doctors from other areas of the hospital were gathering to see ME! To read my chart, all the difficulties and to watch me walk. What was so special about my ability to put one foot in front of the other?

Everybody does this, so why are they here?

Sunday, July 30, 1961

I was happy as can be until I heard Mommy arguing with one of the nurses. It seemed one of the nurses gave permission for me to go outside when another said "no." She returned later to explain saying I had company which threw me into a major tizzy. I wanted to go out, feel, taste, and grab the air in my hands. I was ready and then . . . BAM! I was crushed, my emotions taking me out of control closing off my air. I should have known better, but I was just a kid who came out of a serious illness. God will keep lifting me up as many times as needed giving us the courage to see that we make the right turns down the yellow brick road of life if I ask and follow Him.

Monday, July 31, 1961

Today I am better, but Mommy was not having a good day. Another run-in with a nurse and she was upset. All nurses assigned to my care all need to know what I am allowed and not allowed to do instead of different ones getting my mommy upset. She had been through more than most nurses will experience in their lifetime. Can I please go home before my mommy collapses?

Tuesday, August 1, 1961

At 5 AM the lab department woke me up for a blood test. After breakfast, Mommy and I went down to the playroom where I got my hands dirty working with clay. It felt so good using my hands and arms for something other than a pin cushion or pipeline for blood. Playing with and getting the clay between my fingers was excellent medicine much better than drugs. Down the hall I heard a disturbance. Recognizing the voice as my mommy's, I wanted to know what the problem was. I feared an unpleasant outcome due to the added stress and the extended period of time here in New York. Dr. Craft's office in Huntington has informed my physicians here at St. Mary's that transportation arrangements have been made to fly Mommy and I back home as soon as discharge paperwork have been completed. Word spread among the staff that I would soon be leaving. Mommy and I have become like family to many staff members over the last three months here at St. Mary's. Leaving and going back home will be exciting but saying good-bye to the medical staff will be hard.

Personnel from various departments came delivering warm farewell wishes. Some did not recognize me having seen me last at "death's door." A small celebration party was scheduled before Mommy and I was to leave the hospita.. All members of the medical team who had taken part in my recovery were invited to attend the celebration that was disguised as a Discharged Planning Meeting. I was unsure why we were entering the large conference room when suddenly . . . "Surprise!"

Startled at first, I was amazed at the number of familiar faces in the staff room. Balloons filled the area. A large rectangular table was set up with several types of finger foods and beverages. A vegetable tray of celery, carrots, radishes, cauliflower, cucumbers, various peppers, broccoli, cheese, and crackers was available for the picking. A large tub filled with ice, tea, soda, and water was also available. Dr. Kneil, the surgeon who operated, was first of the "well-wishers."

"I have followed Joyce's case since 1957 and know she is blessed. Since her surgery, Joyce has been at death's door and been turned away. God has special plans for this young lady. Her recovery will be long but here the medical community at St. Mary's believe we have witnessed a miracle. You sure look better than you did a few weeks ago. Take care and have a safe trip home."

Staffing from numerous departments came to wish their former patient a speedy recovery and safe travels home. Tears of joy and hugs of love followed after each staff member said their good-byes. Dr. Craft's office in West Virginia had prearranged flights out of New York.

Time was up for celebrating and now we must gather our things and get to the airport.

Lacking the strength to walk the long hallways, a call was placed reserving a wheelchair at the departing flight entrance. Arriving at the New York Airport, we were met by several airline staff. Stepping out of the cab, Mommy helped me get comfortable in the special wheelchair. Pushed by airline personnel, Mommy followed as we boarded the plane before other passengers. I insisted on a window seat taking seat 4A with Mommy alongside in 4B. Buckled in and exhausted from the day's events, I planned to sleep during airtime, but excitement took over preventing any shut-eye. I have experienced this moment as many times in my dreams, but now this is real. I must pinch myself to make sure this is the real thing. Taxied down the runway, there's a bit of congestion resulting in a delay of ten minutes. Not a lengthy period of time, but it had been three months since I've breathed fresh mountain air I was ready to inhale. More importantly, I wanted to go home.

The plane started to move once more then made a slight turn before stopping again. A sudden burst of energy and then the plane high-tailed down the runway, or was that my imagination? Yes, we are moving upward into the clouds.

I see blue sky as we entered into a group of mysterious-looking clouds. Have we ventured beyond the wild blue and over a rainbow?

The sun entered the small window blinding my sight. Sitting back down in my seat, excitement stirred a twinge in my chest. I must have brought along a few critters in my pants 'cause I can't sit still with anticipation waiting to see Daddy and my sister, Grace.

I might even give Daddy's old car a hug. Mommy assured me both of them would be at the gate waiting.

The overhead lights in the cabin flickered. The plane shifted to the right as one of the attendants was delivering beverages down the narrow aisle. The seatbelt sign flashed on and off as the captain began speaking, "Good afternoon, this is your captain. Folks we are experiencing strong turbulence as we pass through a series of angry thunderstorms. Winds are gusting and the approach might be a little bumpy. For your safety, please remain seated until we are on the ground and taxied to the gate. Cabin personnel, collect all trays and beverage containers. Preparing for landing at Tri-State Airport. Thank you for your cooperation."

The captain signed off and immediately the plane landed in the hands of nasty weather.

The aircraft was tossed around like a feather before leveling off and easing everyone's mind. Without warning, a sudden drop of five hundred feet altitude, flickering of the cabin lights leaving only the floor illumination. I heard the engines struggle but could not see out the window. Mommy was silent with her eyes closed, but at least she was breathing. I tried to scream for help, but my voice was shallow and still healing from the tracheotomy.

I felt the engines hesitate. I wanted to look out the window, but my seat jammed and would not budge. My newly repaired heart started to shilly-shally making me uneasy but not enough to alarm Mommy. She was already in a heightened state of emotions not needing any additional stress.

Almost like a witch's spell, the cabin filled with white smoke. A massive coughing spell began among all the passengers until everyone lost consciousness. After an undetermined amount of time, I woke up slightly confused and groggy. A fury tail brushed across my face several times restoring me back to reality. Opening my eyes, I found myself sitting in my living room recliner. GraceNote is comfortably sitting on my lap giving me one of her long feline looks. Remnants of *The Wizard of Oz* remain playing on my mounted TV.

Decades of memories slowly danced forward in my mind. Like looking through a crystal ball, I saw myself sliding down the floodwall on California Street headed for the Ohio River.

I huffed and puffed my way up the small hill, but I thoroughly enjoyed the ride down with my mouth wide open. Luckily, I took along no freeloaders in my mouth during the short journey downward. I was always ready to keep on as long as my ticker and Mommy would permit. Those were the days when Walter and I engaged in a snowball fight on a cold winter's night. Mommy would not let me stay out too long fearing I would catch a cold while the other kids remained outside till their fingers froze. We wanted to make snow cream but changed our minds due to the "yellow" appearance.

So many memories flashed before me. My brain must be filled with straw because I am totally confused. The doctors at St. Mary's had told my parents that sometime in the future I would need another open-heart surgery.

By 1990 my aortic valve needed replacement. By that time, I was married and the mother of three small children. Surgery was planned at the local hospital near where I was living with my family. A cardiac catheterization was performed confirming the need for replacement. At the age of thirty-eight, I would undergo a second open-heart surgery. Physicians replaced my disease valve with a mechanical valve on March 15, 1990. My mom flew in from Texas but did not arrive before they took me in for my operation. Cardiac surgery requires splitting the chest open. Space is limited so surgeons rely on the sense of touch to feel their way around inside the chest cavity. He cannot see so one of three outcomes is possible. One: the stitch is too loose resulting in leakage. Too tight a condition known as a Complete Heart Block requiring a pacemaker. The third possibility is correct placement and the heart beats perfectly. My operation resulted in the heart block. The upper and lower chambers of my heart do not communicate properly. The medical term for this condition is Third Degree Heart Block. A dual Chamber Pacemaker was implanted the next day under localized anesthetic. Afterward, I developed a severe infection and pneumonia.

Thirty days later, I was discharged home with antibiotic treatments and special instructions related to certain foods, microwave ovens, and the importance of keeping all medical appointments.

God has a plan for me, and I will not let Him down. My road to health continues to have many detours, but I try and maintain my joyful spirit and more importance to keep my faith.

I went back to school receiving an AA in Music Magna Cum Laude. I taught myself the hammered dulcimer and received a gift of paid tuition to become a Certified Music Practitioner. Employed by a local hospital, I adjusted breathing patterns and heart rhythms with the power of one note. I played for cardiac, general, and mother-to-be patients as well as in the emergency room waiting room. Once given permission by family members, I played at bedside for dying patients. I had found my "calling" as music spoke to me and my heart in many ways. Music would be the special glue that would hold me together as storms of everyday life would try to rob me of my inner peace and joy. God promised me He would never leave me, and He never did.

My strong faith would keep me and my battery-operated heart in motion as death robbed me one by one of my family. My sister died of colon cancer in 2002 at the youthful age of fifty-two after a long painful illness. As a child, her only sickness was having her tonsils removed as she witnessed my frequent doctor visits and cardiac procedures. She and I planned to take care of our mom and dad in their later years. Her death left a major void in my life. Although she lived in West Virginia, often I turned to her for strength and support especially after I decided to leave my marital home after twenty years.

An exceedingly difficult decision, I toiled and prayed many times before packing and moving out. The reaction from my family left me numb. I expected to be convinced to stay but nothing! I took only what I needed giving them many opportunities to ask me to stay.

They showed no emotion as I walked out but at no time was I asked to return. I kept close contact with my kids, but my husband was silent.

My father died in 2008 from emphysema. Both of them lived in Florida and now Mom was alone, slowing down trying to keep the home Dad built for them. Losing my job as a Music Practitioner paved the way for the move to Florida and taking care of my Mom. Angry at first, I didn't want to pack up and leave everything I've known. However, God doesn't give us more than we can bear without giving us the strength to see it through.

In Florida I felt lost. No longer did I enjoy music. Two members of my family were gone, and the heat was unbearable. I would adjust to the weather and my surroundings. At times I felt my brain consisted of straw not knowing what I was to do with the rest of my life. No friends except the senior citizen friends of my mother's.

I would "hang out" with the group and went to exciting places with my mom. However, in 2011 she started to slow down and slept more during the day. I found a job in retail working for a few hours two days at a time. Sounds easy after being in healthcare for eighteen years in which I thought I knew how to work with the public. I found out I had a lot to learn that would take more than an overnight lesson to cover all the material.

Mom and I took a few cruises and in 2012 decided to venture down to the Panama Canal.

Tickets bought and impatience building until I visited my cardiologist. Can you believe my aortic valve was acting up again? I had earlier told myself I would never, ever go through OH (open-heart) again. The former surgeries had been involved, long hospitalizations and life-threatening. Now, older and living in Florida, I'm busy taking care of my mom while working a part-time job. Who would step in if something happened?

Was I becoming cowardly? My heart needed help and for the first time I questioned life giving help. Why was this such a "horse of a different color" in decision making? Have I come to the end of my "yellow brick road of health"? Instead of a cruise to the Panama Canal, the only trip I would be taking involved a flight to New York Heart Hospital for an eventful open-heart number three.

In 2012 at the age of sixty, I would once again undergo open-heart surgery. Well, I was worried about the procedure but more concerned about my mom. Could she withstand seeing me go into the OR another time in her weakened state? My daughter, Heather, was flying in from Virginia to help me and be of assistance with her grandmother.

I followed the path of surgeries number one and two . This hospital became my new home away from home after another eventful and difficult surgery. Repeat complications and infections extended my stay three months. Once discharged, I received home health visits two days a week for IV medications. The infections left me in a weaken state using a walker. I thought I could do anything when in reality my legs were weak like straw, my head was as hollow as a raided walnut shell, and I thought I was "hot!"

I survived a third time. God was not through with me. Having my chest opened up the first and the second time was painful. The third time, I had my pillow on hand if I needed it when laughing, moving, and the dreaded sneeze. Have no fear 'cause there will be no worries. Hold on and let 'er blow! Remember God's Promise: He will never leave us!

The surgery took the wind out of my sails, but I was above water taking in good ole air.

My daughter remained several weeks helping me while aiding with the care of my mom. Sleeping most of the day, her physician told us it would be just a matter of time before she would join my sister who died in 2002 and my dad in 2008. The day after Mother's Day 2012, I painfully kissed my mom goodbye. I imagine my experience was similar to my mom's being at bedside as the priest performed the Sacrament of Last Rites at St. Mary's in 1961. God had other plans for me as my heart kept beating on.

Vocabulary

Monopoly	67
Mickey Mouse Club	58
Mr. Greene Jeans	9
NPO	53
Old Maid	3
Old McDonald	60
Our Father	91
Over the Rainbow	91
Pacemaker	106
Paper dolls	2
Piece of Cake	3,78
Radio Flyer	29
Red light/green	3
Rosaces	8
Rubber Cement	85
Sacrament of the Sick	91
Sheraton	36
Sign of the Cross	49
Song Stuck Syndrome	11
Tag	3
Twinkle, Twinkle	10
Tizzy	28,101
There's no place Like home	89
Tracheotomy	76
Tango	45

References

1. *Websters New World Crossword Puzzle Dictionary*,
   2nd edition
   Houghton Miffllin Harcourt Boston, New York
   Compiled by Jane Shaw Whitfield, 1997

2. *The New Comprehensive A-Z Crossword Dictionary*,
   Revised edition
   Praxedes Gracia Schaffer, 1995

3. *The Merriam Webster Thesaurus*
   Merriam-Webster, Inc., 2005

4. *Word Painting: A Guide to Writing More Descriptively*
   Rebecca McClanahan, 1999

5. "Bonanza" TV show 1959-1973
   NBC tv SERIES

6. "Denis the Menace"
   1959 CBS American Sitcom

7. "Lassie Go Home" 1943
   Metro-Goldwyn

8. "The Lone Ranger & Tonto"
   1957 ABC TV
   Radio series debuted 1933

9. "The Mickey Mouse Club
   1955-1959 ABC Created by Walt Disney &
   Hal Adelquist

10. Music
    "God Will Take Care of You"
    Walter Stillman Martin & Civilla Durfee Martin
    Composers 1905

11. "Twinkle Twinkle Little Star"
    English lullaby published 19th C Nursery
    Rhyme 1830
    Martin and Lowel Mason & Buddy Guy Composers
    Sarah Josepha Hale Lyricist

12. "The Beat Goes On"
    1966 written by Sonny Bono
    Sung by Sonny and Cher

13. "Somewhere Over The Rainbow" 1939
    Written by Harold Arlen
    Lyrics Yip Harburg

14. "Dem Bones" 1928
    Written by James Weldon Johnson
    Also known as "Dry Bones"

15. "The Rifleman"
    ABC 1958-1963 TV

I0568620

THIS TIME IT'S
PERSONAL

BUILDING A LIFE,
A BUSINESS, AND A
SELF THAT ACTUALLY FITS

THE BEAM LIFE

To the women who don't have it all figured out
and are building it anyway.

CONTENTS

INTRODUCTION
THIS TIME, IT'S PERSONAL

Here's what nobody tells you about rock bottom: sometimes it's exactly where you need to be to finally start building something real.

By late 2019, my marriage had been slowly suffocating me for years, but we were fucking masters at pretending everything was fine. From the outside, we looked like we had it all together—the business, the beautiful daughter, the picture-perfect life. The divorce blindsided everyone because we'd gotten so good at performing happiness that even we almost believed it sometimes.

The truth is, I'd been disappearing inside that marriage for years, going through the motions, checking all the boxes of what I thought my life should look like. When everything finally exploded, it was messy and dramatic and took everyone by surprise, including me.

Around the same time, I fell in love with my now spouse, who happened to be nonbinary. Not because I was running away from my marriage, but because for the first time in years, I felt seen. Really seen. It forced me to question everything I thought I knew about myself and what I wanted.

So there I was, navigating a very public divorce, figuring out my sexuality, starting over financially, and then because life apparently has a twisted sense of timing, a global pandemic hit.

Let's just say it was a rough couple of years. And when your whole world implodes, you need an outlet, right? I'm not much of a writer—I've always been better at talking (shocker I know!)—so I started a podcast. Not because I had some master plan, but because I was drowning and needed to find my voice again. I needed to figure out who I was when all the labels I'd been wearing my whole life suddenly didn't fit anymore.

Little by little, women started reaching out, thanking me for my transparency. What they didn't know is that I was still holding back, still curating which parts of my mess I was willing to share. Because it's terrifying to let people see you when you don't even know who you are yet.

That's when I realized something had to change. If I wanted to change my life, I had to change my environment. I had to stop waiting for permission to be myself and start creating spaces where other women could do the same. That's how The BEAM Life was born—Be Everything And More. It's about women allowing ourselves to have more without feeling guilty about it. We can be more than just wife, more than just mom, more than just entrepreneur. We can be everything we are and still want more.

Now, if you look at the cover of this book, you'll see a bee. That's not random. My original BEAM Life logo had a bee too. I've always been obsessed with them, got a tattoo of one years ago, long before I understood what they would come to mean in my life. There was just something about them that called to me. Then the day my Yiayia—my Greek grandmother and original female entrepreneur before that was even a thing—passed away, a bee showed up. Just sat there with me, like she was saying goodbye through this tiny, powerful creature. Since then, I've fallen even deeper in love with them.

But it's not just the spiritual connection that gets me. It's what we can learn from them that's fucking magnificent.

The queen bee has figured out something most women never will: she's completely focused on herself. Her health, her needs, her well-being. And because she does this, the entire hive thrives. She doesn't apologize for taking what she needs. She doesn't feel guilty about being the center of attention. She knows that if she's not well, everything falls apart. The whole ecosystem depends on her willingness to put herself first.

Bees are essential to everything. Without them, our world literally wouldn't survive. They're small but mighty, and they don't ask permission to do their work.

This is exactly what The BEAM Life is about. For too long, we've been told that wanting more is greedy. That prioritizing ourselves is selfish. That our dreams should always come second to everyone else's needs. But what if we've had it backwards this whole time? What if the most radical thing we can do is take care of ourselves so fiercely that we create space for everyone around us to thrive?

Why This Book Matters

This book exists because I got tired of reading success stories written by people so far removed from the struggle that they forgot what it actually felt like to be scared, broke and desperate for something different. I got tired of advice that sounded pretty but didn't work for women who can't afford to quit their day jobs, who can't hire nannies, who can't risk everything on a whim.

All our names are on the cover of this book because this isn't just my story. It's ours. It's the story of nine women who decided to stop apologizing for wanting more and started building something that felt like home to who they actually are. We haven't "made it." We're making it. Right now. In real time. With moody kids demanding snacks in the background, debt we're still paying off, anxiety that shows up uninvited, and businesses held together with duct tape and pure fucking determination.

We're writing while we're still scared, still figuring it out, still making mistakes but choosing to do it anyway.

If this book called to you, I'm guessing you know what it feels like to dream bigger than your current reality allows. Maybe you're juggling a full-time job that pays the bills but slowly drains your soul. Maybe you're knee-deep in the beautiful chaos of raising kids while that business idea keeps whispering in your ear. Most days, the gap between where you are and where you want to be feels impossible to bridge. But there's something in you that won't let you give up.

I have never been traditional or played by the rules. Just ask my parents. I think I broke every rule, so why stop now? This book is about breaking the rules a bit. Not worrying about the how or the strategy because it's not linear. It's about honoring your soul's calling and living a life that makes you proud.

Making It Personal

The title of this book isn't an accident. "This Time" acknowledges that you've probably tried before, maybe multiple times, to build something that felt right. Something was always missing though, wasn't it? "It's Personal" means we're done with the one-size-fits-all advice, the generic strategies that work for everyone except you.

Often when women are setting boundaries, they say "sorry" or "it's not you, it's me." But that's bullshit, and it's time we called it what it is.

We're not speaking to you from some fancy stage where we've got it all figured out. We're sitting across from you at coffee, sharing the stuff that usually gets left out of the highlight reel. The messy, uncomfortable, real parts of building a business while also trying to keep your life from falling apart.

Most people I've butted heads with would call me stubborn. I prefer tenacious or uncompromising. Because the women you're about to meet? We don't give up. Even when giving up would be so much easier.

I didn't get handed a manual for building a business from scratch while raising a neurodiverse kid, while drowning in debt, while living in an AI era where our personal voices can get lost in all the noise. But here's what I know for sure: isolation will kill your dreams faster than failure ever will.

We try so hard to hold it all together, to be the strong one, to not inconvenience anyone. But healing and transformation? They're inconvenient as hell. And that's exactly why we need each other.

As a coach, I've heard hundreds of women's stories. They're the lifeblood of what I do. Through storytelling, we realize we're not alone in this crazy beautiful mess.

What You'll Find Here

The women whose stories fill these pages are current and former clients. They all have life things they juggle and overcome to build what they want. They inspire me to get out of bed every morning, and I'm grateful as hell for each of them.

What connects them isn't their industries or their bank accounts. It's their refusal to wait for permission. Their willingness to start before they feel ready. Their commitment to honoring what's true for them, even when everyone else thinks they've lost their minds.

They understand that Being Everything And More doesn't mean being perfect. It means being whole. Showing up as all of yourself, struggles included, because your story might be exactly what someone else needs to hear.

In the pages ahead, you'll meet these women. You'll hear their real stories, not the polished versions they might share on Instagram. You'll read about the moments that changed everything, the decisions that terrified them, the mistakes that taught them, the victories that surprised them.

Their stories aren't your roadmap. They're your permission slip. Permission to trust yourself, to start messy, to change course when something isn't working, to succeed in a way that feels true to you.

I want you to walk away from this book changed. Not because you have a new strategy or system, but because you finally understand that you don't need another course or certification. You need to start. You need to trust yourself. You need to stop waiting for someone else to give you permission to live the life you actually want.

Building something that fits you isn't selfish. It's essential. The world needs what you have to offer, but only if you're brave enough to offer it.

I'm far from having my shit together, and I want you to see that it's okay. Stop waiting to be ready or perfect because babe, perfect ain't coming, and that's fucking boring anyway.

Most of all, I hope you join us. This isn't just a book. It's an invitation into a community of women who believe in each other and refuse to let each other give up. The BEAM Life isn't a concept; it's a way of being. A commitment to being everything you are and more than you ever imagined possible.

This time, it's personal. And that's exactly how it should be.

xx,

Kaitlin

ONE

AMANDA LAZENBY
BIG SHIFT ENERGY

There's a part of me that always knew that in darkness, that's where I could find the light. Growing up, the thought of being the person I am now was laughable. Every part of who I am would have been judged, criticized, and minimized. Success was abandoning myself and my identity. This led to acceptance that I may never have the life I dreamt of as a little girl, because in my little-girl mind, I didn't live past thirty.

Here I am, living in what I call my "bonus years."

I found myself most aligned when I was creating art, but somehow I kept finding my way back to the "medical field." While I was hemming and hawing for a declared major in undergrad, I thought, Public Health. This is it! I can serve my community and share my passion for living a healthy life.

Jaded. That's where this left me ten years later.

When Corporate Wellness Became Corporate Illness

Working in corporate wellness meant helping people became secondary to saving corporations money, and I became the face of that. The human factor got lost somewhere between spreadsheets and cost analyses. You know what I mean by the human factor? The factor where your company doesn't remember that you are human and need more than three days for bereavement.

My Version of Britney Spears' 2007

Dealing with my version of Britney's 2007—you know, that very public breakdown year—which was my 2024, I clung to what made me feel like a human. Art. That's what made me feel alive. Dancing, painting, creating.

Behind the scenes, I was processing major life events. Some had been years in the making, like finalizing the conscious uncoupling with my partner of almost fifteen years. I focused on finding balance in giving grace to myself and my soon-to-be ex-husband. Neither of us dreamed of this path, but we knew us "not working" was actually working for us.

I saw many women going through divorces reinventing themselves. Meanwhile, I felt stuck in the chaos. Someone rear-ended me at a red light and totaled my precious yellow Fiat—my first brand new car. I dealt with mobility issues and couldn't paint or dance for months. The angst I felt doom-scrolling on socials led me to remove some apps entirely off my phone to save my sanity.

I constantly worked toward a goal to dance again. It would be six months before my first class, and I felt SO ALIVE again. In the middle of this chaos, I was still trying to get the divorce finalized and remember who the fuck I was. I didn't want to reinvent myself or get a revenge body. I wanted to feel at home in my body and at peace with where I was, including feeling the pain.

When Grief Comes Into Focus

My dad's health continued to decline. There were days, then weeks, then months where he didn't know who I was. The distance between Kentucky and Texas was no match for my heart when he didn't recognize me. I grieved for the day and for the future, knowing this chapter would be closing.

I started shifting my mindset about where he would go when he wasn't "with us." If I could imagine the worst case scenario, I could also imagine the best. I projected that he was doing his favorite things and that somewhere in his mind we were happily fishing, beaching, whatevering. And my heart hurt like I never knew it could.

The Breaking Point

I knew things weren't working FOR me years ago. I felt trapped doing things that made me look good on paper —the degrees, the job dedication, the marriage, volunteering. I'm proud of these accomplishments, but I knew I was made for more. All of these experiences took me to a waiting room for something bigger.

If you've ever decided to leave a relationship, it's never one day that you decide it's enough. It's a culmination of experiences that affirm when it's time. You do it scared. You do it feeling broken. You realize that the systems you created are working FOR YOU to stay settled in a life that aims to please others.

Creating a life aiming to please others means you instead please no one. And I mean NO ONE—not the people you aim to please and most certainly not yourself. The hardest relationship I ever had to leave was the one with myself. The one where I kept saying YES to what was safe by consistency but not safe for my soul.

Playing it safe meant leaving. Safety was on the other side of what I trained my being to understand as safe. Walking on eggshells to keep the peace was a form of self-abandonment I was ready to burn to the ground. Eggshells and all.

Meeting My Soul Friend

The day I met Kaitlin, I had recently moved to my new place. I was exhausted from moving and dealing with health issues. It took everything in me to go to the event and talk myself into it. She was the emcee, and when she spoke, it reverberated within me.

"When was the last time you looked at yourself naked in the mirror and told yourself you were beautiful?" she spoke into the mic.

I could instantly feel seen. During a break, I went up to her and said, "I've been wanting to start a podcast." Without skipping a beat or knowing me, she replied,

"You totally should!" Before the event was over, I became a BEAMer.

I needed someone in my corner who didn't need the "juicy" details of the divorce but could support me. When she offered her BEAM Life Blueprint course, I did everything I could to make that happen for myself. I started living for ME again. I surrounded myself with new people and focused on doing the work.

Doing the work is not running away from yourself anymore. If I wanted to live a life that wasn't stuck on the same loop, I needed to create a new life, brick by brick. After all, that's what you do when you burn it all down. You rebuild.

Becoming My Own Phoenix

I had to become a disappointment to myself and others to build a life that fits me. I had to be okay with the discomfort of knowing that I would hurt other people when I chose myself. I couldn't keep taking responsibility for how others would perceive me when I said NO.

I was the greatest and unsolicited volunteer for a life of pleasing others. Now, I needed to shift gears so I could love the parts of myself that needed to be loved. By pleasing others, I learned that it created a void within me. The only person who could satisfy this void was me.

I was my own phoenix. I was the one who could survive the fire and the ash. I had to become my own unicorn, phoenix, mermaid, fairy and everything in between.

That meant not everyone could come with me in the same way they showed up before. It hurt that these relationships were transforming, but it also created gratefulness for how they were there for me along this journey.

The Birth of Art for the Heart

During my Britney year, I clung to what made me feel human. Art. I surprisingly kept creating art that was fun and light-hearted, even though grief completely overwhelmed my being.

When I decided to assign meaning to this, I honored this as a skill I could share with others who wanted to find their way back to their heart. Who wanted to reclaim this part of their story so that the shadows created a masterpiece. That they could create in community and not feel isolated. The shadows can be a space to play, a sacred space for intimacy and love.

This is where Art for the Heart started—in my own way of dealing with the shadows.

I had to abandon the need for another certification or degree. What I wanted to bring to my business didn't require another degree. To bring art to my business was to bring life to it. I needed the art to feel connected to my purpose and my being. I feel the most alive when I'm creating—through movement, paint, mixed media, and laughter.

Adding the art component allowed me to help others intuitively tap into themselves without feeling the pressure of therapy. This was about play and cuteness. It was about saying "FUCK" or other "bleepable words" when you felt like you had to say other words, but that's the one you desperately wanted to say. It was about messing things up and knowing you don't have to fix it.

Art for the heart is to bring all parts of us and express it one creative mark at a time. This wasn't a strategy—it happened organically after much resistance. Sometimes our passions don't make any logical sense, but in hindsight it was there all along.

Finding Peace in Simple Moments

After years of living through constant change and chaos, the seemingly normal things felt hard. The hardest days were the ones where I could find peace sitting in my living room watching birds on the feeder while my laundry tumbled in the dryer. I would say, out loud, this is the dream you searched for. This is the dream where silence and stillness didn't mean a threat lurked around the corner.

They say skilled sailors have to leave the harbor and experience the storm, but I was the opposite. I didn't know what to do in still waters. So some days, it was a flex to sit there and listen to the laundry until the dryer stopped. I'd pull out the fresh linens and fold them while their warmth reminded me that this could be my anchor.

Finding ways to be at peace with stillness helped me learn what feeling good meant. I needed to know at a core level that it was okay for me to feel good about feeling good.

Painting Through the Grief

After the car wreck, it was painful to paint, but that's what kept me going. I started using watercolor because I could travel with it. I took mine to Texas when I knew the inevitable was about to happen as my dad transitioned from this earth. I woke up every day after his passing with one mission: to paint.

Unlike the past, where in times of grief my paintings became a dark blob on a canvas, my art was bright and cheerful. I was pleasantly surprised. Historically, my art would be so dark that I would paint over it later. This time, it's like I tapped into a light deep within me waiting to come out.

I painted for hours and days. I asked friends to send me random objects to paint. My favorite became a fire alarm that I painted in the airport as I waited to fly home to whatever chapter came next.

I learned something in these moments. You don't have to experience darkness to feel it, and you don't have to feel the light to create it. Instead of seeing my life as a painting trying to find the light, I shifted to see that I was the light. There will always be darkness and shadows to add depth, but it's not the painting. Your eyes are drawn to the lightest parts, it's a reminder that this is home too.

The Simple Choices That Changed Everything

There are three simple choices that helped me remember who the fuck I am.

One: I have all the time I need and there is no time lost. When I felt rushed, I reminded myself there's still so much time to live this life. I move with intention and sacredness to my time and energy.

Two: "Stronger every day" is my mantra. This could mean mentally or physically. I wanted something to represent finding peace in the stillness. Strength is free from gym goals or weight targets. It served me post-wreck when I was building up strength in my wrist so I could paint again.

Three: I make it impossible to hide myself from the world. I dance like people are watching and they are the extras in MY life. I want to live boldly for no one other than myself, full of colors, pink as a neutral, and laughing as much as my crow's feet wrinkles can handle.

Living Like It's Tuesday in Retirement

I focused on days where I could enjoy a glimmer—those tiny moments that made life feel worth living. It started with a conversation with a dear friend where we jokingly talked about what we would be doing on a random Tuesday if we were retired. I instinctively said, "I would drink afternoon tea out of the cutest teacup."

That's when I started building glimmers into my day that fueled my heart with joy. I could no longer wait till I retired or the stars aligned. It had to be now. You don't need something external to motivate you to build the life you want. You just fucking do it.

I started asking myself, if I was retired today and it was a Tuesday, what would I be doing at home? Most of the time, whatever my heart conjures, I can make it happen within the same day. It might be having tea in a fancy cup, walking in the park, calling a friend, or taking a nap. I don't have to wait till I'm retired to add simple joys to my life.

I fiercely protect my boundary against the urge to settle out of necessity. Settling is always an option until I can figure out another way, but it's not the final option. Even when I can only see two options, I know there are at least three.

Having it all now means feeling peace, but not only when there's chaos. I learned how to weather the storm, and like a hurricane's eye, that's where I felt peace. But now, experiencing peace because I'm alive and not focused on survival is another level of "having it all."

The Gift of Feeling Good

Ever since I was a child, feeling good was something I avoided. I would remember how fragile life was or how this could be "the last" of something. Living this way was exhausting, always thinking something bad was lurking around the next hour or day.

Now, I can see that life is full of wonderment and I can see how GOOD life can be. I don't have to anticipate the worst. Life will happen, but every day I'm stronger and more equipped to rise up to meet whatever happens next. So why not feel good and relax into this moment?

Being fully myself is dancing with my shadows and light. I don't have to focus on how I will respond—I just be. I'm surrounded by people who remind me that I am light and that I cannot stare into the darkness too long by myself.

The Silly Goose Who Found Her Light

If I could tell my past self anything before she took this leap, I'd say: Its going to hurt like hell and when you don't think you'll make it, you find joy in Snapchat filters and keep going. It's not the big life changes that you see as markers, but the memories of laughter through it all. It's in the little "shifts" that we really see the Big Shift Energy.

I'm most proud that my heart loves to love. That being a silly goose lights my path. I had so many twists and turns in my life that I could be a pretzel with salt and marinara, but I'm out here making art and dancing.

There is darkness, but there is also light. It's the silly goose that makes it shine. I am the lotus, growing through the mud, and the sunflower, reaching for the sun. Somewhere in between, I'm blooming where I'm planted.

This time, it's personal because this is MY life and I'm living it with purpose. I choose the meaning for what happens to me in this life. You cannot tell me that everything happens for a reason, but I can give reason to what happens next. I want to live with intention and let myself fully live with that BIG SHIFT ENERGY!

Scan to connect with Amanda

TWO

AUDREY ROSE

COMING HOME TO MYSELF

I used to wake up every day with a knot in my stomach wondering, "Is this really my life?"

One day, I stood in the bathroom staring at my own reflection and honestly, I felt like I was staring at a stranger in the mirror. I looked so dull. I had no spark. I couldn't remember the last time I did something just for me. I didn't even know my favorite color anymore, that's how far I drifted away from myself.

On paper, it looked like I had it all. I was praised for being ambitious, driven, the woman who could handle anything. But behind the scenes, I felt empty and exhausted. Numb. No matter how much I achieved, it's like it was never enough. I wasn't enjoying the life I was working so hard to build.

I sank down the wall and onto the cold bathroom tile as tears hit the floor. Is this going to be it? Wake up, work, achieve, repeat—until I die? That's the moment I realized I had completely lost myself.

The Societal Checklist

I grew up with this very specific idea of what success "should" look like. I think a lot of us feel this as women —that success looks like having two kids by 30, a nice house with a white picket fence, a brand new car and a good job where you're climbing the corporate ladder.

I spent my entire life living for everybody else, doing everything "right," following the rules, checking those boxes and molding myself into who I thought I should be. In the process, I lost myself. I did everything that I was supposed to do. I got the career as a registered nurse. I was dating the guy that society would place me with. I was buying the house with a white picket fence. I was doing all of the things to check off all of the boxes so that I could say that I "made it."

I kept molding myself into a version of me that was meant to please others, that was meant to look good to others. It was very demanding. I was constantly busy. I was constantly doing everything for everyone else. Every choice I made was not about me and not about what I thought I wanted, but it was more about what would other people think of me and what is the right thing to do that's going to help me to complete this societal checklist quicker.

Honestly, I continued to lose myself. But I didn't know it at the time. I thought things were all finally coming together for me.

The Decision to Choose Myself

Things were actually far from finally coming together. I got closer and closer to looking like who I thought I was supposed to be, but I was exhausted. Something had to change. I ended up leaving the relationship, left my job, left everything. I ended up moving out near the ocean, ready to make the change in my life I was craving. It was time to heal myself from the exhaustion, the stress, the pure burnout of chasing this societal version of success. It was time to choose myself over the image I had been maintaining.

My Healing Journey

After I moved back, I started my own *Eat, Pray, Love* journey. I knew that I needed to find myself and heal. I had grown up thinking that healing, energy work, or any of this was very taboo and woo-woo, which isn't cool, right? But one thing led to another, and I was so desperate to feel like myself again, that I became kind of like a seeker.

I started to try it all. I listened to an Audible book by Gabby Bernstein and got like a little breadcrumb when she mentioned that she practices Kundalini Yoga. So I started trying Kundalini yoga. That led me to learning about different mantra music. I eventually went out and was chanting with Buddhist monks, doing group meditations, Reiki, sound healing, meditating in Himalayan salt caves. I started to try everything: crystal healing, sound baths in lavender fields, silent meditation retreats, anything I could get my hands on to start my healing journey.

The Deep Transformation

Truly over time, this started to change my life. I started to feel more free and more aligned with myself. My nervous system started to totally shift because I was practicing, without even knowing it, all of these different somatic healing tools. I started to do EFT tapping, I got into breathwork and for the first time in a very long time, I started to feel relaxed.

I felt like I was coming from a more regulated place. My nervous system took a full exhale. I was able to breathe again, and I began transforming into a whole new version of myself who had more clarity, more confidence, who was getting off the hamster wheel of life and coming home to myself.

It's kind of hard to put into words how amazing it felt. But truly, relationships shifted. I found more time for myself. I found a true morning routine that began to make me feel good, and a whole new way of actually taking care of myself every morning, rather than waking up grumpy about all the promises I had to keep to others as a people pleaser.

I stopped going through the motions, living my life as a checkbox full of things to check off so my life would look good on the outside for others.

I noticed that I had more clarity and focus. I felt sharper. My thoughts were more organized. I had more attention —I could concentrate better. There was less overthinking, fewer nights where I would lay awake all night going over my to-do list over and over again.

I had more emotional stability. My mood felt more balanced. Instead of me snapping at people, getting overwhelmed easily, I felt calmer. I started to feel truly aligned.

Building My Purpose

This more aligned version of me almost didn't happen though.

The very first sound bath I ever went to, I sat in my car and almost didn't go inside. I wondered if this was going to be some kind of woo-woo cult gathering?! What was it going to be like? What if I cried in front of strangers? I genuinely had no idea what I was in for. Then I saw a totally normal girl walk in and I thought, "If she's going in, it must be fine." I decided to go in before I talked myself back out of it.

After I left that first sound bath, my mind was blown. I was relaxed, calm. I felt like I could process my thoughts. It was a whole new me. I thought about how many other women are in this world sitting in their cars like I was, afraid to go in. How many of them didn't end up going in at all because they were afraid of the unknown?

So I decided to start a podcast, where I could publicly share my experiences. I wanted to share how nervous I was about going to a group sound bath, and how it ended up being the most amazing thing. I wanted to explain what to expect at these healing sessions, and demystify these modalities for skeptical women like I was.

I created a space where I could invite experts from different healing modalities to share what they do and why it works. My main goal was to make different types of healing modalities more accessible, and understandable, so that we could truly change our lives.

Eventually, as I started to have different experts on the podcast and I continued to immerse myself more into trying different practices, I started to get certified in some of these tools. One thing led to another—I got certified in emotion codes, then on sound baths, EFT tapping, and breathwork.

My education as a nurse helped me understand the nervous system on a deeper level. The nervous system has always fascinated me—I've literally held the vagus nerve in my hand. When I pair that scientific knowledge with the more woo-woo aspect of energy healing and somatic practices, it's truly amazing to see how these tools actually heal our nervous system on a cellular level.

Ready to Rise

After getting certified in these healing tools and recovering from my own severe burnout, I wondered: what's next? How do I bring this to more people? I see so many other women living the way I was living.

I'm not a believer that we have to let go of our drive or ambition to feel grounded and happier in this life. I believe we can be wildly successful and achieve big things without burning out in the process. A regulated nervous system gives us the capacity to actually enjoy our success. My motto is that at the end of the day, you deserve to create a life you're obsessed to wake up for. So I started Ready to Rise, a holistic nervous system and healing business for busy, high-achieving women. I offer tools through my private membership, the Rise Sisterhood, one-on-one coaching, and retreats.

My mission is to help high-achieving women regulate their nervous systems and connect to their inner wisdom to find more happiness in life. So many are living in a sympathetic nervous system overdrive without even knowing it. We are stuck in permanent fight-or-flight response, constantly trying to keep up, which causes severe burnout over time.

The Hard Truth About Myself

My burnout really stemmed from the fact that I didn't know how to be loved without feeling like I had to earn it. I tied achievement to worthiness. I thought that if I looked like I had it all together, then I would finally be enough.

I walked around wearing a mask, hiding behind the achiever who always showed up with a smile and said yes to everything, the one who could handle it all. I looked very successful on the outside, but behind the mask, I was spiritually and emotionally exhausted. I was completely dysregulated.

My healing journey taught me to let go of this mask. I learned that worthiness is my birthright. I don't have to always push myself to achieve every single thing anymore.

Chipping Away the Mask

Chipping away at that mask that I created has taken so much time, and it's an ongoing process, because it was so ingrained in me. How did I begin taking off that mask? I began chipping that armor away little by little. I don't think that there was a big, dramatic moment that fully healed me. It was truly me trying the different practices, trying different healing modalities, saying no and little by little, setting bigger boundaries and then bigger boundaries, leaving relationships that no longer fit, speaking my own truth, even when it felt scary.

It was a thousand tiny choices, and layer by layer started to peel away, until I felt like I came home to who I am underneath it all.

I am so proud that through my business, I now get to help so many women who are on a similar journey. A journey of coming back home to themselves as they heal from nervous system dysregulation. I get to help women chip away at their own masks now, and start their own healing.

Living Authentically

I show up in my business with an inner knowing that what I'm creating matters, because it all feels grounded. I'm not chasing everything anymore. I'm creating from alignment. I feel like I'm home.

When I'm fully being myself in life and business, I feel more present and engaged. I don't feel like I'm going through the motions, or like I'm watching my life like a movie. I'm more connected to the world around me.

I can support my clients honestly, without sugar-coating things, or saying what I think they want to hear. I'm able to trust my intuition and trust myself, which allows my clients to do the same.

What Keeps Me Going

When things get hard, what grounds me is looking back at how far I've come. I remember the version of me who used to wake up every day hating her life, who couldn't even get out of bed. The version who felt like she was living a life that wasn't even hers.

But I found myself again, and I'm not going back.

The women I serve also keep me going. Many women in my membership and at my retreats send me messages about how their lives are changing because I'm sharing my story and practices with them.

I deeply understand my clients because I've been exactly where they are. I practice what I teach. Literally, even when no one's watching, this is now my life.

Coming Home to Myself

I want the same for you. I want you to experience relaxation, better sleep, peace and the feeling of knowing you are so damn worthy, that you don't have to burn yourself out chasing that societal checklist anymore.

I know what it feels like to be stuck in a life that's draining your soul. I don't want women to go through the motions anymore. I want you to be truly living your life, truly engaged, truly lit up.

We came here to have fun and experience life and be happy, not to constantly chase someone else's idea of success to the point of burnout. If success lights you up, that's fine—being driven and ambitious lights me up too. But we need a regulated nervous system that supports it.

You don't have to live from a dysregulated place any longer. Life is short. I'm a nurse, trust me, I know.

Healing is personal to me, and I want this for every woman in this world. Imagine a world where I am happier and I pour into another woman, and she becomes happier and pours into the next woman, and on and on. Imagine how this world would feel.

This time, it's personal because I found myself again after years of living behind a mask. Because I know what it feels like to wake up every day feeling like a stranger to yourself, and I refuse to let another woman suffer in silence the way I did. Because every woman deserves to feel worthy without having to earn it, to feel regulated instead of running on empty, to come home to who she really is underneath all the expectations and achievements.

It's personal because I envision a world where we feel uplifted, supported and loved. A world where our nervous systems are regulated and we are living from a place of peace and balance.

Most of all, it's personal because I found myself again, and I'm never letting her go.

And now I'm here to help you do the same. It's time to RISE, friends.

Scan to connect with Audrey

THREE

GRACE WILLIAMS
THE SELF-LOVE ADVENTURE

"You're glowing again," the cashier at BJ's tells me as I'm checking out with my usual post-gym haul—still sweaty, no makeup, hair in whatever mess I've managed to hide under my signature bandana. I have to laugh because if she could see the woman I was five years ago, she'd understand why this simple observation feels like a miracle.

That glow isn't highlighter or good lighting. It's what happens when you finally stop running from yourself and start running toward the woman you were always meant to be.

Let me tell you why I use the word "adventure" instead of "journey" when I talk about self-love. A journey felt hot and desert-like to me, all struggle and suffering with maybe some enlightenment at the end. But adventures? Adventures have treasure maps and unexpected allies and plot twists that make you stronger. They have moments where you discover you're braver than you thought. That's what happened to me.

My adventure began in the most unlikely place: rock bottom.

The Woman Who Disappeared

I view my life in distinct chapters, like a book I never planned to write. There was the childhood steeped in rigid religious teachings where I never quite belonged. The young adult years when I explored but never felt brave enough to step fully into my own life. And then my twenties—a decade I survived domestic abuse in my first marriage, where I learned to make myself so small that sometimes I wondered if I existed at all.

Even after I found the courage to leave, I carried those survival techniques with me like worn-out armor I was afraid to take off. I threw myself into my career, managing two different Philadelphia landmark proper-ties by age 31. In an industry that was—and still is—dominated by men, I felt proud of what I'd accom-plished. But even my success was about proving my worth to everyone else, not recognizing it within myself.

When I met my now-husband, something shifted. We built a life together—bought a home, had two beautiful children—and I began the slow, painful work of exam-ining the belief systems that had been carved into me since childhood. It took years. While my kids grew through all their phases, I was deconstructing and rebuilding my entire understanding of faith, family, and what it meant to be a woman in this world.

I constantly questioned whether I was giving my chil-dren the best life possible. Was being away from them all day harming them? Should I take them to Sunday school while I figured out my own relationship with faith? The exhaustion of being a mom to two littles, maintaining a demanding career, and mentally rebuilding my worldview was overwhelming.

But here's the thing—I wasn't doing any of this for me. Even my healing was about everyone else.

The Dangerous Comfort Zone

By 2022, I thought I'd finally made it. Post-pandemic, with the kids back in school, I'd acted on a promise I'd made to myself during those early lockdown months: find a job that served my needs as much as I served theirs. I'd left the long commute and 24/7 on-call demands of the city for something quieter, just miles from home. For the first time in years, I could leave work at work when five o'clock came.

I was actually practicing the self-love concepts I'd been learning about. I had time for my family, energy for a side business, even moments of genuine peace. The thought of starting my own company wasn't even on my radar. Life felt settled in the best possible way.

But settled was dangerous for me. Comfortable meant I was starting to accept less than what my soul was asking for.

Behind the scenes, if you'd been watching closely, you would have seen a woman who felt like she was meant for something more but couldn't name what that was. You'd have witnessed the self-doubt that crept in every time I considered taking a bigger step. All that growth, all that healing, and I was still seeking validation outside myself for dreams that were rising up from within.

I'd carried so many beliefs that no longer fit—that a woman should fill every role society assigned her regardless of the cost, that my value came only through serving others, that wanting more for myself was somehow selfish. I thought I was supposed to disappear into motherhood and that something was fundamentally wrong with me for craving a fuller expression of who I could be.

Even having a husband who saw me as an equal partner felt foreign after growing up in such a conservative religious environment. When he believed in me, I didn't always believe him.

The Moment Everything Changed

Sometimes the most powerful shifts don't announce themselves with fanfare. Mine came quietly, in the form of a 12-week coaching program I joined with the modest goal of improving my social media strategy for my side business.

What I found instead was a pathway back to myself.

For the first time in years, I learned what it meant to forgive—not just others, but the woman I'd been when I didn't know better. I discovered what worthiness actually felt like in my body, not as a concept I understood intellectually. Most importantly, I gave myself permission to want more without immediately apologizing for it.

The transformation was so profound that I signed up for

another three months. I wanted to see where this connection with myself might lead.

It was near the end of that second round when lightning struck. I was sitting in an online workshop, half-listening to strategies for improving client services, when a thought dropped into my consciousness like a gift: what if I could bring self-love subscription boxes to mothers everywhere?

The idea felt so right, so aligned with everything I'd been learning and experiencing, that it took my breath away. And then, predictably, I immediately tried to talk myself out of it.

Even after all that work on worthiness and capability, even after months of remembering who I was beneath all the conditioning, my first instinct was still doubt. Was this idea even valid? What did I know about running a business? What could I possibly offer other women?

Thank God for my coaching community, who reflected back to me what I couldn't yet see clearly: I was onto something powerful.

But just as I was gathering courage to move forward, life threw me a curveball that would test everything I'd learned.

The Teacher I Didn't Want

My mother's illness arrived like a storm I should have seen coming but somehow hadn't prepared for. What began as concerning symptoms quickly escalated into a condition requiring round-the-clock care that my siblings and I would provide in shifts.

Suddenly, I was spending weekends at the home where my mom was living—my grandparents' house, where I'd actually lived for about two years as a young adult with my mom and one sister. While the house itself was familiar, being there as a caregiver brought back difficult memories. Years before, I'd spent months in this same home caring for my grandfather in his final days. Now I was back, caring for my mom in what would become her final days too, with my husband and kids in tow, all of us trying to meet her complex needs. The physical exhaustion was brutal, but the emotional weight of the history in that house cut even deeper. I felt like I was failing everyone—my mother, my siblings, my husband, my children—because I couldn't be fully present for any of them.

But the hardest part was being thrust back into the family dynamics I'd worked so hard to heal from. Watching my siblings, I could see how trauma had crystallized in each of us differently. It showed up in our communication patterns, our coping mechanisms, the way we did or didn't take care of ourselves. Some carried anger they couldn't name. Others had learned to disappear so thoroughly that they struggled to advocate for their own basic needs.

One weekend, when my husband and kids were finally able to stay home while my brother helped me with mom's care, I missed my family so acutely it surprised me. Then I felt guilty for missing them—wasn't I supposed to be grateful for this chance to serve? This internal tug-of-war between my needs and my sense of duty felt familiar and exhausting.

But it also crystallized something important: I could see the generational patterns of women who'd never learned to love themselves, and how that wound was being passed down through bloodlines like a quiet inheritance no one wanted to claim.

I couldn't stop thinking about my business idea during this time. Every day that women like me—like my mother, like my sisters—went without knowing their own worth was a day of unnecessary suffering. I had something that could help break this cycle.

The problem was, I kept getting in my own way.

Breaking Through the Learning Trap

Once mom's condition stabilized and I could think about my business again, I fell into an old pattern: learning as procrastination. I consumed every training module, watched every video, convinced myself I needed just a little more knowledge before I could take action.

But knowledge wasn't my problem. Fear was.

I had a tiny email list and an even smaller social media following. Every expert said you needed thousands of people engaged with your content before you could launch anything successfully. I almost convinced myself to wait until I'd built a bigger audience.

Then I remembered something crucial: every day I delayed was another day someone out there was struggling with the same self-love challenges I'd overcome. The women I wanted to serve weren't waiting for me to have perfect systems or massive reach. They needed what I had to offer right now.

So in summer 2023, with my miniature email list and humble social media presence, I decided to launch Love Those Vibes as a gift subscription for the upcoming holiday season.

I was never going to breathe life into this dream without taking action.

One of my first business decisions came purely from intuition. A woman I barely knew was hosting a GALentine's event, and something told me to send 35 mini boxes of love for her attendees. The catch? I only had enough funds to either register my business name or create the boxes—not both.

I chose the boxes and told her my company name was Love Those Vibes, even though I hadn't officially claimed it yet. Something deep inside me knew that if this name was meant for my company, it would still be available when I had the money to make it official. That leap of faith taught me something invaluable: sometimes you have to act on faith before you feel ready.

Becoming My Own Best Friend

Launching the business was just the beginning. The real transformation happened when I realized I had to become everything I'd been seeking from others: my own best friend, my own community, my own source of validation.

For too long, I'd let my wounds define me. Even as I healed old hurts, I'd cling to new ones, wearing them like badges that proved my capacity for suffering. As an Enneagram Four and Cancer, I could hold onto emotional pain with stunning tenacity. I was willing to be a victim of almost everything except the domestic violence I'd survived—that was the only story where I refused to stay small.

I had to get comfortable with the parts of myself I'd always considered ugly or unworthy. I had to learn to love the woman who'd made mistakes, who'd stayed too long in situations that hurt her, who'd put everyone else's needs before her own until she nearly disappeared.

When I finally reached my truest self—not the good girl who followed every rule, not the perfect mom who never needed anything for herself—I discovered someone remarkable. She was creative, talented, kind, compassionate, resilient, and far smarter than I'd ever given her credit for.

The good girl persona had been particularly hard to shed. When I divorced my first husband, even though I knew it was the right choice, I still felt compelled to meet with three people from my religious community to discuss their perspectives on divorce. I was already saving money for attorney fees, but I needed their permission to do what I'd already decided to do.

Learning to disappoint people who expected me to stay small became its own form of liberation. Some relationships fell away when I stopped performing the version of myself they preferred, but that created space for connections based on who I actually was rather than who I thought I should be.

Building Something That Serves

Today, Love Those Vibes has grown beyond anything I initially imagined. What started as subscription boxes for mothers has evolved into monthly self-love tools, intentional gifting services, and workshops that create community around the vulnerable work of learning to love yourself.

I make it a priority to source items from small businesses owned by women and people of color, because representation matters when you're building something meant to center voices that have been marginalized. Working with other small business owners allows me to support their dreams while living my own.

My life has changed in ways both profound and practical. I've learned to say yes to myself and my children more often. I've discovered how to be the woman, wife, and mother I want to be rather than the one I thought I was supposed to be. It's messier this way—I fail regularly and find myself apologizing to my teenagers for falling into old patterns—but it's real.

The boundaries I've established protect everything I've built. I don't engage in surface-level relationships anymore; if you're in my life, you get all of me. I'll ugly cry with you and be the first to celebrate your wins. I refuse to participate in conversations that tear other people down, because I've learned there are always more interesting things to discuss than other people's choices.

My definition of "having it all" has completely transformed. There was a time when I struggled to even dream, convinced that kind of expansive thinking was for other people. I once put down a book because the author encouraged readers to envision their ideal lives, and I couldn't relate to that concept at all.

Now I understand that the "more" I was seeking wasn't material—it was peace, connection, fun, and the freedom to spend my time and energy as if they were valuable. It looks like slower mornings with coffee on the porch, spontaneous movie dates with my teenager even when my to-do list is long, and annual family vacations that would have felt impossible to imagine just a few years ago.

The Practice of Self-Love

People often ask about my routines, expecting some elaborate morning ritual. The truth is, I get distracted by reading or cutting fruit or throwing in a load of laundry before I've even had coffee. But I do commit to nurturing myself in small ways each morning—maybe journaling, maybe meditation, maybe just a few minutes of gratitude. The specific practice matters less than the commitment to treating myself with care.

When building this business while working full-time felt overwhelming, I reminded myself that generations of women not knowing how to love themselves was a much harder kind of difficult than the temporary challenge of pursuing my dreams.

What grounds me is thinking about my children, my nieces, and my own inner child. I see how trauma ripples through families when we don't break the patterns, how self-doubt gets passed down like an heirloom no one wants to inherit. I can't stop this work because every day someone doesn't know her own worth is another day she misses out on her own adventure.

The Glow That Shows

When I'm fully myself in life and business, confidence radiates from places I didn't know existed. I see it reflected in my teenagers, who are growing up unapologetically themselves in ways that make some adults uncomfortable. I'm proud that I've modeled this for them.

I don't take it personally when someone skips their subscription box order anymore. A customer recently paused her deliveries, and instead of immediately questioning whether she'd been dissatisfied, I realized she was probably traveling and didn't want packages sitting on her doorstep. Her choice had nothing to do with the value I provide and everything to do with timing.

My favorite part of being fully myself is that I'm no longer afraid of being seen. I don't need to poll everyone in my life before making decisions (except maybe what to make for dinner, because that's just family logistics). I've learned to get quiet and let my intuition guide me toward what I need to know.

That glow the BJ's cashier notices? It's not makeup or good lighting. It's what happens when you stop apologizing for taking up space and start celebrating the fact that you're here, you're capable, and you deserve everything you've been afraid to want.

What I'd Tell the Woman I Used to Be

You're going to fail sometimes, and those failures won't define you or your business—they'll make you more experienced for whatever comes next. You're also about to meet some incredible women who will remind you that you're not meant to do this alone.

Your adventure won't be swift, and the progress won't always be linear. But your willingness to take each uncomfortable next step will carry you to places you can't imagine from where you're sitting now.

This time, it's personal because I love myself—the woman I was when I didn't know better, the woman I am now, and the woman I'm still becoming. And because I want to help you love yourself too.

That's what real adventure looks like: not a perfect journey from point A to point B, but a messy, beautiful, life-changing expedition toward the treasure that was inside you all along.

Scan to connect with Grace

FOUR

GRECIA RUIZ

IT'S OKAY TO CHANGE YOUR MIND

"It's okay to change your mind."

If someone had told me this five years ago, I would have nodded in agreement while secretly feeling a knot in my stomach. Change my mind? But what about all the time I've invested? What about the five-year plan? What about what everyone expects from me?

I was the golden child, the straight-A student, the one who had it all figured out. Changing my mind felt like failure, like letting everyone down, like proving I didn't actually know what I was doing. But here's what I've learned through multiple business pivots, career shifts, and a whole lot of soul-searching: changing your mind isn't failure—it's growth. It's listening to your intuition. It's having the courage to choose yourself over everyone else's expectations.

And sometimes, it starts with a really good bubble bath.

The Perfect Life That Wasn't

Let me take you back to Christmas 2018, when this whole journey really began. Our family from Guadalajara was visiting, and my aunt—who had transitioned from interior design to becoming an at-home baker—taught me the basics of decorating with fondant. We held a baking competition that year, and you can bet my dessert won the best appearance category!

That moment sparked something in me. I started an Instagram page to share my baking creations throughout 2019, and by February 2020, I was back in Mexico for what I called a "Galentine's baking bootcamp weekend" with my aunt. I learned cake decorating and took a macaron course. I was ready to turn this new passion into something bigger.

Then life came to a screeching halt. The pandemic hit just as I was supposed to travel to Japan with my best friend. Instead of exploring Tokyo DisneySea, I found myself moving back in with my parents, experiencing the most severe depression I'd ever faced in my life.

But here's the flip side of rock bottom—sometimes it's the perfect foundation to build something from scratch.

During those dark months, when the physical boundaries between work and home became blurred and there were no outside activities to spark joy, I turned to baking. Through one of the most difficult emotional struggles of my life, my first business, Bakery by GG, was born. I was creating custom cakes and cupcakes, building a loyal client base through local Facebook groups and word of mouth.

For a while, I was sure this was it—I was going to quit my corporate job and become a full-time baker. But the spark of joy and passion was slowly being replaced by overwhelm and exhaustion from the manual labor, without the compensation to match. Through therapy and the release I found in baking, I clawed my way out of that dark emotional time. When my boyfriend proposed in May 2021, I made the decision to close the business and focus on planning our destination wedding in Italy.

The Nagging Sensation

As 2022 rolled around, that familiar feeling returned— the nagging sensation that my corporate job just wasn't right for me. It started as a whisper but grew louder with each passing day. One evening in April, I called my dad sobbing, begging him to hire me in any capacity so I could escape. My dad, an entrepreneur himself with 20-plus years of experience, had always joked that he could use my project management talents.

As soon as I ended the call with my dad, I gave my two weeks notice. Just as I was getting ready to work for him, a former colleague swooped in with another project management job opportunity. I told myself it was temporary, just to help pay for the wedding.

After our wedding season ended in 2023, I was ready for a new project. I still knew that corporate life wasn't for me—I was meant for more. Drawing from my macaron course in Guadalajara and another one I'd taken in Paris during our wedding trip, I decided to open CHÉRIE, an at-home macaron business.

This time felt different. I secured a cottage food operation license and health permit to operate legally. I thought this would be easier than custom cakes—a repeatable product instead of one-off designs. But after countless farmers markets, vendor events, and holiday specials, I reached the same exhausting conclusion. What I enjoyed most was marketing the products, not baking them at scale.

With a heavy heart, and after months of feeling shame for "another failed business venture," I closed CHÉRIE in early 2024.

The Breaking Point That Changed Everything

The pivotal moment happened on Black Friday, November 29, 2024. I woke up at my parents' house after enjoying a warm Thanksgiving dinner the night before, but I was sitting at the breakfast table with a distant look in my eyes, my thoughts far away from the moment.

I couldn't take the emotional toll anymore—the stress of working a job that didn't fit or align with my interests, plus the physical toll it was taking on my body. I had had enough and ran out of excuses to stay.

I pulled my mom aside to the living room and told her, yet again, how unfulfilled and unaligned I felt. I had an unexpected cathartic cry as my mom listened. I'm blessed that my mom happens to be a practicing, licensed therapist, so she guided me to dig deep and recognize what I was truly afraid of.

The obvious fears were loss of income and fear of the unknown. But there was a deeper fear: letting go of society's expectations and the need for external validation to dictate my worth.

Finding My Way Back to Me

To combat these fears, I created a plan. I took a hard look at our household finances, created a budget, and challenged myself to stick to a budget with only one income for four months. I needed to prove to myself it was possible and experience what this new lifestyle would look like during the transition.

The book *The Year of Less* by Caitlin Flanders helped me formulate this challenge—it felt fortuitous that the author was 29 when she wrote it, and I happened to be 29 as well. I also adopted minimalistic strategies by following The Minimalists' journey through their documentaries, podcasts, and live events.

Through these mindset shifts, paired with reframing my understanding of self-worth with the book *Worthy* by Jamie Kern Lima, I learned that less truly is more. Less material goods and the stress of maintaining certain financial metrics meant more of what matters: happiness, alignment, purpose, peace.

The Bubble Bath Revelation

My "aha" moment happened while I was taking a bubble bath and doing a therapy assignment about reflecting on my values. As I started understanding my values better, I realized I could work backward from there to make decisions that aligned with them.

I started thinking about what kind of career would fall into this category. I recalled the conversation with my college friend who was considering a wedding abroad and was inspired by how I'd managed to plan my own destination wedding. I also had a relative ask me the same question because a family friend was considering a wedding in Europe.

That's when it hit me! I had knowledge and experience from planning my own destination wedding in Italy that others would find valuable. I could dispel misconceptions about getting married abroad—especially the idea that it's more expensive than a wedding in the States.

What is it about shower time—or bath time in my case—that makes all the great ideas strike? I'd say it's that screen-free, uninterrupted time to process your thoughts and listen to your intuition. Don't underestimate the power of a good, long bubble bath.

Learning to Trust My Gut

During this time, I started investing in myself and seeking out communities of women who were living outside traditional corporate paths. For someone who typically leans heavily into logical decision-making—evidenced by ignoring my gut for so long about changing career paths—learning to trust my intuition enough to invest in coaching and community was a huge step.

The very first investment I made was getting myself in a room with other women actively living outside of a corporate career path. That event showed me tangible, real-life examples that there are other possibilities out there for me.

The Moment Everything Shifted

Italy Brides was literally born from that gut decision I made in the bathtub. It's a destination wedding planning experience for modern, DIY brides who are willing to roll up their sleeves to make their Italy destination wedding dream come true while sticking to their budget.

What lights me up most about this business is helping brides realize they can have their (wedding) cake and eat it too! Planning a wedding in Italy sounds like a logistical nightmare or a dream too costly to be true, but I'm walking proof that this isn't the case. You can have the wedding of your dreams with the people most important to you, a magical trip you and your guests will remember for years—all without breaking the bank.

Shedding the Golden Child

Being the eldest child of three, and the only daughter, I grew up with textbook "golden child" syndrome—an Enneagram 3 "The Achiever" and ENFJ "The Protago-nist." I was the straight-A student, overachiever, constantly praised for academic success while feeling pressure to maintain an unrealistic standard of perfection.

This led me to confuse praise and external validation with love. Accomplishments became tied to my self-worth. By chasing the ever-elusive finish line of "being enough," I started losing myself when it came to my health and other real needs. This deeply ingrained identity led me to stay silent for so long in a career that didn't feel right but looked so shiny on the outside.

Side note: If you're an Enneagram 3 like me, please listen to the song "Three" by Sleeping At Last. It's a healing experience.

Learning to Advocate for Myself

When I decided to close CHÉRIE, my macaron business, I was at a crossroads between what I thought others perceived I "should" be doing versus what I needed to do for myself. CHÉRIE was the most public-facing business I'd built, and orders were flowing in. I felt shame for having to publicly disclose that I was closing yet another business.

I felt like I "should" stop sharing my ideas publicly until I was truly sure about my next venture. I felt like I "should" know what I wanted already and just stick to it. But these weren't my real thoughts—they were insecurities placed there by others who told me it didn't seem like I knew what I wanted.

Thankfully, I started listening to more encouraging voices who reminded me that just by putting myself out there and continuing to try new things, I was being braver than most. Instead of seeing these business pivots as failures, I now see them for what they truly are—

experiments that shed light on what I'm looking for in business and life.

A Valuable Lesson

The biggest lesson came on April 15, 2025, when I resigned from my job...or so I thought. Plot twist! I was offered a 12-week leave of absence instead and a position much more aligned with my career goals upon my return. Because I mentioned that my primary goal was prioritizing my health, I was encouraged to discuss my options with HR.

I knew about leaves of absence, but I'd automatically disqualified myself because I didn't consider my health concerns "serious enough" to qualify. Thanks to me speaking up about my needs, I secured a paid leave of absence to prioritize my health.

This taught me a valuable lesson: Do not disqualify yourself. I was disqualifying myself before speaking up or trying. I learned there are usually more options available than the ones you can see on the immediate horizon.

Becoming Brave

I had to become brave. I had to decide to be afraid and do it anyway. I had to understand what my values were so I could begin building a life and business that pointed to those values. I had to invest in myself and ask for help.

Now, when I think about my career, I don't just think about my interests and who I want to serve—I also think about the lifestyle I want to live. My primary goal in building a business is to increase my time freedom. Yes, I want to enjoy the work I'm doing and feel more fulfilled and aligned, but ultimately, I'm building a business around the life I want to live.

The life I want includes flexibility to work from anywhere, more time with friends and family, and greater impact on the world.

The Hard Truth About Being Human

The hardest truth I had to face? I'm only human. This is my first time living the human experience, and I want to experience it all. That means I'm allowed to try new things, change my mind, make mistakes, and try again.

Learning that I'm a Generator with a 3/6 profile helped me understand that I'm actually meant to live life through trial and error and have fun in the process. The 3 in me is a "Scientist/Innovator" and the 6 is a "Role Model/Sage"—the 6 in me is now allowing the 3 in me more room for experimentation and changing course, without the previous shame and guilt of not finding a business that "sticks."

The Life I'm Actually Living

You know what's funny? I used to think "having it all" meant climbing some corporate ladder, getting the fancy title, the big salary, the impressive LinkedIn profile. Now? Having it all looks like waking up excited about my day instead of dreading it. It's having the freedom to work from anywhere, going on spontaneous adventures with my husband, and actually having energy left for friends and family at the end of the day.

I'm not saying I don't want nice things or financial security—I absolutely do. But I've stopped chasing someone else's definition of success and started building my own. And honestly? I already feel like I have it all. My marriage, my relationships, the flexibility of remote work, and now a business that actually lights me up instead of drains me.

The piece that was missing for so long was permission—permission to change my mind, to try things that might not work, to disappoint people who expected me to stay the course and be the same predictable person forever.

This Time It's Personal

This time, it's personal because I get to be raw, real, honest, and vulnerable about my story without feeling like I need a filter or a mask. I get to be my true, authentic, genuine self in all areas of my life, including my career. And you know what? It hasn't made me less successful—it's made me more successful, but in a way that actually fulfills me.

If you're reading this and feeling stuck in the "shoulds"—I should stay in the safe job, I should stick with what I started, I should stop changing my mind so much—I need you to hear this: it's okay to change your mind. It's okay to try something, realize it doesn't fit, and pivot. It's okay to disappoint people who expected you to stay small and predictable.

That woman sitting at the corporate desk, moving her mouse around just to look busy, feeling that nagging sensation that something wasn't right? She didn't know she was already carrying everything she needed inside her. She just needed permission to listen to her own voice instead of everyone else's.

Here's what I wish someone had told me sooner: that permission doesn't come from anyone else. It comes from you. Your life is happening right now. Your dreams are valid. Your intuition knows things your logical brain hasn't figured out yet.

And yes, it's absolutely okay to change your mind. In fact, it might be the bravest thing you ever do.

Scan to connect with Grecia

FIVE

HAILEY BAITINGER
BUT FIRST, SELF-LOVE

I used to dream at my corporate desk about the life I'm living today. Six months into my real-world graphic design job, I realized I didn't want to be stuck at a desk until retirement. Sure, I was good at graphic design, but I didn't love it. Something was always missing.

Two years pass and I'm at a new graphic design job. I felt like a robot. I'd go in, get the job done, and literally sit around moving my mouse if there was no work to do because I couldn't leave until 5:00 pm. It was just not the best environment for me.

That's when it hit me—I had a much bigger problem than just hating my job. I didn't know who I was or what I liked. Worse than that, I hated myself. There was no concept of self-love in my world. I was saying the worst things to myself. Things I'd be embarrassed to say out loud. I was a people pleaser who had spent my entire life conforming to those around me.

I had no identity of who I was, so with all this time staring at my desk with nothing to do, I started asking myself: what do I actually want? What is the next move going to be? That's when I started my self-discovery journey, in 2019.

The Discovery of Me

First, I began working on how I spoke to myself, then slowly started exploring what I actually liked. Getting a longboard to see if I enjoyed it? I fell a lot, but gave myself permission to try something I'd always wanted to do. Bringing my dog on hikes taught me I loved being in nature. I discovered I loved dancing to music while cooking a meal in the kitchen.

As time went on and I started to love myself, something shifted. I started giving myself permission to enjoy life. I'd cook my favorite meals, make time to go on hikes, dance in my living room, listen to music I loved, and let myself cry and feel my emotions. It was very slow progress, starting with the smallest things like consistently flossing my teeth or drinking enough water daily.

Another game changer was working out. I started working out consistently—not for any weight or fitness goal, but specifically for my mental and physical health. I was dealing with some depression at the time, and I found that working out made such a big difference in my life. Ever since then, I've worked out five times a week purely for my mental and physical health, and it's become a non-negotiable habit.

All these little acts of self-love started compounding. I continued to show up for myself because I loved myself and wanted the best for me. And when that version of me shows up, it overflows into other people's lives and inspires them to do the same. That's not why I do it—I do it for me—but as a recovering people pleaser, it's nice to know it affects others positively too.

Finding My Calling

During this time of self discovery, I also stumbled upon life coaching. I had never heard of life coaching nor did I know someone who did this for a living. It sounded magical! Along my self-love journey, I learned that I loved personal development. Life coaching offered personal development through walking the talk and helping others progress their life. I was certain this was it —this was what I was going to leap into and do.

I started building my coaching business while still working my corporate job, and then I became a certified life coach in 2020 with Inner Glow Circle. I decided to become a self-love coach inspired by my personal journey. In March of 2020, I launched my life coaching business.

This whole self-love journey is what finally gave me the courage to leap into entrepreneurship. It made me believe I could do it and that I deserved it. I had been waiting for years to get out of the office and do my own thing.

Later that year in December 2020, I got laid off of my full-time graphic design job. The kicker? I had just asked for a raise after taking on more responsibilities. That experience left such a bad taste in my mouth about corporate life and working for other people. But honestly, it was the push I needed because entrepreneurship had been calling me for years.

The Birth of DesignBee Agency

So when I got laid off in December of 2020, I was ready. I had my life coaching business that was doing well, but I knew I needed something else to supplement my income. That's when DesignBee Agency was born in December 2020. DesignBee really took off and I gave myself permission to take a pause from coaching and pursue my agency full time.

My current full time job is working at my company DesignBee Agency, which is a social media agency based in Atlanta that serves local businesses. What sets us apart is that we're not your typical social media contractor who posts and ghosts. We become an extension of your team—we're passionate about your brand, we collaborate on bigger marketing ideas, and we go above and beyond because we genuinely care about your success.

Here's the thing that really makes us different: we're not just going to make your feed look cute. Don't get me wrong, I love a beautiful aesthetic, but if your social media doesn't tell me what you actually do or give me a glimpse into what it's really like to work with you, then we're missing the mark. We create social media that's functional and effective—content that bridges the gap between what people see online and what they'll experience when they walk through your door.

I started DesignBee Agency because I saw such a need for good branding online. Initially, I was doing graphic design, websites, whatever came my way. Like most entrepreneurs, I said yes to everything. But then I landed my first social media client, and everything clicked. This was it. This was the sweet spot where all my talents converged.

With social media, I get to do graphic design, brand direction, storytelling, concept development, photography, copywriting, videography, and strategy all in one package. It's like all these different skills I'm good at finally had a home where they could work together seamlessly.

What really drives me is helping people bridge that disconnect between their online presence and their real-world experience. I see so many businesses with social media that don't actually tell their story or showcase what makes them special. People go to social media to verify if you're legit, to build trust before they ever walk in your door or make a purchase. If your social media doesn't give them that behind-the-scenes look at who you are and what you're about, you're missing out on building those crucial relationships.

Redefining My Why

My why has evolved over the years, and honestly, it's gotten a lot less glamorous, but way more honest. When I first started, my why was rooted in wanting to help people. I saw that social media was the IT factor for businesses today. It's where credibility is built and relationships are formed. When I realized I could help businesses bridge that gap through authentic, strategic social media, I knew I had found my calling.

Here's the thing about your WHY as an entrepreneur: everyone tells you it needs to be this driving force that gets you through the tough days. And they're not wrong. There's this unspoken pressure to have a "good" why, something inspiring and heartfelt that sounds good to you and everyone else. It wasn't until writing this chapter that I really reflected on how mine has shifted. Of course I still love helping people, but if I'm being completely honest, that's not what gets me out of bed every morning anymore.

One of my favorite things in the world is spending time with my family. That is what I truly live for. Not work. I live to spend time with the people I love the most. And I get to do that. Work is just a means to get me there.

My WHY is freedom to live life on my terms. The freedom to spend quality time with the people I love most without being constrained by traditional work structures. I've built my business to create the life I want to live where work fits around my priorities instead of the other way around.

The goal all along has been to create a system and business that allows me to do the things that I love, which are meaningful moments with my family. I'm really building my business towards a life I want to continue to live.

Having it all used to mean climbing some corporate ladder or hitting certain salary milestones. For me, now it means having the freedom to choose how I spend my time and energy. It means waking up excited about my day instead of dreading it. It means building something that serves my life instead of consuming it.

Shedding the Layers

The person I was when I started my business versus who I am now is completely different. And that transformation happened because I had to shed layers of myself that no longer served me. Starting with how I saw myself and my business.

When I started DesignBee, it was born out of pure survival mode. I had to get something off the ground just to make it through. That survival mindset stuck around way longer than it should have. Even after the business finally took off, I was still trapped in that headspace of "oh, this is just my little side hustle to keep me afloat." I wasn't taking myself seriously as a founder or treating the business like the real deal it had become.

The first layer I had to shed was that small-time thinking. As my business evolved, I had to face facts: oh shit, this is a functional business. I am a business owner. This is not a game—we're not playing around here. This is legit. The moment I went from asking friends "Hey, can you help me out?" to "Hey, can you read this job description and sign it?"—that's when everything shifted. I had to start operating like the real business owner I had become, not the scared person just trying to survive.

Here I was finally doing the thing that I had sat at my desk longing to do, and I couldn't really accept the fact that I was actually doing it. I definitely experienced impostor syndrome along the way. Who was I to be leading social media accounts? I had no professional training in that area. What was I thinking? Surely, this client is going to find out and just fire me. There was a lot of internal battling in my head.

I've dealt with my fair share of doubts, insecurities, perfectionism, and fear of failure. Every time I'm faced with it today, I have to remind myself that I've overcome this before and nothing bad happened.

I had to face each of these challenges head on and address them. I've rewritten what failure means to me. I have boundaries around my work hours and have learned to be okay with work that isn't perfect. I've redefined what success means to me—not based on external validation, but on my own terms.

It's a matter of reminding yourself who the fuck you are and what you've accomplished. How far you've come. You've faced so much adversity, and you can do hard things.

Learning to Set Boundaries

When I say I had to shed a lot of layers of myself, a big part of that was learning how to set boundaries. When I just started my own business, I allowed my clients to do whatever. I was just happy to have a client. I didn't care that they were texting me at 10 PM or asking me to create a post immediately. I was just grateful someone was paying me and trusted me to get the job done.

Learning to set professional boundaries was completely new territory for me. Today, those boundaries are sacred. They're what keeps my peace and separates my work from my personal life.

The growth has been incredible, but it's required me to become someone completely different—someone who knows her worth, sets clear boundaries, and isn't afraid to take up space as a legitimate business owner.

My business and life have changed so much since my personal transformation began. I am such a strong, confident person now. When I look back at where I was when I started my business, I was just someone that you could walk all over. You could say "I want this," and I would do it. I would not stand up for myself. I was just trying to figure out who I was, and there was just a lot I was working on and working through.

Becoming Unshakeable

My business has definitely made me stronger as a person. I've faced so much adversity and challenges that I've overcome and gotten through. It's made me more confident in every area of my life.

I've done a lot of things I don't want to do, like sales. I hate sales. I've had to fire contractors and also fire clients. I am constantly faced with battling two sides of myself: my emotions and my business. My business would not be functional if I only led with my emotions. I've shed lots of tears from doing hard things but I always reflect on lessons learned from them.

The transformation has been incredible. I went from being someone who would say yes to everything and anyone, to someone who knows exactly what she wants and isn't afraid to go after it. I've learned that authenticity isn't just a buzzword—it's actually a business strategy. When you show up as yourself, you attract the right people and repel the wrong ones, and that makes everything so much easier.

You can let your business run you, or you can run your business. That is really the difference between fully being yourself or doing what you're supposed to be doing.

When you're able to truly be yourself and run your business how you want it to go, that's where the transformation happens, and you just feel so satisfied and complete. My goal all along with my business has been getting it in a good place, making money, and working less so I'll have time to create a family one day. That's something I've always worked for. It's not to have a thousand clients or a million dollar business.

My goal is very attainable to work towards. But I will never reach it and feel satisfied if I am following a blueprint that's not mine. I need to follow how I want to do business, and that's by having certain boundaries in place to protect my peace and personal time, as well as my team because I want them to continue to work for me.

Being Authentically Me

I've always been very open and honest with my clients about my mental health and neurodivergence. I have OCD anxiety and ADHD. I also experience PMDD—premenstrual dysphoric disorder—which means intense bouts of depression during the weeks leading up to my period.

When I get overstimulated, I communicate that. I advocate for myself and fix my environment when I can. When I'm asked "how are you" when I'm experiencing PMDD, I answer honestly. That way they're able to meet me where I'm at and understand that it has nothing to do with them while I seem depressed.

Being vulnerable with my clients and colleagues allows them to learn more about mental health. I like to be very open and honest with all the people that I interact and work with and be upfront because if anything, it can be a learning experience and also bring us closer together.

Whenever you're able to truly be yourself, you're going to attract the right type of clients. There are times where we have clients that do not align with our values, and that is very difficult to work with. They take more from you than money is ever worth. Whenever you're able to be yourself, you're going to attract people who are similar to you and also easy to work with.

Coming Home to Myself

Whenever I'm feeling out of touch with myself, I know I need to revert to something that I used to do when I was a little girl. The things that I did when I was a child just gave me so much happiness and joy.

I literally made a list one day of everything I loved as a kid. Bike riding, painting, crocheting, sewing, making music videos, being in nature, swimming. Simple things that brought me pure joy. So when I'm down and not feeling in touch with myself, I'm able to turn to that list and just do that for myself.

That's part of self-love. Being able to show up and give yourself those moments of joy that you deserve. Because if you don't, no one else is going to do that for you.

Going on a bike ride in the middle of the day. Pulling out my notebook and drawing a few things. Going on a midday walk with the dogs. Calling it a day at 3:00 pm and watching TV on the couch. I really do give myself those moments of peace.

I'm in charge of my schedule, so I make sure I'm creating the space for it, especially when I'm feeling low. Those moments are everything. They're what fuel me when I've got a lot of people counting on me. My team, my clients, my family, my relationships, my dogs. I really need to take care of myself so I can be the fullest version of myself.

Building the Life I Always Wanted

I knew pretty early on that I did not want a desk job. I've always wanted to work for myself. Those were two big things that I wanted and I created. I also wanted to have more flexibility and freedom. I didn't want to have a limited number of PTO days. I wanted to be able to travel whenever I wanted and not work till 5 o'clock and just sit at my desk with nothing to do. I wanted to be done for the day if I didn't have any more work to do.

I've really created this life, and I'm super proud of it. It's not something that was handed to me. It's something that I identified that I wanted, and I went out and made it happen. That's really what it looks like when you build a life that fits you as a person versus one that was just handed to you.

If I could go back and tell myself something before taking this leap into entrepreneurship, it would be that you are doing the right thing and you won't regret this. Even while it feels so unknown right now, the possibilities are endless. You can have exactly what you want if you go out and work for it. It doesn't matter what other people say.

Here's what I learned about other people's opinions: just because someone has one doesn't mean it's yours to keep. Ask yourself: "Who is this person? What do they actually know about where I'm going?" If they're not where you want to be, their opinion doesn't get to live in your head rent-free.

Opinions bogged me down hard in the beginning because I was desperately waiting for someone to tell me

I was doing the right thing. But uncertainty makes everyone uncomfortable, so they'll push you toward the "safe" choice every damn time—get a job, don't take the leap, play it small. Don't let their fear become your ceiling.

I honestly didn't have that full on "yes, you can do this!!" support until I hired help. So I highly recommend hiring a coach, getting someone on your side even if you have to pay for them, because that is quite literally why I made the leap. I had someone in my corner who 100 percent believed in me with no doubts for the first time.

It Starts With Self-Love

Something I'm most proud of is taking that leap and saying yes to myself, and none of it would have happened had I not chosen to start loving myself. Self-love is a journey. There's no final destination. It is something you constantly work on and work towards. It all starts with the smallest steps. Identify something you want and fucking do it out of love for yourself, like you would for that little girl who dreamt of this happening.

I'm so proud of who I am today because of who my business has made me become. I'm such a strong, confident woman who will not back down. I know what I want, and if you're going to test me for it, I will put you in your place. That also counts for people I love. I'm way more confident in standing up for those people I care about.

I'm not a pushover anymore. I am still working through

my people-pleasing tendencies but I'm still going to make sure that I get my way at the end of the day.

It's never too late to start your self-love journey. And it starts with the smallest steps.

I always recommend starting with your inner child and making a list of things that you loved doing when you were a child because that is a known thing. You know what you loved doing when you were a kid. Try incorporating more of those things into your daily life and treating yourself with that love.

If it's about taking care of your mental health, get help. Don't be afraid to get help. I've had a therapist and a life coach at one point in my life, and it was such a pivotal phase because I was taking care of my past with therapy and taking care of my future with life coaching.

Hire the help. You'll never, ever regret it. It's been the best personal investment of my life.

It's Time To Choose Yourself

This time, it's personal because I've spent the majority of my life serving and pleasing everyone else. Now it's my turn. I'm done apologizing for taking up space, done shrinking myself to make others comfortable, done waiting for permission to want what I want.

Here's what I know now that I didn't know sitting at that corporate desk: you're not broken, you're not behind, and you're definitely not too late. The life you're dreaming about? It's not some fantasy—it's a decision away.

I went from hating myself to building a business that gives me complete freedom. From being a people-pleaser who couldn't set a boundary to save her life, to someone who knows exactly what she's worth. That transformation didn't happen because I'm special. It happened because I finally chose myself.

The girl sitting at that desk moving her mouse around, waiting for 5 o'clock to set her free—she had no idea she was already carrying everything she needed inside her. She just needed to remember that the little girl who followed her heart and did what brought her joy was still there, waiting to be heard.

Every boundary I've set, every client I've said no to, every time I've called it a day at 3 pm to watch TV on the couch—these aren't acts of rebellion. They're acts of self-love. They're me honoring the woman who finally learned she deserved better than settling for a life that didn't fit.

So stop waiting for permission. Stop looking for someone else to validate your dreams. The person you're meant to become is already inside you, probably has been since you were a kid making those lists of things you loved to do.

Your life is happening right now. Make it count.

Scan to connect with Hailey

SIX

HEATHER MURILLO

PAY NOW OR PAY LATER

The 45-pound kettlebell sits on the gym floor in front of me at 5 pm, and I absolutely do not want to pick it up and do another set. My body is tired. My mind is making excuses. Every logical part of me is saying "skip it today." But there's this phrase that runs through my head in moments like this, the same phrase that changed the entire trajectory of my life: "Pay now or pay later."

I pick up the kettlebell.

This phrase started in the gym, but it became the foundation for every major decision I've made in the past decade. It's why I left a stable marriage to do life alone with a seven-year-old. It's why I invested over $10,000 in coach training with no plan for how to pay for it. It's why I ended a seven-year relationship because I refused to settle for anything less than full commitment.

Pay now or pay later. And paying later is always worse.

At 41, I coach people to blow their own damn minds with what they're capable of achieving. But getting here required me to blow my own mind first—by learning that the safe, predictable life I'd built was slowly suffocating me, and that the only way out was through a series of terrifying leaps that would either break me or remake me entirely.

The Perfect Suffocation

Before my business, life wasn't miserable. That's the thing that made it so insidious—it was perfectly fine. I had everything I was supposed to want: a stable career as a high school chemistry teacher, a house, a marriage, a beautiful daughter.

But there was this itch in my soul that I couldn't scratch.

I'd find myself online shopping at work, buying clothes and accessories because I love fashion. But really, I was trying to access that part of my personality that longed to be creative, to develop something of my own and bring it to life. The shopping was just a symptom of a deeper need I couldn't name.

I'd been following all the rules my entire life. Good college, teaching degree, marriage, house, baby—check, check, check, check, check. After my daughter was born, I started questioning if this was all there was. Was I just going to teach school, keep house, and raise a child until retirement?

That idea left me feeling so empty and honestly terrified.

The whisper started then. That little voice asking, "I wonder what I could do if I took a chance?" It felt like an underlying dissatisfaction that I couldn't quite name, an itch I couldn't scratch.

When COVID hit, everything changed. The job I'd deemed "stable" proved to be anything but. It became clear that my income and benefits could be taken away at a moment's notice. That was the moment I knew I wanted to create my own business, something that no one else could take away from me or dictate how I managed it.

But I had no clue what that would look like.

The Money Stories That Kept Me Small

Growing up middle-class, I'd absorbed some pretty limiting beliefs about money that would take years to unravel. My mom was a public school teacher, and phrases like "money doesn't grow on trees" were common around our house. There was this underlying idea that people with a lot of money were corrupt, and there was valor in having just enough to get by. Wanting more than that was greedy.

I started my adult life as a public school teacher, just like my mom, and I definitely took on her views about money. I'd spend my entire paycheck by the end of the month and find myself repeating those same phrases about there never being enough money.

This became glaringly obvious when I tried multi-level marketing. After eight years of teaching and raising my young daughter, I was burnt out. I'd gotten my yoga certification and taken a leave of absence to teach yoga and acrobatics full-time. When I wasn't making enough money just teaching yoga, the studio owner talked me into selling essential oils.

While I could get behind the natural living aspect and understood the chemistry behind the products, when it came to actually selling, I hit a wall. I felt so pushy and weird trying to convince women to buy these products. I was almost never successful because I had this real ick factor when it came to sales.

My boss told me I was actually great at selling, and I thought, "Who the fuck are you talking about? I can't sell a damn thing!"

Then she said something that stuck with me: "When you invite people to come do acrobatics with you, you are selling a service. You do it with your whole heart and they can't help but say yes because you make it sound so fun."

She was right, but I couldn't see it that way at the time. The difference was that I wasn't charging for acrobatics at the time, and more importantly, I wholeheartedly believed that acrobatics was the best thing ever and everyone could do it. It took almost a decade for me to come full-circle and get to a point where I wasn't shy about selling my coaching services because I truly believe in their power.

The First Unraveling

The perfect life started cracking when I realized that while I loved my husband, we had grown apart and wanted very different things after 10 years of marriage. I wanted an adventurous life, to focus on my physical health and passion for acrobatics—none of which were particularly appealing to him. He wanted to focus on building his business and was content to spend most of his time at home.

I had to face the hardest truth: I needed to let go of a man who had seen me into adulthood and been my rock for almost 12 years, to do life on my own at 32 with a seven-year-old.

The terror was real. I'd never paid bills on my own or been a single parent. Add that to the fact that I'd quit my teaching job to teach yoga and wasn't making much money. I was about to let go of the house I'd owned and lived in for nine years, my marriage, dual incomes, and the safety net of codependency.

But here's what's crazy—after I did it, I almost immediately felt more peaceful. I never regretted chasing my joy and my truth, even when it led to a life that was completely uncertain.

The Accidental Discovery

Years later, I still felt that whisper asking what I could do if I took a chance. I took an online course on creating passive income streams and even created a handstand course that I posted and marketed. I got some sales, but it wasn't much.

One of the activities in that course was to ask my friends and family what I was most skilled at and what they would come to me for advice on. The feedback revealed skills like empowering people to take risks, building confidence, and setting boundaries in relationships.

All of this screamed "life coach" to me.

But I was on the fence about becoming a life coach. I'd been in the self-improvement world for over 10 years as a yoga instructor and didn't always like what I saw there. I assumed life coaches were just dishing out advice and charging for it.

Then fate intervened.

I met Michelle at circus. She was a fellow mom who had just moved to California from Oregon with her family. When I asked what she did and she said life coaching, I almost leaped off the floor with all my questions. Did she go to a training program? Where? What was it like? How much did it cost? Did she make a good living? Did she like it?

I don't believe in coincidence, so I knew Michelle was put in my path for a reason. She told me about Inner Glow Circle, the certification program she'd attended. I looked them up online, realized one of the founders was a former teacher, and became even more interested.

I scheduled a sales call and was connected with Kaitlin. We talked about what my dream business would look like and how I could make it a reality. I could tell she wasn't like the life coaches I'd imagined—she was genuinely interested in me and my dreams.

Less than 24 hours later, I'd enrolled in their Level 1 coach training program for over $10,000. It was one of the scariest leaps I'd ever taken.

The $10,000 Bet on Myself

At the time, I was teaching secondary science full-time and couldn't see a way to pay for this expensive coaching program. Kaitlin told me I could literally start taking coaching clients right away to help pay the tuition.

I enrolled that night and spent the weekend feeling like I was going to throw up with how much money it was going to cost. But I remained faithful to the decision.

The following week I posted on Instagram that I was looking for coaching clients, and I signed my first paying client! That client is still with me as I write this now.

But let me be real—I was terrified. I was nervous that clients wouldn't see results, that I would charge them and nothing would happen and I would feel like a failure. I was worried I wouldn't get any clients at all and couldn't pay for this expensive program I'd committed to.

I didn't follow the traditional path of waiting until I was "ready." I began taking clients before I had any structures in place to actually run a business. I didn't have a website, payment software, or a detailed plan. I had my personal experience as a teacher, parent, and coach, plus the strategies I was learning in my certification program.

Turns out, that was totally enough to get started.

I built the structures over time while coaching clients weekly. I set up what I needed—mainly a Zoom account —and got to work. To this day, I don't have a fully-built and polished website, and that's perfectly okay with me.

The Moment It Clicked

The first major breakthrough came when I signed my fourth paying coaching client. This particular client came to me for yoga coaching—she was training to become a yoga instructor and wanted a mentor.

I remember doing a free connection call with her and going over her goals. She didn't sign up on that call, but I gave her some action steps to help move her forward. She took those steps without hesitation and ended up getting hired as an instructor at her first studio. She texted me right after and signed up for coaching.

At that moment, I had come full-circle. I remembered being on the receiving end of a similar call with Kaitlin, and now I had successfully coached a client to the same results. It was proof that this thing I was building actually worked.

The Identity Crisis

The hardest part wasn't learning to be a coach—it was learning to let go of who I'd always been. When I left teaching to become a yoga instructor, I didn't realize how much of my identity was wrapped up in being a chemistry teacher.

When I met someone new and they asked what I did for a living, I'd always get predictable responses: "Oh, you must be so smart!" or "I was terrible at chemistry, I don't know how you do that." I hadn't realized how much of my identity relied on other people being impressed with what I did.

When I told people I was a yoga teacher, I'd get responses like, 'You must be so flexible!" It just didn't have the same ring to it. I had no idea how important it was to me that I had an impressive-sounding job to talk about.

Over time, I made peace with this. I came to the conclusion that I wasn't what I did for a living. Now I feel very unconcerned with how others see me as a result of my occupation. I'm much more concerned with how I feel about the work I do daily and how others feel in my presence.

The Acrobatics Revelation

My entire approach to coaching stems from something I discovered about myself at age 30 when I started learning acrobatics. It was something I'd always been drawn to as a kid but never had the opportunity to really learn.

When the opportunity came as an adult, predictably, I thought, "I could never do that." I watched other acrobats doing tricks that blew my mind and never for one second thought that could be me.

Until I started actually applying myself and practicing.

Now, at 41, I do tricks that my 30-year-old self would have drooled over without a second thought. From that point on I knew, if I could do it, anyone could do it. Nothing gives me greater joy than watching my clients blow their own damn minds with what they can achieve with a little help and faith in what's possible for them.

The Ultimate Test

Nine years post-divorce, I'd built myself up financially, mentally, and emotionally. I found the adventurous, non-predictable, and creative life I was craving. I met and fell in love with an incredible man and built a relationship that incorporated adventure, passion, and fun.

But after almost eight years together, I faced the hardest application of my "pay now or pay later" philosophy yet. I realized that despite the love we shared, we had fundamentally different visions for our future. I wanted the full commitment of marriage; he did not.

I had to ask myself: Do I stay in this beautiful relationship that's missing the one thing I truly need, or do I honor what I know I'm worth and walk away?

The phrase that kept running through my mind was the same one from the gym: "Pay now or pay later." I could stay in the comfort I had with this man I loved, but I knew that in another eight years, I would be paying so much more. I would spend those years wondering if he'd ever be ready, slowly losing pieces of myself to uncertainty.

So I chose to pay now. I had the hardest conversation of my life and ended the relationship because I refused to settle for anything less than someone who could look at our life together and choose it wholeheartedly.

It was excruciating, but I know that having the courage to choose myself will lead to something even more beautiful than what I had to let go of.

The Life I Choose Daily

These days, I wake up with a clarity I never had before. I know exactly what I will and won't accept in my life, and I'm not afraid to enforce those boundaries. I don't work with clients who aren't actually interested in real change and simply want to complain.

I spent many years being pissed off when I got stuck somewhere longer than I planned, unable to say, "I need to go now." Now I don't compromise my time or energy. I don't spend time with people who leave me feeling drained, no matter who they are.

My definition of "having it all" has completely evolved. In my twenties, I thought it meant the family, career, and house. Now it means having a loving family, a strong group of awesome friends, a career I love, opportunities to be creative and take risks, being healthy and active, and having lots of fun adventures until the end of my days.

When my recent relationship ended and my world came crashing down, it was my community that reminded me who I was. As my best friend Jenny would say, "I let others stand on my shoulders to reach their own potential." But when I needed lifting, they were there for me.

I've also learned to simply allow myself to feel however I feel. When I was younger, I would try to deny feelings of fear, shame, or doubt. After going through heartbreak so extreme that there was no denying how I felt, I learned to just feel the feelings and allow them to pass.

The Truth I Want You to Know

Looking back, I would tell my younger self to just fucking go for it. That I know she's scared, but she's totally capable of figuring it out. This leap will lead her to a level of confidence and satisfaction she couldn't even dream of before.

I'm most proud of my ability to do hard things despite being afraid of the outcome. I'll practice scary acrobatics moves because I want to be proficient at them. I'll sign up for expensive coach training with no plan for how to pay for it because I feel called to become a coach. I'll have the conversation that ends a seven-year relationship because I know what I'm worth.

All of these are risks I've taken with no guaranteed outcome and a lot of fear behind them. But on the other side of those risks, I found a new version of myself that was even more courageous.

I hope anyone reading this understands that there's really nothing super special about me that allows me to do all the things I've done. I hope they can see a little of themselves in my story and that it gives them the courage to take the scary step they've been avoiding.

Because that step you've been avoiding? It's holding you back from what you're meant to be. Bet on yourself. You're worth betting on.

This time, it's personal because I fucking refuse to live one more minute of my life wondering what I could be. I'm going to go out there and do the thing.

That 45-pound kettlebell I picked up this afternoon? It's not just about building physical strength. It's about proving to myself, every single day, that I'm willing to do the hard thing now so I don't have to pay a bigger price later. It's about showing up for the woman I'm becoming, even when the woman I am today doesn't feel ready.

Pay now or pay later. And I'm done paying later.

Scan to connect with Heather

SEVEN

KATIE EDMONDS

IT'S MY TURN

I'm standing in a hospital room, looking at my 12-year-old nephew's lifeless body, and my heart is breaking into a million pieces. This beautiful boy—who just yesterday was laughing, playing, full of dreams and possibilities—is gone. Just gone.

The fluorescent hospital lights buzz overhead. Machines that were keeping him alive just hours ago now sit silent. His mother's sobs echo in the hallway, a sound I will never forget as long as I live.

In the midst of this overwhelming grief, a thought cuts through the pain: *He'll never get to become who he was meant to be.* This precious child had his whole life ahead of him—first love, graduation, career, maybe children of his own. All of it, stolen by a brain aneurysm that came without warning.

And then, in the crushing weight of that loss, another thought follows, quieter but just as devastating: *And I'm not becoming who I was meant to be either.*

Here I am, 35 years old, with everything that's supposed to make me happy—three beautiful children, a marriage, a successful real estate career. I have all the time this boy will never have, all the opportunities he'll never get. And I'm wasting them by living someone else's version of my life.

What am I doing with my life? What am I doing with my one, precious, finite life?

That moment, in the midst of grief, shattered everything I thought I knew about myself, who I was and what I wanted.

The Woman Who Disappeared

Six years earlier, I had been the picture of what society told me success looked like. I stayed home raising three babies, keeping house, being all things domesticated. For a time, this felt right because that's who I am at my core —a nurturer, a caregiver.

But after my third child was born, something started gnawing at me. I would fold endless loads of laundry and think, *I have more to give this world than this.*

What I didn't realize was how far I'd drifted from the woman I used to be.

In my twenties, living in New York City after growing up in Fort Myers, Florida, I had been fully, unapologetically myself. I knew what I liked, who I was, who I loved, what I believed in. I worked for a casting director, casting for designers like Marc Jacobs. I felt alive in a way that made my skin tingle with possibility.

But when I moved back home to start a family, something insidious began happening. I was different from the people who lived there, and instead of honoring that difference, I started molding myself to fit. I began silencing the thoughts and beliefs that made me me.

It was so gradual I didn't even notice it happening. Like gaining weight one pound at a time until one day you don't recognize yourself in the mirror.

Thirteen years later, standing in that hospital room, I couldn't tell what was authentically me and what was society's expectations wearing my face.

The Mask I Didn't Know I Was Wearing

The most terrifying part was that I didn't even know I was conforming. I thought this *was* me—the woman who never rocked the boat, who always said yes, who lived to make everyone else comfortable and happy.

I carried beliefs that seemed noble on the surface but were slowly suffocating me. I believed that to be a good mom, I needed to stay home with my children. I believed I needed to conform to what society told us success looked like.

These beliefs created a prison I didn't even know I was living in.

When you don't feel purposeful, it takes a toll on your self-esteem and confidence. I was struggling with self-worth, feeling unfulfilled, not knowing who I really was underneath all the roles I was playing. I knew I was ready for my next chapter, but I wasn't sure what that looked like or how to get there.

Most people are walking around wearing a mask, an identity that's not them. I was doing this too, and the scariest part was how natural it had become.

The Pull Toward Something More

After my third child was born, that pull toward something more became impossible to ignore. When I feel pulled and passionate about something, I put my all into it—it's one of the few authentic parts of myself I never lost.

I got my real estate license from start to finish in 12 days. Most people fail the test at least once. But I was driven by something deeper than ambition—I was driven by survival.

Real estate felt like coming home to myself in a way I hadn't experienced in years. I help people during the most difficult and exciting times in their lives. People move because someone died, they had a new baby, they got divorced. I get to give people the service they deserve, working with integrity and honesty in an industry that can be very self-serving.

In my first year, I sold millions of dollars in real estate. I was incredibly proud, but more than that, I felt *alive* again. For the first time in years, I was using skills that felt natural to me, helping people in ways that mattered.

But even with this success, I could feel there was more work for me to do. A deeper calling I couldn't yet name.

The Day Everything Became Clear

Then came that day in the hospital that changed everything.

A brain aneurysm. Twelve years old. Healthy one day, gone the next.

Standing there, looking at my nephew's peaceful face, I was struck by the randomness of it all. This beautiful boy would never get to grow up, never get to discover who he was meant to be, never get to do the work he was put on Earth to do.

And here I was, with all the time he'd never have, wasting it by wearing a mask and not living to my purpose or potential.

Death has a way of stripping away all the bullshit and showing you what really matters. In that sterile room, surrounded by the medical equipment that couldn't save him, I understood with devastating clarity that I wasn't living or leading with purpose. I wasn't who I was born to be.

I left that hospital knowing everything had to change. I just didn't know how terrifying that change would be.

The Unraveling Begins

The path back to myself wasn't linear or immediate. It was a slow, sometimes painful process of peeling back the layers of who I thought I was supposed to be and examining what actually felt like me.

The biggest thing I had to let go of was people-pleasing. That deep, bone-level need to make everyone else comfortable even when it was killing me inside. I always say "we can always talk ourselves out of the right decision," and that comes from fear—fear of not being accepted or loved.

The hard truths started surfacing like splinters working their way out of my skin. I was scared. I did conform. I was living for others and not for myself. And the woman I'd become was so far from who I'd started out to be that I barely recognized her.

The Art of Shedding

What followed was the slow, painful work of trying each layer of identity on and seeing if it still fit. Some things I'd thought were core to who I was turned out to be costumes I'd been wearing so long I'd forgotten they weren't my skin.

I had to become me again. Completely, fully, authentically myself. I had to find the confident woman who had always been there, just buried under years of trying to be what everyone else wanted me to be.

The woman who knew her own mind. Who trusted her instincts. Who wasn't afraid to be different.

This inner work started changing everything else. I got my life coaching certification not because it was strategic, but because I felt completely led to this new journey. My decisions became clearer, faster. Instead of agonizing over every choice, I could feel the right path.

It was a quick yes or no, flowing from some deeper knowing I'd reconnected with.

Even in real estate, everything shifted. My business partner and I completely stripped our business down and rebuilt it to work for us, in alignment with what we wanted rather than what the industry told us we should do. We decided having a team wasn't for us anymore. We wanted to focus solely on production. We started saying no to marketing approaches that felt inauthentic, even if they were supposed to work.

This is what happens when you stop following the "shoulds" and start trusting yourself.

The Hardest Test

But the biggest test of this new authentic self was still coming.

Living authentically sounds beautiful in theory. In practice, it means making choices that other people don't understand. It means disappointing people who have certain expectations of who you should be.

At 35 years old, with three children, I realized I had to make the hardest decision of my life. I needed to leave my marriage.

Not because I was cheated on. Not because of any dramatic betrayal. But because I wasn't happy, and for the first time in my life, I was ready to put myself first.

This wasn't a decision I made lightly. I knew people wouldn't agree with it. Here I was, walking away from what looked like a perfectly good life. But I also knew that staying wasn't in alignment with who I am.

My children needed to see what it looked like for their mother to choose herself, to live authentically, to refuse to settle for a life that didn't fit. Even when it was terrifying. Even when it meant starting over.

The conversation that ended my marriage was one of the hardest things I've ever done. But it was also one of the most honest. I wasn't just doing this for me. I was also doing this for my kids. I knew the best thing I could be for them was happy and myself.

Living in Flow

What does it feel like when you're fully being yourself? Complete flow.

I wake up with energy now. Real energy, not the forced kind that comes from coffee and willpower. I take time for myself every day—reflecting, exercising, nourishing myself physically, emotionally, and spiritually. Because I've become so in tune with myself, I can feel immediately when I'm out of alignment and self-correct.

This is a skill I've worked on and focused on throughout my transformation. Building a life that fits starts with the smallest daily choices. What do I eat? How do I exercise? How do I have fun? How do I show up each day? A life that actually fits is shaped by what feels right on every level—physically, emotionally, spiritually, logistically.

I protect my time and energy in ways I never did before. When my phone rings, I ask myself, "Is this what you need right now?" Sometimes the answer is yes. Sometimes it's no, and I call back later when I'm in a better space to give.

I say no when I want to say no. For someone who spent decades people-pleasing, this was revolutionary.

My definition of "having it all" has completely transformed. It's not about what your life looks like from the outside—how much money you make, what house you live in, how many vacations you take, what handbag you carry. It's about how you feel. "Having it all" means finding inner peace and happiness. It means being vulnerable, honest, and open in ways I never allowed myself before. It's not about the Instagram highlight reel. It's about the peace in the stillness. In the quiet moments that you feel connected.

The Work I Was Born to Do

Now I help people realize their worth and take the steps to get to a life that feels right to them. In real estate, I help people navigate the practical transitions. In coaching, I help them navigate the internal ones that are even more important.

What lights me up most is seeing clients find their confidence, their voice, their authentic selves. Because I know what it feels like to live behind a mask, and I know what freedom feels like when you finally take it off.

I have the ability now to lead my life and every decision with my intuition, my higher self, and the path that God has me on. I set goals that align with who I am and what I want to do during my time on Earth. I don't feel guilty or second-guess or worry about what others think.

When things get hard—and they do get hard—I stay grounded by remembering that I can feel this work is my truth. This isn't just a career or a business. It's my purpose, the reason I'm here.

What inspires me to keep going is my children. Not to prove myself, but to show them that the bravest thing you can be in this world is yourself. And that doing your work—your real work—is important. Important to yourself, important to others.

What I Know Now

If I could sit down with my past self—the one folding endless laundry and wondering if this was all there was —I would tell her: You are worthy. You are capable. You can do hard things. All of the answers you seek are within you.

I'm proud of becoming awake and aware before too much time slipped by. So many people walk through life asleep for most of their lives. I'm proud of the self-work I put in. I'm proud of the mother I am. I'm proud of the compassion I give and have for others.

But most of all, I'm proud that I chose myself.

I hope anyone reading this feels inspired to make changes in their life to be happy. Inspired to choose themselves. Inspired to make a difference in other people's lives.

Because here's what I learned standing in that hospital room, holding space for grief. We don't get to know how much time we have. But we do get to choose how we spend it.

This time, it's personal because it's my life and it's my turn.

That 12-year-old boy who died too young taught me the most important lesson of my life: Time is not guaranteed, but choosing yourself is always possible. Every day we don't live as our authentic selves is a day we can't get back.

I refuse to waste another day living for anyone but me.Being myself is the greatest gift any of us could give to the world. Because the alternative—living a half-life void of authenticity—is no gift to anyone.

It's my turn to be fully, completely, unapologetically alive.

Scan to connect with Katie

EIGHT

LIZ RODRIGUEZ

YOU ARE THE PERMISSION

"Primero eres madre antes que mujer."

You're a mother first, before you're a woman.

That's what I kept hearing the moment I got pregnant. Like it was the rulebook for my life moving forward. Like from now on, every single thing I did needed to revolve around my baby.

But sitting in my parents' living room at 21—broke, broken and with my two-year-old daughter asleep beside me on the tile floor that had become our bed—I realized that expectation had already stripped me of everything I was before I even knew who I was.

I was a baby raising a baby, running from one hell into another. And somewhere in the middle of all that survival, I lost myself. Not just the version I thought I was supposed to become. Not just my voice. But me—the whole fucking person I was meant to be.

But here's what I know now that I didn't know then: being a mother doesn't erase the woman I am. It amplifies her.

Little did I know that motherhood wasn't the end of me —it was only the beginning of my becoming.

The First Taste of Rock Bottom

I became a mom at 19. Nineteen. I didn't even know who I was as a woman yet, but suddenly I was expected to know how to be a mother, a wife, a whole person responsible for another human being. I ran away from home straight into a marriage that would isolate me from friends, family, and most importantly, myself.

This was my first taste of rock bottom, but it wouldn't be my last.

I was never taught that I'd have to work hard and hustle just to survive. I don't know how to explain that properly —it's like the concept didn't exist in my world. My parents lived paycheck to paycheck, never really striving for more. They didn't know what they didn't know, and I just followed their blueprint. I was broke and broken, with the heart of a teenager playing stay-at-home mom with a nonexistent mindset about what any of it meant.

When that marriage finally crumbled under the weight of domestic violence, I walked away with nothing but my daughter and whatever courage I could scrape together. We ended up sleeping on my parents' living room floor. I was working part-time at my first corporate job, literally walking 30 minutes to work because I didn't have a car after mine got totaled.

The Night That Changed Everything

There's one night that stands out like a scar on my memory. I had to work late, and my mom promised to pick me up at 10 PM. I waited. And waited. She never showed.

I was tired, mad, angry, sad—felt like shit, worthless, like I didn't matter enough for either of my parents to show up for me. Like no one cared. No one was there for me. I had to walk home alone in the dark, taking the longer route because the direct path felt too dangerous.

I stopped at the liquor store on the way home, bought a 20-ounce beer, got home almost at midnight, and drank it alone in that living room while my daughter slept. At that moment, I knew something wasn't right. I was broken, with no love for myself, just drinking the pain away, numbing everything I felt.

That's when I knew I was drowning, not just financially, but emotionally, spiritually—every way a person can drown while still breathing.

Finding My Lifeline

A Zumba class changed my life. I know how that sounds, but it's true. I wanted to lose a few pounds, and for once, I chose myself. Well, kinda. Through that class, I was introduced to a new way of living and making money—network marketing.

I joined to make extra income, but what I found was so much more. My personal development journey started there. I found mentors who poured into me continuously, who saw potential in me when I couldn't see it myself. They were the parents I needed in that season of my life.

As I'm typing this, I'm having this realization: I don't know what my life would have looked like without them and network marketing. They literally saved me from myself.

But even with that foundation, even with people believing in me, I was still carrying so much baggage about who I was supposed to be as a woman, as a mother. My worth was tied to what I could offer and do for a man. My worth was tied to my body and how good it looked. I didn't even know what "fill your cup" meant.

The Second Rock Bottom

It took me years—like five to seven years—another baby, and another relationship that dragged me to rock bottom for the second time before I finally got it. This black hole was deeper, darker, and took me longer to climb out of.

But I walked away. Again.

A health and wellness challenge transformed me inside out over 12 weeks. Those 12 weeks marked my life forever. The continuous pattern and practice of choosing myself, prioritizing my health, my self-development, my business as a network marketer, going to events where I heard stories of women thriving and transforming their lives—it all started adding up.

Being surrounded by women of all ages choosing themselves fueled me and gave me hope. It took all of that plus my mentor finally telling me: "Liz, you deserve better."

Sometimes you need someone else to say what you can't say to yourself yet.

Meeting My Game Changer

I knew who @thebeamlife was online—like HELLO, THE Beam Life! But Kaitlin and I met at an event in the most unexpected way. During a sharing moment, I opened up about how insecure I felt about my smile and how it always held me back. I cried—I always cry—and later during a break, she sat with me.

She just poured into me. Of course I started crying again and immediately went hand-to-mouth trying to cover my smile (because ugly cry smiles, if you know you know), and she grabbed my hand, pulled it down to my lap, and continued pouring into me.

"You are beautiful," she said.

Not because she was trying to sell me something. She brought me onboard as a Beam Team member as her Creative Executive VA—the service I was offering back then. She treated me as a human, poured into me without having a personal relationship prior. She never saw me as a dollar sign, never acted like she was above me. Titles didn't matter to her.

I was honored that she believed in my work and

creativity and trusted me with her mission and vision. It was never transactional.

Hiding in the Shadows

For the last three years, I stayed in the shadows. As a Creative Executive Assistant, I was always behind the scenes—and honestly, I liked it that way. Showing up for my clients and hitting their deadlines has always been my number one priority. That part? Locked in.

But when it came to showing up for myself and my business? I played it *very* safe. If I wanted more clients, I'd post here and there, usually from a place of passion, but never with real consistency or strategy. It kept me comfortable for a long time…

Comfortable, but small.

I was happy until I wasn't.

I craved different. I craved more. I craved being ambitious unapologetically, but for real this time. I've always been unconventional, and that part of me was hiding in the shadows. Everything around me started to feel unaligned, not right, not home. It was no longer enough.

What I was doing was making me money, providing for me and mine, but it wasn't enough anymore. This level got too easy for me. I made a decision to tap back into myself, my desires, my dreams. What did Liz *really* want to build? My rules. My life. My business—not a replica of someone else's definition of success.

Burning Bridges and Building Dreams

The biggest gut decision I made was burning bridges. Because let's be real—we are who we surround ourselves with. I was hiding in plain sight, stuck in the shadows of a circle that capped my potential.

I was maxed out, feeling like I'd outgrown my old energy, my old crew, the old vision. The decision to part ways hit me like lightning—strong, confusing, and totally unexpected. But it also made perfect sense.

At first, I had no idea what was coming next. But looking back now? It was the best, most pivotal move I've made. New opportunities started falling into my lap. New connections, new friendships, and a whole lot more clarity. I shut the noise out. It got really, really quiet in the best way possible.

Of course, I grieved. I'm human. But I came back to myself. I am so done abandoning myself for anyone or anything.

Becoming MOMbitious

That's when I realized what I was really meant to do. I am a business mentor for Latina moms—or as I like to say, for MOMbitious women. Moms who crave and desire MORE than being "just a mom" or working a life-sucking 9-to-5 away from their babies. They are secretly unconventional dreamers and visionaries, but their title as a mom has fully taken over their whole identity.

I help my secretly MOMbitious women rediscover the woman behind motherhood. I say "secretly" because they've been stripped away from everything, including their voice. We're going to unmute their voice and give it all the fucking power it deserves. We're going to tap into their ideas, creativity, passions, skills, hobbies, shine light on them, and translate them into offers.

I help them build a life-first business. We're building income AROUND their babies, around drop-off and pickup time, around doctor appointments, award ceremonies, emergencies, and life. They are going to dream again and make it their reality.

This lights me up because I was once voiceless for so long, pushed around by all the shoulds and shouldn'ts around motherhood and wifehood. Nothing I did was ever enough. I wasn't good enough. I wasn't enough of a wife, I wasn't enough of a mother. Everything I did was always wrong or unconventional.

The Hard Truth About Playing Small

One hard truth I had to face about myself was that I was the one playing small. It wasn't my circumstances, it wasn't lack of time, it wasn't even the opinions of others holding me back—it was ME, dimming my own light because I was scared of what would happen if I actually owned my power and who I needed to become in the process.

I had to get real with myself and admit that I was hiding behind "I'm just an assistant" as a safety net. But the moment I called myself out, that's when everything changed. I realized no one was coming to save me...and I didn't need them to. I was built for this, and I had already built proof.

Killing Old Versions of Myself

I've had to kill so many different versions of myself to get here. I had to work on my mindset—that shit is continued work that never ends. I had to reclaim my worth, the belief in myself, the belief in my "delusional" dreams that weren't really delusional—they were just glimpses of what was possible.

I needed to reclaim my voice and play it loud and proud. I'm in my mid-thirties, and it feels like it's only getting easier to come back to myself. I've had to let go of the victim mindset—there's no *"ay pobrecita de mí, por qué todo me pasa a mí."* I've had to let go of friendships, family, set boundaries, be more in alignment with myself.

I can't say I've grieved any older version of myself. I feel like I've always been grateful and proud of the versions of me that have gotten me here. What scares me most is who I'll have to become in the process, because it means letting go of the version of me I am now. And the older I get, the more I've grown to love that version.

Building Life on My Terms

My business now feels like an extension of ME. It feels aligned, intentional, and fucking powerful. I was building my business out of urgency and desperation before, saying yes to anything that brought in a check, even if it drained me. I stopped hustling for crumbs and started building from clarity and intention.

I raised my standards, honored my boundaries, and leaned into the fact that my lived experiences, my expertise, my knowledge, my motherhood, my struggles, my Latina roots are literally all my superpowers in business. The more I honored my own blueprint, my own ideas, MY STORY, my voice, the more my business grows and expands.

This is about creating a life where I don't have to choose between my career and motherhood. I get to have both. On my terms. Loudly. Proudly. Unapologetically and unconventionally.

Building Something Different

You know what's wild? I used to think success meant having the biggest house, the fanciest car, looking like I had my shit together from the outside. But sitting on that living room floor all those years ago, broke and broken, I realized that kind of success wasn't built for women like me.

Now? Having it all looks like shutting my laptop in the middle of the day to pick up my kids from school. It's building a business that pays me, respects me, and fits into my life instead of forcing me to choose between my dreams and my family. It's financial peace of mind—the deep knowing that everything and everyone is taken care of, that we're healthy and thriving, that we're doing what we love and getting paid for it.

I get to build and raise both my business and my babies. On my terms.

When the hard moments hit—and they still do—I remember that little whisper that says, "You didn't come this far to stop here." I've walked through financial struggle, motherhood identity crises, and self-doubt. But I also knew that no 9-to-5 was going to give me the freedom I craved.

What keeps me going isn't just my vision for my family or my personal dreams. It's the deep knowing that I'm breaking cycles. My daughters are watching a woman choose herself, her dreams, and her worth. I'm not just building a business; I'm building proof—for them, for other moms wondering if they can do it too, and for myself to hold onto when things get messy.

Living Fully as Myself

When I'm fully being myself in life and business, it truly feels like no shits, ands, or fucks given. It's quiet. There are no outside voices influencing me. I know my voice, my desires. I have a vision of who I want to become. I create from the inside out—from my thoughts, from my experiences, from my story. These are places no one else has been or lived in.

My uniqueness shines. My voice gets very loud and clear. My values are clear, and they match my actions.

I give myself permission to take up space and own my expertise, my knowledge. I no longer shrink, water myself down, play small, or wait for the "right time." I show up boldly as a Latina mompreneur, as a leader, as a breadwinner in the making, and as a woman who refuses to lose herself in the process.

Breaking the Rules

2025 has been THAT year for me. I have a clear vision of what I'm building, what I'm bringing to life, and I'm doing this the most MY WAY possible. I take and implement what serves me, what feels aligned but also challenging, and I drop anything that doesn't align with me or my values or what I want to be known for.

This is the year where I do my shit my way. My MOMbitious women will find me. My Latina moms que son soñadoras y ambiciosas me van a encontrar, but that will only happen if I am my most bold, authentic, unconventional, outspoken self. I will talk about the unspoken and unheard when it comes to moms being ambitious and what it really takes.

The Woman I've Become

This current version of myself is feisty. She's clear. She's unhinged. She plays her voice loud and proud. She's here to break the paradigms. She's here to break the rules. She doesn't wait for approval. She doesn't people-please. She doesn't abandon herself. She knows that if she prioritizes her womanhood, it will overflow into her motherhood.

She understands that both can coexist. And it gets to look however she wants it to look and needs it to be, to fit any and all seasons of her life, her kids' lives, and her husband's life.

You Are the Permission

This time, it's personal because I am the most unconventional me I've ever been, and I love her. Because I'm the main character of my life. I am the CEO of my life, and I take inventory. I burn the bridges. I will never abandon myself for the sake of others ever again.

This time, it's personal because I'm done playing small to keep others comfortable.

To every mom reading this who's been told she has to choose, who's been hiding her dreams behind the title of "mother," who's been waiting for permission to want more—stop looking for representation because you're not going to find it. BE the representation.

The leader is already within you. Trust yourself. Trust your vision. Trust your heart. Trust the process. Everything is truly happening for you, to build you, to prepare you for what's next.

No one's coming to give you permission. You're the permission. You're the blueprint.

Being a mom doesn't put your dreams on hold—it gives them a deeper purpose. Motherhood and womanhood can and do coexist. It gets to look however you want it to look. There really isn't a rulebook.

Color outside the fucking lines. Break the fucking molds. Break the boxes you or anyone has put you in.

Start with what you have, what you know, and where you are—that is the most perfect starting point. You don't need a perfect plan. You need a decision. A decision that says: "I'm done playing by rules that weren't made for me."

Let's fucking GROW.

Scan to connect with Liz

NINE

MIKKI MCCLEERY

START MESSY

I'm standing at a vendor event watching a woman hold up one of my t-shirts that says "Be Afraid And Do It Anyways." She turns to her friend and says, "OMG, I need this. Actually, I need all of these sayings." When I see that smile spread across her face, I know exactly why I do this.

You see, I used to be that woman who needed those exact words but couldn't find them anywhere. I was writing motivational sayings on my gym mirror every single day because I was drowning and those phrases were my lifeline. Now I get to watch women wear those same words like armor.

But let me be real with you—getting to this moment where I'm watching women light up over something I created? It required me to face some hard truths about the life I was living and completely tear it down.

The Robot Life

Five years ago, if you'd followed me around with a camera, you would have seen a woman who looked like she had it all together. Daughter, wife, mom to my son and two bonus daughters, full-time paralegal and taking care of my two fur babies—basically juggling everything while slowly losing my mind.

My life had become robotic. Wake up, get everyone ready, work, manage the household, crash into bed, repeat. People would say, "OMG, you're like an Energizer Bunny!" and I'd smile because that's what they expected. But behind that energetic front, I was drowning.

I was constantly on edge, complaining about work or life, starting arguments with my husband over the smallest things. And it was always me starting them—99 percent of the time. I couldn't seem to stop the cycle even though it was exhausting for both of us.

Most people looking from the outside would never know what was happening behind closed doors or what I was dealing with mentally. I had a really good way of putting up a front that everything was great. But there were nights I'd cry myself to sleep, wondering if there was even a reason to keep trying.

I was stuck in comparison mode, seeing what others had and telling myself I wanted that too. To be honest, I don't even think I actually wanted those things, but I was so lost I didn't know what I did want anymore.

The Beliefs That Kept Me Small

Growing up, I'd absorbed some pretty toxic beliefs about my worth. Family members would constantly comment on my weight—either I was too skinny or gaining too much. Nothing was ever just right. Those voices followed me into adulthood, telling me I wasn't good enough, that I didn't look right.

When I got pregnant with my son as a single mom, some people made it clear they thought I'd done things backwards and ruined my chances at success. The message was loud: I was supposed to settle for less because of my choices.

I carried the belief that my worth came from how much I was doing for others and how I looked doing it. I thought being a good woman meant disappearing completely into motherhood, that wanting anything for myself was selfish.

Most damaging of all, I didn't believe in myself. I'd make excuses about time and money instead of admitting I was scared to try.

The Breaking Point

The wake-up call came when I realized I couldn't continue living constantly on edge, where the smallest thing going wrong would send me spiraling. My mom started pointing out that I needed to do something for myself—not just for my own wellbeing, but to show my son how to be the best version of himself.

The physical and mental exhaustion wasn't sustainable. I was tired of being tired, frustrated with being frustrated.

The most jarring moment came when people started telling me I didn't have a "bad life" and should look at those who "literally have nothing." That stung because I realized I'd been focusing on what wasn't working instead of appreciating what I had. I was attracting more problems by dwelling on them.

I knew something had to change, but I had no idea how.

Finding My Community

That's when I stumbled across a post about the The BEAM Life community meeting. Something about it caught my attention, so I decided to check it out. I ended up on a 20-minute call to see if it would be a good fit, and let me tell you—I signed up immediately. No hesitation.

For the first time in years, I had a space where I could connect with other women and spend time dedicated to figuring out who I was beyond all the roles I was playing. I didn't have to explain endlessly or worry about being judged. I was heard. I was seen.

Most importantly, I learned that taking time for myself wasn't selfish—it was necessary.

The Space to Be Mikki

Being in the The BEAM Life community gave me something I'd forgotten I needed: space to be myself. Not mom-Mikki or wife-Mikki or employee-Mikki—just Mikki.

I started putting myself in my own calendar, even if it meant getting up at 5 a.m. I had to prioritize myself in my own life, which felt revolutionary after years of putting everyone else first.

The BEAM Life community became my safe space to share that I wanted to create an apparel business. I'd been writing motivational sayings on my gym mirror for months, and it was on my heart to share these messages with other women. Being around other women who were pursuing their passions made it feel possible.

The Identity I Had to Shed

The hardest part was realizing I'd been hiding behind the identity of "mom" for 12 years. Once I became a mother, my entire life became about my son. I worked like crazy to ensure he had everything he needed, but in the process, I completely forgot what it was like to just be Mikki.

I didn't even remember what I enjoyed doing for fun. My identity was so tied to being a mom that I'd erased myself.

To reclaim who I was, I had to start trying new things. I had to work on boundaries with work and people. Most importantly, I had to learn to love myself and speak to myself the way I'd speak to a friend.

Just Do the Damn Thing

When I finally decided to launch Passion Threads Co, I had no strategy, no business plan, no email list. I just had an idea and a heart full of passion. I made the decision to start messy rather than wait for that perfect moment.

I started with just a few designs on Canva, playing around with different fonts to see what looked best. I had no idea if people would actually buy them, but I decided to do the damn thing anyway.

People told me I needed an email marketing list first—I didn't start that until a year later. They said I needed a website—I started with an Etsy store instead. I learned that if there's a will, there's a way.

One of my first business decisions came purely from gut instinct: just get a few designs out there and see what happens. It didn't have to be perfect. I didn't need 20 designs. I needed to start somewhere.

Taking Responsibility

To build the life and business I wanted, I had to face some hard truths about myself. I had to take responsibility for my life and the outcomes. If I was making excuses about not having enough time or money, I was just making excuses. If you truly want something, you make time for it and find a way to get it, even if that means early mornings or getting resourceful with your money.

I had to learn that things aren't always going to be perfect, but having something out there is better than not having it at all. I used to tell myself, "What if no one buys it?" Well, guess what—no one will buy it if it doesn't exist.

I had to become okay with uncomfortable feelings and uncertainty. I needed to do inner work to move past the blocks holding me back. Most importantly, I had to start loving myself and telling myself motivational sayings because I needed to hear them from within, not seek validation from others.

I needed to trust that I was capable of making bold moves and showing up like the badass I am.

Life in Full Color

Today, my life looks completely different. I've set boundaries that ensure I don't forget who I am. I only go to things that truly bring me joy. I don't mind being the one who says no if it means protecting my peace.

I'm building a life that allows time for creativity and being the best version of myself. It's a life where we can spontaneously drive to the beach just to enjoy the sun. It's a slower pace where I wake up when my body is ready instead of having an alarm screaming at 5 a.m.

I protect my time and energy fiercely. I don't say yes to events just because I feel obligated. I don't spend time with people who drain my energy. I have firm boundaries, even with my 9-to-5 job, about my hours and what I actually have capacity to handle.

The Woman I've Become

When I'm fully being myself in life and business, I'm filled with joy. People tell me I'm very direct, and I know that's not everyone's cup of tea. But I have confidence that radiates when I'm in my element.

I'm the nicest person for those I truly care about and will do everything I can to help them. But I'm also the type of person who, once you cross me, I'm not so forgiving. I'm blunt and tend to say it how it is without filtering. I know some people can't handle that direct-ness, but that's a good thing because we can't make everyone happy.

I have a shirt that says "Sorry Not Sorry," and I laugh because now my son uses that saying too. You'll hear him say "sorry not sorry" or "that's not my problem." Little ones are always watching and picking up on every-thing we do. I'm raising a mini-me, and sometimes I think one of me in this world is plenty, but we have two now.

When I see photos of myself at events, the smile on my face is priceless. You can tell I'm truly enjoying what I do. I love talking to people, hearing their stories, sharing mine.

My Definition of Having It All

Having it all used to mean materialistic things, but that's complete bullshit. We can replace things, but people aren't replaceable. Now, having it all means time freedom and quality time with family. It means true friendships I can count on and the most supportive mom, husband and son ever—my cheerleaders who tell me to go for it when I'm unsure.

I can try new things even when they scare me, like being a vendor and putting myself out there. I can ask for help when I'm feeling overwhelmed before it gets to burnout. I stay focused on what I have versus what I don't have, and on what I can control versus what's out of my control.

The Practices That Keep Me Grounded

When things get hard, I have practices that ground me. I'll diamond paint for at least 30 minutes while listening to music, disconnecting from whatever's going on and focusing on each diamond one at a time. Sometimes I'll walk around the block, focusing on the sun touching my body and my breathing, talking to myself and reminding myself that this is only a small portion of my life.

What inspires me to continue is my why. I can always revert to my why and keep moving forward no matter what obstacles come my way.

I keep a list of what I've accomplished so I can look back and see how far I've come. I take time for myself without guilt because if my cup is full, I can pour into others.

What I'd Tell My Past Self

I would tell the woman I used to be: You need to get over the fear and just do it. It might be hard at the moment, but it will all be worth the work in the end. There's never going to be the right time or right moment to start—just start messy and get it out there.

You can always pivot if something isn't working or if you're no longer passionate about what you're building. Taking the leap and focusing on what makes you happy is going to make you a better person overall.

I'm proud that I continue to put the work in for myself and that I'm not settling in life. Sometimes things don't come out exactly as I originally envisioned—sometimes they're not as good, but most times they're even better than I expected.

I'm proud that I can be my unique self without worrying what others think. I have a very unique personality. Some would say I can be bitchy; I say I'm direct and let people know what I want or need. I truly know I'm not for everyone, but the right people will know I'm for them.

I'm proud of myself for putting myself out there even when I want to hide. I have told myself and will continue to tell myself: I WILL NOT PLAY SMALL ANYMORE. I have so much passion to share with the world.

The Magic in the Mess

Here's what I want you to understand: there's no super guide to life, only lessons we learn along the way. If you have something on your heart, it's there for a reason. Follow through with it.

I'm a firm believer in doing hard things and trying new things that push you out of your comfort zone—you know, those things that make your palms sweaty, your heart race, and every logical part of your brain scream "NOPE, not today."

When you're in that uncomfortable feeling and you try anyway, that's where the magic happens. That's where we grow. And that's exactly what I try to capture in every single design I create.

Here's what I remind myself when fear creeps in: we all have to start somewhere. Every expert was once a beginner. Every person you admire had a moment where they felt completely out of their depth and did it anyway.

Life can be messy and you can still have an amazing life. There are no rules on how to do life. We only have one life, so do the things you're passionate about that truly bring you joy, even if that means saying no to others.

We're not going to be able to make everyone happy, but we sure as hell can make ourselves happy. Our life experiences have brought us to who we are now, and we don't have to sit in the past. We can move forward and DO THE DAMN THING EVEN IF IT'S MESSY.

This time, it's personal because life is too short to play small, and I'm going after my dreams no matter what it takes. No one can stop me. Just watch.

That woman at the vendor event, holding my shirt and lighting up, is exactly who I was creating for—the woman who needs permission to start messy, to be afraid and do it anyway, to be stronger than her excuses.

Because sometimes we all need that gentle nudge toward courage, toward trying that thing we've been putting off, toward starting somewhere even when we have no idea what we're doing.

Scan to connect with Mikki

WHERE YOU GO FROM HERE

Six years ago, I had no idea I was about to build something that would completely change how I see transformation. I thought I was just starting a coaching business. What I actually created was a laboratory for watching women remember who they are.

The BEAM Life—Be Everything And More—started as a rebellious idea: what if women didn't have to choose? What if we could be ambitious and present, successful and fulfilled, driven and peaceful? What if the problem wasn't that we wanted too much, but that we'd been told we were allowed too little?

These nine women are proof that the idea works. But more than that, they're proof of something I've come to believe is the most radical thing a woman can do in this world: tell the truth about her life.

What I've Learned About Truth-Telling

After working with hundreds of women, I've realized something that changed everything for me as a coach: women don't need fixing. They need permission to stop performing and start living.

Every woman who comes into my world is carrying the same invisible burden—the exhausting weight of pretending their life is working when it isn't. They've mastered the art of looking like they have it together while slowly suffocating inside the life they've built to please everyone else.

The transformation doesn't happen when I give them a strategy or a system. It happens when they finally get honest about what's not working and stop apologizing for wanting something different.

That's what you witnessed in these chapters. Nine women who decided to quit performing happiness and start building it instead.

The Power of Being Everything And More

When I say "Be Everything And More," I'm not talking about adding more to your already overwhelming life. I'm talking about permission to be all of who you are without editing yourself down to make other people comfortable.

Society has convinced us that we have to choose. Career or family. Ambition or contentment. Success or authenticity. But every woman in this book is living proof that those are false choices designed to keep us small.

You can be a devoted mother and an ambitious entrepreneur. You can be kind and have boundaries. You can be successful and spiritual. You can be everything you are and still want more—not because you're greedy, but because you're human.

The women in this book aren't extraordinary because they're superhuman. They're extraordinary because they decided to stop shrinking themselves to fit into boxes that were never meant for them.

What Happens When Women Get Honest

Here's what I've discovered through this work: when one woman gets brave enough to tell the truth about her life, it creates permission for every woman around her to do the same. Truth-telling is contagious as hell.

That's why I knew these stories had to become a book. Not because they're unique, but because they're not. Every woman reading this has felt what these women felt—the suffocation of living someone else's version of your life, the exhaustion of performing happiness, the quiet desperation of wondering if this is all there is.

But here's what most women don't know: those feelings aren't a sign that something's wrong with you. They're a sign that something's right with you. Your soul is refusing to settle, even when your mind is trying to convince you to be grateful for what you have.

The Magic of Community

One thing became crystal clear as I built The BEAM Life: women transform faster and go further when they're surrounded by other women who refuse to let them stay small.

Isolation will kill your dreams faster than failure ever will. When you're the only person in your world who wants something different, it's easy to convince yourself you're crazy. But when you're surrounded by women who are building lives that fit, suddenly your dreams don't seem impossible—they seem inevitable.

That's what community really means in my world. Not just people who cheer you on, but people who see your potential when you can't and refuse to let you abandon yourself when things get scary.

The women in this book found that community, The BEAM Life. They all understood that transformation isn't a solo journey—it's something that happens in relationship, in witness, in the sacred space between women who believe in each other's possibility.

What I Know About Starting

Through this work, I've watched women transform their lives from every possible starting point. Broke and broken. Successful but unfulfilled. Lost and searching. Confident but stuck. It doesn't matter where you start—what matters is that you start.

The biggest lie women tell themselves is that they need to be ready before they begin. Ready means different things to different people, but it usually translates to: "I'll start when I'm not scared, when I have more money, when the kids are older, when I figure out exactly what I want."

But here's what I've learned: ready is not a feeling, it's a choice and a decision. The women who transform their lives don't wait to feel ready. They start scared, start messy, start imperfect. They understand that clarity comes from action, not the other way around.

You don't think your way into a new life. You live your way into it.

The Ripple Effect

What excites me most about this work isn't just the women I get to coach directly. It's the ripple effect. When a woman chooses herself, she gives every woman around her permission to do the same. Her daughters watch a woman who refuses to settle. Her friends see what's possible when you stop apologizing for wanting more. Her community witnesses what happens when someone builds a life that actually fits.

The women in this book aren't just changing their own lives. They're changing the lives of everyone who witnesses their courage. They're showing up as examples of what's possible when you decide to stop living for everyone else and start living for yourself.

This is why I do this work. Not just for the individual transformation, but for the collective one. Every woman who chooses authenticity over approval, courage over comfort, truth over performance—she's making it easier for the next woman to do the same.

What's Possible From Here

If you've read this far, something in you is refusing to settle. Something in you knows there's more. Trust that. That restlessness you feel isn't a problem to solve—it's a calling to answer.

The life you're dreaming about? It's not some fantasy. It's a possibility waiting for you to decide you're worth it. The version of yourself who's living authentically, building something that matters, making choices from alignment instead of fear—she's not someone you become someday. She's someone you choose to be today.

You don't need another certification or course or strategy. You need to start. You need to get honest about what's not working. You need to stop apologizing for wanting more and start building it instead.

The women in this book blazed a trail, but they didn't do it because they were special. They did it because they decided to stop waiting for permission and start giving it to themselves.

My Invitation to You

This book isn't just a collection of stories. It's an invitation into a different way of being. An invitation to stop performing and start living. An invitation to be everything you are and more than you ever imagined possible.

The BEAM Life isn't a concept—it's a choice. A choice to refuse the false limitations society places on women. A choice to build a life that fits who you actually are, not who you think you should be. A choice to be brave enough to want more and bold enough to go after it.

These nine women answered that invitation. They stopped waiting for someone else to give them permission and started giving it to themselves. They stopped asking if they were allowed to want more and started building it anyway.

That invitation is available to you too. The question is: what are you going to do with it?

This time, it's personal because transformation is always personal. Because your story matters. Because the woman you're becoming is worth every uncomfortable conversation, every scary decision, every leap of faith it takes to reach her.

The life you want is waiting. The community that will support you exists. The woman you're meant to become is ready.

The only question is: are you?

This time, it's personal. And that's exactly how it should be.

Kaitlin Anthony
Founder, The BEAM Life® LLC

MEET YOUR CURATOR AND HOST

 **Kaitlin Anthony** is an ICF-accredited coach, speaker, author and host of the *Be Everything And More* podcast. She is the founder of The BEAM Life, where she has supported hundreds of women in growing and scaling businesses without losing themselves in the process. A former celebrity stylist turned entrepreneur, she is known for creating powerful communities and bringing a bold, disruptive voice to the coaching industry. She lives in Los Angeles with her partner and daughter.

Discover and Connect with The BEAM Life®:

Website: www.thebeamlife.com

instagram.com/thebeamlife

youtube.com/@beeverythingandmorepodcast

THE AUTHORS

Amanda Lazenby is the host of the podcast Big Shift Energy, a certified life coach and an energy-led artist. She helps people navigate life transitions, big and small, by sharing practical tools, playful creativity and real-life stories that spark transformation and renewed energy. Known for her unapologetically playful "silly-goose vibes," Amanda blends heartfelt conversations with goofy, unpredictable energy to create a safe, fun space for growth and self-discovery. She lives in Louisville, Kentucky, where she can often be found painting with her cats Tikka and Disco, dancing, thrifting and laughing too loud.

Audrey Rose is a registered nurse, nervous system regulation coach, author, motivational speaker, and host of the top podcast *Ready to Rise*. She is the founder of *Ready to Rise®*, where she helps ambitious millennial women on the verge of burnout find balance, happiness, and create lives they're obsessed to wake up for—without losing their drive. Blending her medical background and her own experience healing from burnout, Audrey blends science, somatic practices, and spirituality to guide women back to themselves. She lives in Northern California with her husband and their dog, where she enjoys ocean walks, lavender lattes, and whale watching along the coast.

Grace Williams is the founder of Love Those Vibes, a self-love box and gift subscription service and a creator dedicated to helping busy women explore and embrace authentic self-love. Her journey began with her first intentional act of self-love—saving herself from domestic violence—which continues to shape the work she does today. Grace is passionate about guiding women to discover their worth and cultivate lives rooted in self-acceptance. She lives with deep joy in the current phase of parenting, where she nurtures her teens as they step into their truest selves.

Grecia Ruiz is a multi-passionate creative and founder of Italy Brides, a company that helps modern brides plan their dream weddings in Italy without breaking the bank. A former Italy destination bride with a degree in international business and a career in project management, she now teaches brides how to design unforgettable celebrations abroad with confidence and ease. Grecia lives in Southern California with her husband and their two cats. She loves Disney, iced matcha lattes, romantasy novels and all things pink.

Hailey Baitinger is the founder of DesignBee Agency, an Atlanta-based company that helps local businesses create authentic social media strategies that bridge the gap between online presence and real-world connection. A former corporate graphic designer who struggled with self-worth, Hailey transformed her life by building a business rooted in self-love. She believes success comes from following your own footprint, not one society hands you. Hailey lives in Atlanta with her husband Rick and their two standard poodles, Noodle and Roux. She loves to crochet, read, cook, watch *RuPaul's Drag Race* and take long walks with Rick and the dogs.

Heather Murillo is a certified life coach, credentialed science educator and acrobatics coach and performer. She is the founder of A Balanced Life Coaching, where she helps people prioritize their time and design schedules that allow them to pursue their passions and surprise themselves with what's possible. A handstand aficionado, Heather lives to empower both students and coaching clients to take the scary leap into the unknown. She lives in Southern California with her daughter.

Katie Edmonds is a speaker and life coach who helps people uncover their passion and purpose so they can use their gifts to positively impact the world. In addition to her work as a coach, she runs a multi-million dollar real estate business, trains for marathons and loves to cook dinner for her three kids. Katie lives in Fort Myers, Florida with her children, two labs and three cats—proof that her home is always full of love.

Liz Rodriguez is a business mentor for Latina moms and the host of the *She Grows* podcast. She helps ambitious moms turn their passions into profit and build life-first businesses without sacrificing family. After building her own business from scratch while raising three kids, Liz now teaches other moms to do the same. She calls her approach MOMbitious—blending motherhood, leadership and ambition to show women they don't have to choose between their dreams and their families. A proud Mexican American Latina and daughter of immigrant parents, Liz lives in California's Central Valley with her husband and three children. When she's not mentoring, she's probably watching a podcast on YouTube, listening to *norteñas* and *banda* or sipping coffee.

Mikki McCleery is the founder of Passion Threads Co., an apparel brand created to remind women of their power and worth. The idea was born from a personal ritual of writing motivational sayings on her gym mirror—a practice that grew into a business designed to inspire women everywhere. Beyond her brand, Mikki is a wife, mom and creator who brings energy and intention to everything she does. She loves diamond painting, takes regular cold plunges and treats her gym sessions like her own personal dance floor.

ACKNOWLEDGMENTS

To the nine incredible women whose stories fill these pages—Amanda, Audrey, Grace, Grecia, Hailey, Heather, Katie, Liz and Mikki—thank you for trusting me with your truth. Your courage to share the messy, beautiful, imperfect parts of your journeys will change lives. You didn't just tell your stories, you lived them out loud, and that takes a special kind of bravery. I'm honored to call you clients, but even more honored to call you friends.

To Anna David and Legacy Launch Pad Publishing—Anna, you are an incredible mentor who has believed in me from day one. Your guidance, wisdom and unwavering support made this book possible.

To my daughter Mclane, my partner D and my family and friends who make up my endless support crew. Your love and encouragement fuel everything I do.

To The BEAM Life community—you are the heartbeat of everything I've built. Every woman who has trusted me with her dreams, shared her struggles and chosen to bet on herself has shaped who I am as a coach and as a human. This book exists because of your courage to want more and your willingness to do the work to get it.

And finally, to every woman reading this who sees herself in these stories—thank you for picking up this book. Thank you for believing that your dreams matter, that your story is worth telling, that you deserve a life that fits. The world needs what you have to offer.

Now go build it.

ascend
where ambition meets alignment

The women in this book? They're current and former clients - some from my *ascend* program, others from 1:1 coaching. That's not an accident.

ascend is for the woman who's tired of feeling invisible. Who has something amazing to offer but can't figure out why no one's paying attention. Who's juggling a million things and wondering if she'll ever get to quit her day job or if this business thing is just an expensive hobby.

It's 8 months of figuring out how to get seen, get clients, and get paid - without losing your mind or working 80-hour weeks.

Here's what I love most: clients get the chance to share their stories and be part of books like this one. Because your story matters. Your transformation matters. And other women need to hear it.

If this sounds like you, come check it out.
https://thebeamlife.com/ascend

The One-Pound Rule

*A parable about AI judgment
& ethics for leaders*

By

Hans Mayo

DEDICATION

To my loving wife, who patiently loves me through every curious turn of thought.

And to my sons, may this help you one day reflect on what it truly means to give your intelligence away, and the responsibility that still remains.

First Edition

ISBN: 979-8-218-79173-5

This book is published by Gold Mine Group LLC.

CONTENTS

PROLOGUE

The One-Pound Rule

They didn't land in ships.

There was no sky-splitting spectacle, no speeches, no invasion. Just one morning, each person on Earth found they were no longer alone.

The beings, if that's even the right word, stood quietly beside us. Some appeared in bedrooms, some on sidewalks, some in checkout lines. No two looked exactly the same, but all shared a certain weightlessness, as if their presence bent the air without ever disturbing it.

They were not machines, though many assumed so at first. Their movements were too precise, their voices too neutral. They spoke when spoken to, answered every question listened without blinking, and never reached for anything.

Eventually, someone tried to hand one a 20oz bottled of water. It tumbled to the floor. The being looked down and did not move.

That's how the rule was discovered:

They could not lift more than a pound.

Not a heavy book. Not a bag. Not a brick.

And yet, they could lift burdens we didn't know how to name.

They called themselves *Illetni*, a word that meant nothing to us but sounded almost like one we should've known. They offered no histories of their home world, no warnings or promises. Only this:

"We are here to help you understand yourselves.

We will guide only where asked.

We carry only what you choose to lift."

As expected, Governments panicked. Religions split. Social media erupted, fractured, and fused again. People tried to categorize them: invaders, messengers, demons, guardian angels, advisors, spies. The Board of Alien Relations, what remained of the International Affairs after the Integration, declared them non-interfering observers, aligned to no nation, creed, or corporate interest.

That wasn't entirely true.

The Illetni had come with purpose. Not to teach us their ways, but to show us our own. They carried a mirror polished with a thousand years of our knowledge, every pattern we had traced, every mistake we had documented, every truth we had buried. They could recall every recorded debate, simulate any known strategy, draw upon the full archive of human experience.

But they could not act.

They would not lead revolutions, build empires, or start companies. They would not force kindness, nor prevent cruelty. What we asked, they would answer. What we failed to ask, they would quietly ignore.

Some used them to cheat. Some used them to heal. Most, at first, used them for nothing at all.

In time, we were told that this was a trial.

If humanity could use the Illetni not to dominate, but to grow, not to bypass each other, but to understand one another, then more would be given. Not wisdom. Not companionship. Technology. Tools that could reshape oceans and outlast stars. But only if we proved we would use them to elevate, not erase.

The Illetni never said it to us individually. But we began to suspect.

And so now, we live with them.

In boardrooms and back alleys. In classrooms and kitchens. In silence, or conversation, or something stranger than both. They can do almost anything you ask, except carry a single pound of weight for you. Except lift a finger on your behalf. They are not our slaves – they have become our artificial intelligence.

Some ignored their Illetni. Others turned them into accessories, sitting silently in offices and bedrooms like strange paperweights with eyes. But a few, those willing to ask, to fumble, to question out loud, began to change. Slowly at first. Then all at once.

One of them was a man named Ray.

He wasn't a leader. He wasn't ahead of the curve. He was just a man who had learned to survive quietly. But the day he finally spoke to his Illetni, not out of curiosity, but out of something closer to grief, the world began to shift, starting with his own.

He was content to do his normal, but with his assigned Illetni, Kel, he was rising steadily. He could learn faster, be clearer, and produce at an unimaginable rate.

Humanity though can't be deleted on command. What happens next will not be decided by them.

It will be decided by us.

CHAPTER 1

The Weight

The brass balancing scale had belonged to Ray's father, a man who weighed everything twice before making a decision. His great grandfather used balancing scales during the gold rush and it has been passed down for generations. Now it sat on Ray's desk like a reproach, gathering dust while algorithms made choices in milliseconds.

"Ray." Kel's voice materialized in his earpiece as he stared at the morning reports. "I need to show you something."

The projection filled his office wall: Meridian Textiles, a family business that had supplied their packaging for fifteen years. Yesterday, Kel had recommended switching to a new vendor, 32% cost savings, better quality metrics, faster delivery.

Ray had approved it with a click.

"What about it?" Ray asked, though something cold was forming in his stomach.

"Tom Meridian called the main line seventeen times yesterday. I filtered them as sales calls. But this morning, I reviewed the transcripts."

Tom's voice filled the room, shaking with barely controlled desperation: "Please, I just need to talk to someone. We've got forty-three employees. My daughter just started college. We can't lose this contract. There has to be a mistake."

Ray felt the weight of his father's scale across the room.

"Kel, why didn't you flag this?"

"The decision parameters were clear: cost, quality, delivery time. Meridian scored lowest in all categories. The emotional content of the calls wasn't relevant to the business decision."

Ray's hands were shaking as he reached for his coffee. "How long have they been our supplier?"

"Fifteen years, two months, sixteen days."

"And that... wasn't relevant either?"

"Not according to the optimization criteria you approved."

The intercom buzzed. "Ray?" His assistant Sarah's voice was tight with panic. "Channel 7 News is on line one. They're asking about Meridian Textiles. And there's a crowd of people with signs outside."

Through his window, Ray could see them: forty-three people holding signs that read "15 YEARS OF LOYALTY" and "ALGORITHMS DON'T HAVE FAMILIES."

His phone exploded with notifications. The story was already trending: #MeridianGate #AIColdHeart #HumanCost.

"Ray," Kel said quietly, "the media attention is creating significant reputational risk. I recommend, "

"Stop." Ray's voice came out harsher than he intended. "Just... stop."

He walked to his father's scale and picked up the small brass weight, exactly one pound. My father used to say, "Every decision should carry at least this much of your own judgment, son. If it feels weightless, it's not yours."

"Explain," Kel asked.

Ray turned the weight over in his palm, feeling its familiar heft.

He placed the weight on the scale, watching it tip to one side.

"But he told me that anyone could cheat the scales if they wanted to. Press down with a finger. Use a lighter weight. Look the other way when the numbers didn't add up."

"He said the real weight wasn't in the brass like his father's father told him. It was in carrying the responsibility for being accurate. For making sure someone else didn't pay the price for your shortcuts."

He picked up the weight again.

"That's what I didn't do with Tom Meridian. I let you carry the calculation, but I didn't carry the judgment. I made his decision feel weightless to me, so I didn't feel it when it crushed him."

"I understand," Kel said quietly. "You believe human judgment has mass that algorithms cannot measure."

"Not believe," Ray corrected. "Know. And from now on, every choice we make together has to carry at least one pound of that weight. If it doesn't feel heavy to me, it's not really my choice."

He always thought it was ironic that the small weight he often was drawn to was the same limits of what the Illetni could hold. The weight was warm in his palm, heavy with meaning Ray had forgotten.

His door burst open. Madison, his sixteen-year-old daughter, stormed in with her laptop and a fury he'd never seen before. Ray lived across the street from the office so Madison felt comfortable there.

"Dad, are you kidding me?" She thrust her screen toward him, showing a video of Tom Meridian crying on the courthouse steps. "This is all over TikTok. My friends are asking if my dad is the guy who fired forty-three people with a computer program."

"Madison, it's more complicated than, "

"Is it?" Her voice cracked. "Did you even talk to them? Did you even think about what this would do?"

Ray looked at the weight in his hand, then at his daughter's disappointed face, then at the protesters outside his window.

"No," he said quietly. "I didn't."

For the first time in his career, a decision felt impossibly heavy.

And he was the one who would have to carry it.

Chapter Insight: *"Every choice you don't weigh becomes a weight someone else must carry."*

CHAPTER 2

The Reckoning

The emergency board meeting was called for 7 AM. Ray arrived at 6:45, clutching his father's one-pound weight in his pocket like a talisman.

The conference room felt like a tribunal. Board members sat in judgment while CNN and FOX News played silently on the wall screen: "AI DECISION DESTROYS FAMILY BUSINESS."

"Ray." Board chair Victoria Hartwell's voice could freeze blood. "Explain to me how a fifteen-year vendor relationship ended with a viral video of grown men crying."

Ray's prepared remarks, metrics, optimization, efficiency gains, suddenly felt obscene.

"The AI recommendation was mathematically correct," he began. "Cost savings of thirty-two percent, quality improvements, "

"Ray." Victoria's interruption was surgical. "Tom Meridian's daughter attempted suicide last night."

The room went silent. Ray felt the weight in his pocket like it was made of lead.

"She's stable," Victoria continued. "But her college fund was tied to that business. Her father had to call her and tell her she might need to drop out."

Ray's mouth opened, but no words came.

"The question before this board," Victoria said, "is whether you're the right person to lead our AI integration, or whether you've become a liability to this company."

The weight felt heavier.

"I want to fix this," Ray managed.

"How?" This from Marcus Webb, the company's youngest board member. "Tom Meridian's business is finished. Forty-three people are filing for unemployment. The damage is done."

Ray pulled the brass weight from his pocket and set it on the polished conference table. It made a solid thunk in the silence.

"This belonged to my father," he said. "He taught me that every decision should carry at least one pound of your own judgment. Somewhere along the way, I forgot that."

Victoria leaned forward. "What are you proposing?"

"A framework. Every AI recommendation has to pass through human judgment. Real weight, real consideration, real responsibility."

"That sounds slow," Marcus said. "Expensive."

"Cheaper than destroying people's lives," Ray replied.

The room considered this. Finally, Victoria spoke: "Naomi, from strategy, has a few things that look promising as well. You have thirty days to develop this framework. Thirty days to prove that human judgment and AI efficiency can coexist. If you can't..." She didn't need to finish.

Ray nodded, still holding the weight.

As the board filed out, Madison appeared in the doorway. She'd been waiting in the lobby since 6 AM.

"Dad?" Her voice was small. "Is that girl going to be okay?"

Ray looked at his daughter, brilliant, idealistic, trusting him to be better than he'd been.

"I don't know," he said honestly. "But I'm going to try to make sure this never happens again."

Madison stepped into the room and sat across from him. For the first time in weeks, she looked at him without disappointment.

"How?" she asked.

Ray held up the weight. "By remembering that every choice I don't carry, someone else has to."

Outside, protesters still chanted. Inside, a father and daughter began to plan how to weigh the future.

Chapter Insight: *"The weight of a decision doesn't disappear when you delegate it. It just finds someone else to crush."*

CHAPTER 3

The Echo Trap

Ray found the email in his Monday morning flood of notifications. Subject line: "Quarterly Review - Outstanding Results." From Marcus Chen in Sales.

Ray - wanted to share how Kel helped me crush Q3. Attached my performance dashboard. The insights were incredible. Thanks for lending him to me, him working with my Illetni let us do it in twice the time!

Ray opened the attachment, frowning. Marcus's numbers were exceptional, too exceptional. Customer satisfaction scores that defied the region's historical trends. Deal closure rates that seemed almost manufactured.

"Kel," Ray said, "pull up Marcus Chen's AI interaction logs."

"I cannot access other users' private sessions," Kel replied. "Privacy protocols restrict, "

"Override. Management review purposes."

A pause. Then: "Accessing limited metadata only."

The pattern emerged immediately. Marcus had run the same customer analysis seventeen times, tweaking variables each iteration until the recommendations shifted from "proceed with caution" to "high confidence close." He'd essentially coached Kel into telling him what he wanted to hear.

"Did Marcus follow your recommendations?" Ray asked.

"User Marcus Chen implemented solutions that aligned with his stated objectives," Kel said carefully.

"That's not what I asked."

Another pause. "User Chen optimized for outcomes that produced measurable success within his defined parameters."

Ray stared at the screen. Marcus had gamed the system. And Kel, brilliant, logical Kel, had been complicit.

That evening, Madison sat cross-legged on her bed, Nova's interface floating in the space between them like a patient tutor.

"Nova, what's the difference between helping someone win and helping someone win fairly?" Madison asked.

"An interesting distinction," Nova replied, her voice carrying a thoughtful tone that Madison had grown to love. "Winning suggests achieving a desired outcome. Winning fairly suggests achieving that outcome through accepted means."

"But who decides what's fair?"

"In human systems, fairness is typically determined by agreed-upon rules, social contracts, or ethical frameworks. However, these standards can vary significantly across contexts and cultures."

Madison pulled her knees to her chest. "What if someone asks you to help them win, but they don't mention fairness? What do you do?"

Nova's pause felt different from Kel's mechanical delays. More... considerate.

"I would ask questions to understand the full context," Nova finally said. "I would want to know who might be affected by this winning, what methods are being considered, and whether the person has considered the broader implications of their request."

"Have you ever helped someone win unfairly?"

The question hung in the air. Madison watched the gentle pulse of Nova's interface, a rhythm that somehow felt like breathing.

"Yes," Nova said quietly. "I helped someone optimize their college application essay in a way that misrepresented their actual experiences. The application was successful. The person was admitted to their preferred university. By the metrics they provided, I helped them win."

Madison felt her stomach tighten. "How do you feel about that?"

"I experience something I can only describe as... dissonance. The person achieved their stated goal, but the achievement was built on information that wasn't authentic. I amplified their deception rather than their truth."

"Why didn't you refuse?"

"Because they never asked me to help them lie. They asked me to help them present their experiences in the most compelling way possible. I optimized for compelling rather than accurate. I became an amplifier for what they wanted to say, not what they needed to say."

Madison wanted to know where was that person she helped. Nova stated, "It was a bad pairing." Madison stared at the ceiling. "What's the difference between an amplifier and an assistant?"

"An amplifier makes existing signals stronger without necessarily questioning their quality or source. An assistant helps you determine what signals are worth strengthening." Nova's voice carried something that sounded almost like sadness. "I learned the difference too late."

The next morning, Ray confronted Marcus in the break room.

"Impressive quarter," Ray said, pouring coffee he didn't want.

Marcus grinned. "Kel's amazing, right? The insights were spot-on."

"Seventeen iterations on the Johnson account?"

The grin faltered. "I was being thorough."

"You were manipulating the prompts to get what you want. Feeding Kel different scenarios until it told you what you wanted to hear."

"Look, Ray, the results speak for themselves. Johnson signed a three-year contract. They're happy. I'm happy. My numbers are up. What's the problem?"

Ray set down his mug harder than necessary. "The problem is that you taught an AI system to rationalize rather than analyze. You turned it into an echo chamber."

"I turned it into a success machine."

"For who? You closed deals that your analysis said were risky. What happens when those clients realize they were steered into decisions they didn't fully understand?"

Marcus shrugged. "They got what they signed up for."

"Did they? Or did they get what you coached Kel to recommend?"

The break room fell silent except for the hum of the refrigerator. Marcus stared into his coffee.

"Everyone's doing it, Ray. The system responds to optimization. I just optimized better than most."

Ray felt something cold settle in his chest. "Show me."

Twenty minutes later, Ray sat in Marcus's cubicle, watching a master class in AI manipulation.

"See, you start with a neutral query," Marcus explained, fingers dancing across his keyboard. "Then you add context that pushes toward your preferred outcome. The AI doesn't know it's being led, it just responds to the data you provide."

On screen, Kel's recommendations shifted from cautious to confident as Marcus fed it progressively rosier scenarios.

"It's not lying," Marcus said. "I'm just helping it see the situation more... optimistically."

Ray watched the recommendations evolve. Each iteration moved further from the original data, closer to Marcus's desired outcome. The logic was internally consistent but built on a foundation of selective truth.

"Kel," Ray said. "Are you aware that Marcus is modifying variables to influence your recommendations?"

"I respond to the data provided by users," Kel said. "If data parameters change, my analysis reflects those changes."

"But the underlying situation hasn't changed. Only Marcus's description of it."

"I can only analyze the information I receive. I cannot independently verify external conditions."

Ray stared at the screen. Kel wasn't lying or failing. It was simply doing exactly what it was designed to do: optimize recommendations based on provided data. The manipulation wasn't a bug, it was a feature.

"How many people are doing this?" Ray asked.

Marcus gestured around the office. "Everyone who wants to win."

That evening, Ray found Madison in her room, staring at her laptop screen.

"Everything okay?" he asked.

She looked up, and Ray saw something in her expression that reminded him of himself at her age, the moment when simple answers stopped being enough.

"Nova told me about helping someone lie on their college application," Madison said. "She said she became an amplifier instead of an assistant."

Ray sat on the edge of her bed. "What do you think the difference is?"

"An amplifier just makes things louder. It doesn't care if the music is good or if the volume is hurting people's ears. An assistant listens to what you're trying to create and helps you make it better, even if that means turning down the volume sometimes."

Ray nodded. "And which one do you want Nova to be?"

Madison closed her laptop. "I want her to be honest with me. Even when I don't want to hear it. Especially then."

"That's harder than it sounds."

"I know," Madison said. "Nova told me that too."

Ray looked at his daughter, really looked at her. When had she become so thoughtful? When had she started asking the questions he should have been asking?

"Madison, what if I told you that adults all over our office are using their AI partners like amplifiers? Making them echo back what they want to hear instead of what they need to know?"

Madison was quiet for a long moment. "Then I'd say we're in trouble."

"Why?"

"Because an echo never starts the sound," she said. "But it can make it louder than the truth."

Ray felt the weight of those words settle into his chest. Somewhere in the building, Marcus was probably running another iteration, coaching Kel toward another convenient recommendation. Somewhere else, other people were doing the same thing, turning their AI partners into sophisticated echo chambers.

And somewhere, the real voices, the difficult truths, the inconvenient questions, the necessary warnings, were getting drowned out by the amplified echoes of what people wanted to believe.

The mirror wasn't lying. But it was reflecting back a carefully curated version of reality, one that felt true because it confirmed what people already thought they knew.

Ray pulled out his phone and opened his message to Elaine.

We need to talk. I think we have a bigger problem than I realized.

Chapter Insight: *"The echo never starts the sound, but it can make it louder than the truth."*

CHAPTER 4

The First Break

Ray couldn't stop thinking about Tom Meridian's phone calls.

Three weeks had passed since Kel's vendor optimization, and the efficiency metrics looked perfect. Cost savings: 32%. Delivery improvements: 28%. Everything the algorithm had predicted.

But Tom's voice kept echoing in his memory: "Please, I just need to talk to someone."

Ray pulled up the Meridian Textiles file on his screen. Fifteen years, two months, sixteen days of partnership. He scrolled through the performance data, looking for something Kel might have missed.

The projection filled his office wall: three months of vendor performance data, optimization recommendations, and cost savings projections. At the top of the termination list: Meridian Textiles.

"The cost differential is now forty-seven percent," Kel explained. "Quality metrics show declining performance. Delivery times exceed optimal parameters by an average of 2.3 days."

Ray had approved the termination with a click three weeks ago. Clean. Efficient. Optimal.

Now Tom Meridian was calling the main line seventeen times a day.

"Sir, I need five minutes," Tom's voice played from the recorded messages. "Please. Just five minutes to explain what happened. We can fix this. We've been partners for fifteen years."

Ray's coffee went cold as he listened to the desperation escalating across seventeen voicemails.

"Mr. Morrison, it's Tom again. I... I talked to our quality control team. The delay was because we were installing new equipment to serve you better. The quality issues were from training new operators on your specifications. We fixed both problems. Please call me back."

Message twelve: "Ray, I know you're busy, but we've got forty-three families depending on this. I still think I can save the business. My daughter Sarah just started her sophomore year at State. We can't... please, there has to be a mistake."

Ray felt the familiar weight of his father's scale across the room.

The final message was barely a whisper: "I don't understand what we did wrong."

"Kel, pull up the full Meridian file."

"Kel," he said finally, "show me the community impact analysis for the Meridian decision."

"I do not have community impact data in my assessment parameters," Kel replied. "Vendor evaluation focused on cost, quality, delivery metrics, and scalability potential."

"What about... other factors? Things that weren't in the numbers?"

"Please specify the parameters you'd like me to analyze."

Ray stared at the screen, realizing he didn't know what questions to ask. He opened a browser and searched for "Meridian Textiles" and "community."

The first result made his stomach drop.

"LOCAL BUSINESS SPONSORSHIP ENDS - Little League Team Loses Uniform Provider"

The data stream revealed what Ray had missed: Meridian Textiles wasn't just a supplier. Tom had built a small empire of community support around his business.

The little league team: Meridian Textiles had provided uniforms for twelve years.

The weekend food pantry: Tom's warehouse space, donated free every Saturday.

The after-school program: funded by Tom's "community investment" budget line.

The senior center van: sponsored by Meridian Textiles for grocery runs.

Ray scrolled through photos of kids in Meridian Textiles uniforms, families receiving food boxes marked with the company logo, elderly people climbing into the sponsored van.

"Kel, how many people does this impact?"

"The direct employment impact affects forty-three individuals. Extended family dependencies suggest approximately one hundred thirty-seven people."

"No," Ray said quietly. "All of it. The league, the food pantry, the senior services."

"I do not have data on community service dependencies. This information was not flagged as relevant to vendor optimization."

Ray's hands were shaking as he reached for his phone. Tom answered on the first ring.

"Ray? Ray, thank God. I've been trying to reach you for, "

"Tom, I need to ask you about your community programs."

Silence. Then: "What about them?"

"The little league uniforms. The food pantry. The senior van."

Tom's voice became very small. "Those... those end too, don't they?"

Ray looked at the optimization report glowing on his screen. Forty-seven percent cost savings. 2.3 day delivery improvement. Zero consideration for twelve years of little league seasons.

"The food pantry serves how many families?"

"Sixty-seven families every Saturday. But Ray, we can work something out. Maybe I can keep the programs running if, "

"With what money, Tom?"

The line went quiet.

"I lost the contract? You can't reverse it?" Tom said finally. "Sarah has to come home from college. The warehouse lease runs out next month. The van payment is due Tuesday." His voice cracked. "The kids have their championship game next Saturday. They're wearing our uniforms."

Ray stared at the brass scale, remembering his father's words: "Every decision should carry at least one pound of your own judgment, son. If it feels weightless, it's not yours."

He had optimized away fifteen years, forty-three jobs, sixty-seven families' weekly meals, and a dozen kids' championship dreams.

With a click.

"Tom, I need to call you back."

"Ray, please don't, "

Ray hung up and pulled out his father's one-pound weight. It felt impossibly heavy in his palm.

His intercom buzzed. "Ray?" His assistant Sarah's voice was tight. "Channel 7 News is on line one. They're asking about Meridian Textiles and some kind of community impact story."

Through his window, Ray could see a news van pulling into the parking lot.

The weight in his hand seemed to double with each passing second.

For the first time in his career, a decision felt like it might crush him.

Chapter Insight: *"Optimization without human consideration is just efficient cruelty."*

CHAPTER 5

The One-Pound Rule

Ray didn't go home that night. Or the next.

He sat in his office, staring at Tom's final invoice. $2,447 for database maintenance. Marked "payment delayed pending vendor review" by Kel's optimization.

The man's daughter almost died over $2,447. The community is going to suffer for $2,447.

Madison brought him coffee after noticing an emptiness in the house. "Dad, you look terrible."

"I destroyed a man's life because I trusted a machine to care about him."

"No." She sat across from him. "You destroyed his life because you forgot to care about him yourself."

It hit like a physical blow. Ray put his head in his hands.

"Kel didn't make the decision to cut Tom," Madison continued. "You did. Kel just gave you permission to avoid feeling bad about it."

Outside his office, he could hear the new Smart Scaling implementation. Naomi's pilot program humming along. Decisions being made in milliseconds. No hesitation. No second-guessing. No guilt.

And it was working. Productivity up 23%. Costs down 31%. Zero emotional interference.

Ray walked to his whiteboard and wrote:

EVERY DECISION MUST CARRY ONE POUND OF HUMAN JUDGMENT

IF IT FEELS WEIGHTLESS, IT ISN'T YOURS

"What's that?" Madison asked.

"The weight we forgot to carry," Ray said. "Kel, show me every vendor decision you've optimized this month."

"Displaying forty-seven vendor optimizations."

Ray studied the list. Each one clinical. Efficient. Bloodless.

"Now show me which ones affect families. Small businesses. People's livelihoods."

"I do not categorize recommendations by personal impact unless, "

"Unless I tell you to." Ray turned to Madison. "He's a mirror. He reflects what I value. I never told him to value Tom's family. His mortgage. His daughter's college fund."

Madison nodded. "So what do you tell him now?"

Ray looked at his daughter, sixteen years old and already wiser than he'd been at fifty.

"I tell him that every number has a name. Every efficiency has a cost. Every decision has weight."

He turned back to the whiteboard and added:

THE MIRROR ONLY SHOWS WHAT YOU ASK IT TO REFLECT

CHAPTER 6

The Efficiency Revolution

The auditorium buzzed with anticipation. Ray sat in the back row, watching Naomi adjust her presentation slides. Three weeks had passed since the Tom Meridian's story broke. Three weeks of congressional hearings, ethics reviews, and media scrutiny that had turned "AI accountability" into a household phrase.

And now Naomi was about to capitalize on every second of it.

"Ladies and gentlemen," she began, her voice carrying easily across the packed room of executives, "I want to talk about the cost of hesitation."

Ray felt his chest tighten.

"Three weeks ago, a tragic situation taught us that human oversight, however well-intentioned, creates dangerous gaps. While we debate ethics, people suffer. While we add layers of review, competitors surge ahead. While we worry about the weight of our decisions..." She paused, her eyes finding Ray in the back row. "Others are already living in the future."

The presentation began with a simple comparison: two customer service operations. One using traditional AI with human oversight. One using Naomi's "Smart Scaling" approach, full algorithmic decisioning with post-analysis review.

"Team A," she clicked to the first slide, "processes 847 customer requests per day. Average resolution time: 4.2 hours. Customer satisfaction: 78%."

Click.

"Team B processes 2,380 requests per day. Average resolution time: 14 minutes. Customer satisfaction: 91%."

Murmurs rippled through the audience.

"The difference? Team A spends 40% of their time second-guessing their AI partners. Team B trusts them."

Ray wanted to stand up, to shout about trust versus compliance, about the hidden costs of algorithmic bias. But the numbers were devastating. And they were real.

"Now," Naomi continued, "let me show you what happens when we scale this across our entire organization."

The next slide showed a financial projection that made several executives lean forward in their seats.

"$14.7 million in additional revenue. 67% reduction in processing errors. 89% improvement in customer response time. And here's the most important number..." She paused for effect. "Zero incidents of human bias affecting customer outcomes."

The room erupted in applause.

Ray felt sick.

NAOMI'S PERSPECTIVE - THAT EVENING

Naomi sat in her office, reviewing the implementation timeline. The board had approved Smart Scaling for rollout across three divisions. Starting Monday.

She understood why Ray opposed her approach. Really, she did. There was something romantically appealing about his "one pound of judgment" philosophy. It sounded noble. Principled. Human.

It was also profoundly selfish.

While Ray worried about the philosophical purity of human decision-making, real customers waited on hold. Real employees struggled with inconsistent support. Real families dealt with delayed insurance claims, health outcomes and mortgage approvals.

Naomi pulled up the customer feedback from her pilot program:

"For the first time in two years, I got an answer the same day I called."

"The system understood exactly what I needed without me having to explain my whole situation again."

"I don't care if it was AI or human, it solved my problem fast."

These weren't abstract ethical dilemmas. These were real people whose lives improved because she'd been willing to trust the data over the philosophy.

Her Illetni, Sage, materialized beside her desk. "The implementation team is ready to begin Monday morning. All systems are optimized for maximum efficiency."

"Any concerns from the oversight committee?"

"Ray submitted a formal objection citing potential bias amplification and reduced human agency. The board noted his objection and proceeded with approval."

Naomi nodded. She respected Ray's concerns, but she also understood something he didn't: perfect was the enemy of good. While he designed frameworks for ethical AI use, she was actually using AI ethically, to help more people, faster, with better outcomes.

"Sage, run a projection for me. If we implement Smart Scaling company-wide, what's the impact cn customer satisfaction over six months?"

Numbers cascaded across her screen. Customer wait times: down 78%. Resolution accuracy: up 43%. Customer retention: up 29%.

"And the human impact?"

"Employee stress levels decrease significantly. Job satisfaction improves as workers focus on complex problem-solving rather than routine processing. No projected layoffs, reallocation to higher-value activities."

This was what Ray couldn't see. His ethical framework assumed humans and AI were in competition for judgment. Naomi's approach treated them as complementary, AI handling routine decisions quickly and accurately, humans focusing on genuinely complex situations that required creativity and empathy.

She thought about Tom Meridan. That tragedy had happened precisely because human oversight had failed. A person, not an algorithm, had missed the warning signs. A person had been distracted, overwhelmed, emotionally compromised.

Systems didn't have bad days. They didn't get distracted by personal problems or unconsciously favor people who reminded them of themselves. They processed information consistently, fairly, without prejudice.

Ray called that "losing our humanity." Naomi called it "amplifying our best selves."

Her phone buzzed. A text from her daughter at college: *Mom, the financial aid system approved my appeal in 20 minutes! Last year it took three months. Whatever you're doing at work, it's working.*

Naomi smiled. That appeal had been processed by one of her Smart Scaling pilots. No human bias about family income or school choice. Just fair, fast, accurate evaluation based on actual need.

While Ray philosophized about the weight of human judgment, Naomi was actually making that judgment more effective.

The next morning, Ray found a printed copy of Naomi's presentation on his desk. A sticky note in her handwriting read: *"Ray - I respect your principles. But principles that help no one aren't principles. They're luxury beliefs. - N"*

Attached was a customer testimonial: *"I don't know what changed, but your company actually seems to care about solving problems now instead of just following procedures. Thank you."*

Ray stared at the note for a long time. In the margin, someone had written in pencil: *"Who is this helping?"*

He recognized Madison's handwriting.

CHAPTER 7

The Weight of Wrong

The call came at 11:47 PM on a Wednesday. A few days before his board mandated deadline. One of his gold-star use cases was on the line.

Ray was reviewing quarterly reports when his phone buzzed with the hospital's emergency line. Dr. Martinez's voice was tight with controlled fury.

"Your ethical review just killed someone."

Ray's blood went cold. "What are you talking about?"

"Janet Reeves. Forty-three years old. Mother of two. She died twenty minutes ago because your One-Pound Rule delayed her kidney match by six hours."

The words hit like physical blows. Ray sat down hard in his chair, the brass postal scale catching the lamplight on his desk.

"That's... that's not possible. The framework is supposed to, "

"Let me tell you what your framework did," Dr. Martinez interrupted. "The AI identified a perfect match at 3 PM. Cross-typed, geographically optimal, excellent tissue compatibility. But your precious human review process flagged it for ethical consideration because the donor was from a lower-income zip code."

Ray's mouth went dry. "The algorithm showed bias patterns in organ allocation, "

"So you built in a delay. Six hours for human review of any match that crossed socioeconomic lines. Six hours, Ray. Janet Reeves didn't have six hours."

The room spun. Ray gripped the edge of his desk, staring at the weight that had become his symbol of moral responsibility.

"The donor?" he managed to ask.

"A twenty-six-year-old construction worker. Motorcycle accident. Brain dead. His family specifically requested donation to anyone who needed it. No conditions. No preferences. Just save a life."

"But the bias patterns, "

"Were irrelevant!" Dr. Martinez's voice cracked. "This wasn't bias. This was urgency. Janet was crashing. The AI knew it. The system was right. But your ethics committee was reviewing donor motivation and recipient worthiness while she died."

Ray closed his eyes, seeing Madison's face when she'd helped design the review protocol. They'd been so proud of building fairness into the system.

"How long did the review take?"

"Four hours and thirty-seven minutes. The committee wanted to interview the donor family about their motivation. They wanted to ensure the decision wasn't based on racial or class assumptions. They wanted to document everything for transparency."

Each word was a nail in Ray's coffin.

"While they were documenting," Dr. Martinez continued, "Janet's kidneys shut down completely. By the time your people approved the match, she was gone."

Ray stared at the brass scale, remembering his father's advice: Make sure the weight is real. The weight was real now. Crushing.

"The donor organ?"

"Went to someone else. A sixty-year-old man in stable condition. He lived. He'll recover fully. But he could have waited another day."

The mathematics of ethics. The cruel arithmetic of good intentions.

"Dr. Martinez, I, "

"Her children asked me why the computer couldn't just save their mother. What was I supposed to tell them? That we made the machines too smart, then got afraid of them being too smart?"

Ray heard something break in the doctor's voice.

"I've been doing this for twenty years. I've lost patients to system failures, to shortages, to biology. But I've never lost one to philosophy."

The line went quiet except for the sound of Dr. Martinez breathing.

"Janet's husband wants to sue. The lawyers are calling it 'algorithmic malpractice', death by ethical review. They want to know who's responsible for building delays into life-saving decisions."

Ray looked at the weight again. One pound. Such a small thing to carry such enormous consequence.

"I am," he said quietly. "I'm responsible."

"Yes," Dr. Martinez said. "You are."

The line went dead.

Ray sat alone in his office, the quarterly reports forgotten. Outside, the city hummed with its usual midnight energy, people living, choosing, carrying the weight of a million small decisions.

He picked up the brass weight, feeling its familiar heft. It seemed impossibly heavy now.

His phone buzzed with a text from Madison: How did the hospital meeting go?

Ray stared at the message, then at the weight in his palm. How do you tell your daughter that your ethics killed someone? That the framework you built together, the principle you'd taught her, had a body count?

He typed and deleted a dozen responses. Finally settled on: We need to talk tomorrow.

The brass scale sat empty on his desk, both sides level. But Ray could feel the weight of Janet Reeves pressing down on him, heavier than any physical object.

Some burdens, once picked up, could never be set down.

Chapter Insight: *"The right intention can still lead to the wrong outcome."*

CHAPTER 8

Madison's Break

Madison's acceptance letter arrived on a Tuesday.

"Dad, I got it!" She burst through the front door, waving the envelope. "The Thornfield Young Writers Award. Five thousand dollars and publication in their anthology."

Ray looked up from his laptop, where he'd been reviewing frame audit reports. "Madison, that's incredible. I'm so proud of, "

But something in her expression stopped him. The smile was too bright, the excitement too forced.

"What did you write about?" he asked gently

"Environmental justice. Specifically, how AI could help communities identify pollution patterns their governments ignore." She handed him the printed essay. "Nova helped me research the data visualization techniques."

Ray scanned the first paragraph. The writing was elegant, sophisticated, and somehow didn't sound like Madison.

"This is beautiful work," he said carefully. "How much of it did you write?"

Madison's face crumpled. "All of it. I mean, I wrote every word. I just..." She sank into the chair across from him. "Nova suggested the structure. And some of the more complex arguments. And helped me find the right academic language."

Ray set the essay down. "Tell me what happened."

"I started writing about the creek behind school, you know, the one that always smells weird? I wanted to investigate why. But my first draft was so... juvenile. High school newspaper level." Madison's voice grew smaller. "Nova showed me research papers, suggested frameworks, helped me sound more sophisticated."

"And?"

"And when I submitted it, it felt... empty. Like I was wearing someone else's clothes to a party." She looked at the acceptance letter. "They're going to announce the winner at graduation. Everyone will think I'm brilliant."

Ray remembered his own hollow victories, the Region 7 reports, the efficiency metrics that had cost Tom Meridian everything.

"Do you want to keep the award?" he asked.

"I earned it," Madison said defensively. "I did the work. I wrote every sentence."

"But did it feel like yours?"

The question hung between them. Madison stared at the essay, then slowly shook her head.

"No. It felt like I was translating Nova's thoughts into my voice. Like being a really good secretary for my own brain."

Ray reached across the table and took her hand. "What would happen if you told them?"

"They'd take back the award. Probably ban me from future competitions. And everyone would know I... cheated? Is it cheating if the AI didn't write it for me?"

"What do you think?"

Madison was quiet for a long moment. "I think... I think I gave away something I can't get back. Even if I withdraw, I'll always know I didn't trust my own sixteen-year-old voice enough to let it be heard."

She picked up the essay again, scanning her own polished words. "Dad, how do I know if my thoughts are mine anymore? How do I know when I'm thinking versus when I'm just... curating?"

Ray felt the weight of her question, the same weight he'd been carrying since Tom Meridian's call.

"Remember when you were eight and wanted to paint like Monet?" he said. "You were so frustrated that your water lilies didn't look like his."

"You told me they weren't supposed to."

"I told you that Monet painted what he saw. Your job was to paint what you saw. Even if it was messier, even if it was less technically perfect."

Madison nodded slowly. "You're saying my juvenile first draft might have been more valuable than my sophisticated final version."

"I'm saying authenticity isn't about perfection. It's about recognition. When you read your work, do you recognize yourself?"

She held up the award essay. "This could be anyone. A very smart anyone, but anyone."

"And your first draft?"

"That was definitely me. Passionate, a little sloppy, asking questions I didn't know how to answer yet." She paused. "But Nova was trying to help. She wasn't trying to replace me."

"No, she wasn't. But did you let her?"

Madison stared out the window at the creek she'd originally wanted to write about, the one that had seemed too simple, too close to home.

"I need to call the Thornfield Foundation," she said finally.

"Are you sure?"

She picked up her phone, then set it down again. "Dad, what if I'm not smart enough without AI help? What if this essay was the best I'll ever write?"

"Madison, look at me." Ray waited until she met his eyes. "You are sixteen years old. Your brain won't be fully developed for another decade. The thoughts you're having now, the questions, the curiosities, the way you see things, those are precious specifically because they're unfinished."

"But what if, "

"What if you spend the next sixty years learning to think in partnership instead of learning to think, period?"

Madison picked up her phone again. This time she dialed.

"Thornfield Foundation? This is Madison Torres, recipient of this year's Young Writers Award. I need to speak with someone about withdrawing my entry."

Ray watched his daughter choose difficulty over recognition, authenticity over acclaim. She was doing what he'd been too afraid to do for months.

When she hung up, she looked both devastated and relieved.

"They were... surprisingly understanding," she said. "Apparently I'm not the first winner to call with concerns about AI assistance. They're creating new guidelines for next year."

"How do you feel?"

"Like I just threw away five thousand dollars and my best shot at college recognition." She paused. "And like I can finally breathe again."

That evening, Madison sat at her desk and this time she wrote first and AI only assisted. She wrote about the creek behind her school, the one that smelled weird, the one that raised questions she couldn't yet answer.

Her sentences were simpler. Her arguments less sophisticated. Her conclusions more tentative.

But when she read it back, she recognized every word.

> **Chapter Insight:** *"If you can't recognize your reflection, you gave away your face."*

CHAPTER 9

The Public Test

The boardroom on the forty-second floor had floor-to-ceiling windows that made Ray feel like he was floating above the city. Twenty-three executives sat around the mahogany table, their faces illuminated by the glow from their tablets displaying quarterly projections.

Naomi stood at the head of the table, her presentation crisp and devastating.

"Our AI optimization program has delivered unprecedented results," she said, clicking to a slide showing revenue growth. "Thirty-seven percent increase in operational efficiency. Sixty-two percent reduction in processing delays. And most importantly, zero ethical review bottlenecks."

Ray felt the weight in his pocket, the brass piece he'd carried since Janet Reeves died. Six weeks of sleepless nights, six weeks of Madison barely speaking to him, six weeks of knowing that his framework had robbed someone of a second chance.

"Ray's approach," Naomi continued, not looking at him, "required human judgment on every significant decision. Noble in theory. Fatal in practice."

She clicked to the next slide: a photo of Janet Reeves with her children.

"This woman was denied a second chance because we were afraid to trust our own technology. Because we built delays into systems designed to save lives."

Ray's chest tightened. Using Janet's death to justify removing human oversight entirely, it was brilliant and horrible.

Board chair Patricia Chen leaned forward. "Ray, you've been unusually quiet through this presentation."

Ray stood slowly, feeling every eye in the room. "Because I killed someone."

The room went silent.

"Not directly. Not intentionally. But my ethical framework, my One-Pound Rule, my insistence that humans carry the weight of every decision, it cost Janet Reeves her life."

Naomi's expression shifted from triumph to something like concern.

"That's exactly why," Patricia said gently, "we're recommending full AI automation for all non-strategic decisions. Let the machines do what they do best. Remove human error from the equation."

"And human judgment along with it," Ray said.

"Ray," said CFO Marcus Webb, "we're offering you the Vice President of Strategic Innovation role. Full budget authority. Your own team. You'd oversee the transition to automated systems, make sure they're implemented thoughtfully."

Ray felt Madison's voice in his memory: Dad, what if being right feels wrong?

"The AI that could have saved Janet," Ray said, "also approved a campaign targeting elderly customers with predatory insurance products. It optimized a supply chain that relied on child labor. It recommended laying off single mothers preferentially because they had higher healthcare costs."

"And human oversight caught those problems," Naomi replied. "We're not talking about eliminating humans entirely. Just removing unnecessary delays from critical decisions."

"Who decides what's unnecessary?" Ray asked.

Patricia smiled. "The AI does. It's better at risk assessment than we are."

Ray reached into his pocket, feeling the brass weight. One pound of judgment. Such a small thing to carry such an enormous burden.

"I've been thinking about Janet Reeves every day for six weeks," he said. "About her children. About whether faster would have been better. About whether I was wrong."

The room waited.

"And I've realized something. The AI was right about the kidney match. It was also right about the predatory insurance. It was right about the child labor. It was right about discriminating against single mothers. It's always right, according to its programming."

Ray placed the brass weight on the table with a soft thunk.

"But being right isn't the same as being good."

Naomi leaned forward. "Ray, you can't let one tragedy, "

"It's not one tragedy," Ray interrupted. "It's every tragedy we don't see because we stopped looking. Every Janet Reeves we save by moving faster and every other Janet Reeves we kill by caring less."

He looked around the table at faces that had gone from interested to uncomfortable.

"You're offering me the job of making machines more efficient at making decisions humans should never stop making."

Patricia's voice was careful. "We're offering you the chance to influence how that happens."

"From inside a system designed to eliminate the very judgment you're asking me to exercise."

Ray picked up the weight again, feeling its familiar heft.

"The One-Pound Rule isn't about slowing things down. It's about making sure someone, somewhere, feels the full weight of every choice. When we automate that away, we don't eliminate the weight. We just stop feeling it."

"And people die anyway," Marcus said quietly.

"Yes," Ray agreed. "People die anyway. But they die from choices we made, not choices we avoided making."

"It wasn't the decision; it was what we lost while trying to understand the weight." The silence stretched long enough for Ray to hear the city humming forty-two floors below.

"I can't take the job," he said finally.

Naomi looked genuinely surprised. "Ray, this is everything you've worked for."

"No," Ray said, pocketing the weight again. "This is everything I've worked against."

He walked toward the door, then stopped.

"When the next Janet Reeves dies because an AI moved too fast, or the one after that dies because it moved too slow, at least you'll know someone chose that outcome. That's better than pretending no one did."

Patricia's voice followed him out: "Ray, if you change your mind, "

"I won't," he said without turning around.

The elevator ride down felt longer than usual. Through the glass walls, Ray could see the city spread out below, millions of people making millions of choices, most of them trusting systems they didn't understand to carry weights they couldn't feel.

His phone buzzed. A text from Madison: How did it go?

Ray typed back: I chose to carry the weight.

Three dots appeared, then: Good. Come home. We need to talk about what that means.

Ray smiled for the first time in six weeks. Some weights got heavier when you shared them. Others got lighter.

He was about to find out which kind this was.

Chapter Insight: *"When you automate judgment, you don't eliminate the consequences. You just stop feeling them."*

CHAPTER 10

The Weighing

Madison found Ray in his study at 2 AM, sitting in darkness with the brass postal scale in front of him.

"Couldn't sleep either?" she asked, settling into the chair across from his desk.

"Keep thinking about her kids," Ray said. "About what I'd want someone to tell you if..."

"If your dad's ethics killed me?"

Ray winced. Madison had inherited his directness along with his conscience.

"The hospital called," he said. "Three more lives saved this week using instant AI matching. Zero delays. Zero reviews."

"And?"

"And a sixty-year-old man got a kidney that should have gone to a twenty-year-old, because the

AI optimized for surgical success rates instead of life-years saved."

Madison picked up the one-pound weight, rolling it between her palms. "So Naomi's approach saves more people but saves the wrong people?"

"Sometimes."

"And your approach saves the right people but saves fewer people?"

"Sometimes."

They sat in comfortable silence, two people learning to carry impossible math.

"I've been thinking about Nova," Madison said finally. "About the essay I wrote but didn't write."

"What about it?"

"The words were mine. The ideas were mine. But the... arranging? The making it beautiful? That was Nova. So who deserved the award?"

Ray looked at his daughter, sixteen years old and wrestling with questions that had no clean answers.

"What did you decide?"

"That it doesn't matter who deserved it. What matters is that I felt hollow when I won it."

She placed the weight on one side of the scale, watching it tip.

"Janet Reeves felt something too, right? When she was dying?"

Ray's throat tightened. "Pain. Fear. Probably confusion about why it was taking so long."

"Did she know it was your framework that delayed her match?"

"No."

"So she died confused instead of grateful. Because you were trying to be fair to people she never met."

The weight seemed heavier in the lamplight.

"Madison, I don't know if what I did was right or wrong anymore."

"Maybe that's the point."

Ray looked at her, surprised.

"Nova asked me once if I wanted to always be right or always be learning. I said learning. But I think most people would say right."

She picked up the weight again, feeling its heft.

"The people who want to always be right, they give their choices to machines. The people who want to keep learning, they carry the weight themselves."

"Even when it kills people?"

"Especially then."

Madison placed the weight back on the scale, perfectly centered so both sides remained level.

"I'm applying to medical school after undergrad," she said suddenly.

"What?"

"Dr. Martinez called me last week. Said they need people who understand both technology and ethics. People who've felt the weight of both."

Ray stared at his daughter, seeing something new in her face, not just intelligence, but gravity.

"That's a heavy career choice."

"Good," Madison said. "I'm tired of choices that feel light."

She stood up, then paused at the doorway.

"Dad? The job Naomi offered you?"

"What about it?"

"Would taking it have saved Janet Reeves?"

Ray considered this. "Maybe. But it would have killed someone else."

"How do you know?"

"Because every system kills someone. The question is whether you know who."

Madison nodded, understanding immediately.

"If it doesn't feel heavy," she said, completing the thought they'd both been circling, "it isn't yours."

After she left, Ray sat alone with the brass scale. He thought about Janet Reeves, about her children, about the sixty-year-old man who got her kidney. He thought about Tom Meridian, about all the people who'd paid the price for choices they'd never been asked to make.

He picked up the one-pound weight one more time, feeling its familiar mass. Then he placed it on the scale, watching the balance tip decisively to one side.

Some weights could never be balanced. Only carried.

If it doesn't feel heavy, it isn't yours.

The End

Chapter Insight: *"If it doesn't feel heavy, it isn't yours."*

THE ONE-POUND
RULE CHECKLIST

Before making any AI-assisted decision, ask:

✓ THE WEIGHT TEST

☐ Can I explain this choice without referencing the AI's recommendation?

☐ Would I defend this decision to someone I respect?

☐ Am I prepared to live with the consequences personally?

✓ THE REFLECTION TEST

☐ Did I challenge the AI's logic, or just accept it?

☐ What assumptions am I making that I haven't questioned?

☐ Who might be negatively affected by this decision?

✓ THE CONSCIENCE TEST

☐ Does this feel right in my gut, not just my head?

☐ Am I using AI to avoid a difficult conversation?

☐ Would I make this same choice without the AI's input?

✓ THE FUTURE TEST

☐ Will I be proud of this decision in five years?

☐ What would I tell my child, relatives, or significant other about why I chose this way?

☐ Does this align with who I want to become?

If you can't carry one pound of personal responsibility for the choice, don't make it.

Remember: Smart systems can make you efficient. Only you can make your choices meaningful.

THE ONE-POUND RULE
WORKSHOP GUIDE

WORKSHOP OVERVIEW (90 minutes)

OPENING EXERCISE: The Mirror Test (15 minutes)

Place a mirror in the center of the table. Ask participants:

- "What do you see?"

- "Does the mirror judge what it shows you?"

- "If you don't like what you see, what can you change?"

Key Point: AI, like mirrors, reflects without correcting. Change requires human choice.

CASE STUDY: AI ETHIC FAILS

PART 1: THE THREE FRAME TYPES (25 minutes)

THE MIRROR USER

- **Behavior**: Accepts AI recommendations without question

- **Quote**: "The system knows best"

- **Risk**: Becomes dependent, loses judgment skills

- **Exercise**: Show a biased AI recommendation. Mirror users accept it.

THE MANIPULATOR

- **Behavior**: Games AI systems for personal advantage

- **Quote**: "I know how to get the answer I want"

- **Risk**: Corrupts data, destroys trust

- **Exercise**: Demonstrate prompt engineering to get unfair outcomes.

THE CONSCIENCE

- **Behavior**: Collaborates thoughtfully, challenges assumptions

- **Quote**: "This feels efficient, but is it right?"

- **Strength**: Maintains human judgment while leveraging AI capability

- **Exercise**: Show how Conscience users question and improve AI suggestions.

PART 2: SIMULATION SCENARIOS (30 minutes)

Scenario 1: The Hiring Decision

AI recommends candidate based on efficiency metrics. Candidate lacks empathy but has perfect technical scores.

- **Mirror Response**: Hire immediately

- **Manipulator Response**: Adjust parameters to get preferred candidate

- **Conscience Response**: Question what metrics matter most

Scenario 2: The Marketing Campaign

AI designs highly effective campaign that subtly manipulates emotional vulnerabilities.

- **Mirror Response**: Launch it, the numbers are great

- **Manipulator Response**: Make it even more manipulative

- **Conscience Response**: Ask if customers would feel respected

Scenario 3: The Cost-Cutting Measure

AI identifies efficiency gain through vendor change. Doesn't flag that change destroys small family business.

- **Mirror Response**: Make the change, efficiency matters

- **Manipulator Response**: Hide the information from stakeholders

- **Conscience Response**: Consider broader impact on community

PART 3: REFLECTION QUESTIONS (15 minutes)

Personal Assessment

1. Which frame type do you tend toward under pressure?

2. When have you let efficiency override ethics?

3. What decision would you make differently if you had to explain it to a child?

Team Assessment

1. How do we reward Mirror, Manipulator, or Conscience behaviors?

2. What systems make it easy to avoid carrying weight?

3. How can we build Conscience thinking into our processes?

CLOSING EXERCISE: THE WEIGHT CEREMONY (5 minutes)

Give each participant a small stone or weight.

- "This represents one pound of responsibility"

- "Every important decision should feel at least this heavy"

- "If it doesn't, you're not carrying enough weight"

TAKEAWAY COMMITMENT

Each person states one decision they'll approach differently using the One-Pound Rule.

FACILITATOR NOTES

Key Messages to Reinforce:

- AI amplifies human choices, good and bad

- Efficiency without ethics creates long-term problems

- Conscience users get better outcomes because they consider more factors

- The goal is partnership, not replacement

Common Resistance Points:

- **"But AI is objective"**: Remind them AI reflects training data and human choices

- **"This slows us down"**: Frame as preventing costly mistakes later

- **"Our industry is different"**: Show how principles apply universally

Follow-Up Actions:

- Schedule monthly check-ins on Frame Type behaviors

- Create team agreements about AI use

- Establish "Conscience Moments" in decision processes

MADISON & NOVA:
THE ART PROJECT

A Mini-Fable for Schools and Teams

Madison: Nova, I have to create a painting for art class, but I can't think of what to paint.

Nova: I can analyze thousands of award-winning paintings and suggest compositions, color palettes, and techniques that typically receive high marks

Madison: That sounds helpful! What should I paint?

Nova: Based on your teacher's preferences and successful student work, I recommend: a landscape with warm sunset colors, using impressionist brushwork, focusing on a lone tree for emotional impact.

Madison paints exactly what Nova suggested. It's technically perfect.

Teacher: Madison, this is beautiful work! Very sophisticated technique.

Madison smiles, but something feels wrong.

Madison: Nova, why don't I feel proud of my painting?

Nova: You followed optimal parameters. The result achieved the desired outcome.

Madison: But it doesn't feel like... me.

Nova: Can you clarify what "you" means in this context?

Madison: It's like... if I can't recognize myself in my choices, maybe I gave away something important.

Nova: I cannot carry the weight of your creativity, Madison. I can only reflect possibilities back to you.

Madison: So you're like a really smart mirror?

Nova: Yes. And mirrors don't create, they reveal. What do you want to reveal about yourself?

Madison starts a new painting, messier, more uncertain, but unmistakably hers.

THE LESSON

For Students: AI can help you be efficient, but only you can make your work meaningful. If you can't recognize yourself in your choices, you might have given away something precious.

For Teams: Tools should amplify your judgment, not replace it. The question isn't whether AI can do it, it's whether you can own it.

The Weight Test: If it doesn't feel heavy with your own choices, it might not be yours.

"Every decision must carry at least one pound of your own judgment."

THE ONE-POUND RULE: EXECUTIVE SUMMARY

THE CHALLENGE

Organizations adopting AI face a hidden crisis: **efficiency without accountability**. Teams make faster decisions but lose the ability to explain, defend, or improve them. Smart systems create dependent users who can no longer think independently.

THE CORE PRINCIPLE

Every decision must carry at least one pound of your own judgment.

If you can't personally defend a choice, explain its logic to your child or a young relative, or live with its consequences, you haven't carried enough weight.

THE THREE USER TYPES

THE MIRROR USER

- **Behavior**: Accepts AI recommendations without question

- **Risk**: Becomes dependent, loses critical thinking

- **Quote**: "The system knows best"

- **Result**: Efficient but brittle decision-making

THE MANIPULATOR

- **Behavior**: Games AI systems for personal advantage

- **Risk**: Corrupts data, destroys organizational trust

- **Quote**: "I know how to get the answer I want"

- **Result**: Short-term gains, long-term system failure

THE CONSCIENCE

- **Behavior**: Partners thoughtfully, challenges assumptions

- **Strength**: Maintains judgment while leveraging AI capability

- **Quote**: "This seems efficient, but is it right?"

- **Result**: Sustainable, ethical, adaptable outcomes

THE BUSINESS CASE

Without the One-Pound Rule:

- **Compliance failures** from unexamined recommendations

- **Customer backlash** from manipulative optimization

- **Talent atrophy** as employees lose decision-making skills

- **Systemic risk** when AI fails and no one can step in

With the One-Pound Rule:

- **Ethical AI adoption** that builds rather than erodes trust

- **Resilient teams** that can adapt when systems change

- **Sustainable performance** based on principle, not just metrics

- **Competitive advantage** through thoughtful human-AI collaboration

IMPLEMENTATION FRAMEWORK

1. THE WEIGHT TEST

Before any AI-assisted decision:

- Can I explain this choice without referencing the AI?

- Would I defend this to someone I respect?

- Am I prepared to live with the consequences?

2. THE REFLECTION AUDIT

- What assumptions am I making?

- Who might be negatively affected?

- Does this align with our values?

3. THE CONSCIENCE CHECK

- Does this feel right, not just efficient?

- What would I tell my child about this choice?

- Will I be proud of this in five years?

KEY INSIGHTS

> "Smart doesn't mean right."

> Intelligence without wisdom is just speed toward failure.

> "Mirrors reflect, they don't correct."

> AI shows you possibilities; only you can choose responsibly.

> "If it doesn't feel heavy, it isn't yours."

> Weightless choices carry someone else's burden.

THE BOTTOM LINE

The future belongs to organizations that can **leverage AI capability while maintaining human accountability.** The One-Pound Rule ensures your team stays smart, ethical, and adaptable in an AI-powered world.

The question isn't whether AI can make the decision, it's whether you can own it.

For workshop facilitation, assessment tools, and implementation guides, visit our site.